The Blessing

GIVING THE GIFT OF
UNCONDITIONAL
LOVE AND ACCEPTANCE

John Trent, Gary Smalley,
and Kari Trent Stageberg

W Publishing Group

An Imprint of Thomas Nelson

Published in Nashville, Tennessee, by W Publishing Group, an imprint of Thomas Nelson.

Thomas Nelson titles may be purchased in bulk for educational, business, fund-raising, or sales promotional use. For information, please e-mail SpecialMarkets@ThomasNelson.com.

978-0-7852-2905-6 (TP)
978-0-7852-2597-3 (eBook)

Library of Congress Cataloging-in-Publication Data

Trent, John, 1952–
The blessing: giving the gift of unconditional love and acceptance / John Trent and Gary Smalley. — Rev. and updated by John Trent.
p. cm.
Includes bibliographical references.
ISBN 978-0-8499-4637-0 (trade paper)
1. Families—Religious life. 2. Child rearing—Religious aspects—Christianity. 3. Blessing and cursing. I. Smalley, Gary. II. Title.
BV4526.3.T74 2011
248.8'45—dc22 2011004971

Printed in the United States of America

Contents

A New Edition . . . with Grateful Thanks   v

Part 1: Understanding the Blessing

Chapter 1:   The Importance of Asking Why   3
Chapter 2:   Celebrating with Your Blessing Team   10
Chapter 3:   The Lifelong Search for the Blessing   22
Chapter 4:   "Bless Me—Me Also, O My Father!"   30
Chapter 5:   A Life-and-Death Choice   38

Part 2: The Five Elements of the Blessing

Chapter 6:   Our First Look at the Five Elements
of the Blessing   51
Chapter 7:   The First Element: Appropriate
Meaningful Touch   58
Chapter 8:   The Second Element: A Spoken or
Written Message   79
Chapter 9:   The Third Element: Attaching High Value   97
Chapter 10: The Fourth Element: Picturing a Special Future   117
Chapter 11: The Fifth Element: An Active,
Genuine Commitment   134
Chapter 12: First Steps: A Written Blessing   153

Part 3: Living the Blessing

Chapter 13: Your Blessing   171
Chapter 14: Blessing Your Kids and Grandkids   185

CONTENTS

Chapter 15: Blessing Your Spouse   218
Chapter 16: Blessing When You're Single   235
Chapter 17: Blessing Your Parents   252

Part 4: Turning Hurt into the Blessing

Chapter 18: Blessing Others, Even When It Hurts   269
Chapter 19: I've Blessed Them, and It's Not Working   276
Chapter 20: What If I Didn't Get the Blessing?   284
Chapter 21: Your Next Step Is Living the Blessing   298

Notes   305
About the Authors   312

A New Edition . . . with Grateful Thanks

As you get ready to dive into this new edition of the book and experience, let me start out by thanking my patient, loving wife, Cindy, for being such a huge help as always in supporting every word I write. By the time this book comes out, we will have been married forty years. What a blessing God has given me every day, year, and decade.

In addition, you'll notice there are three names on this new edition of the book. I'm honored to have and to keep Gary Smalley's name on the cover. Gary was my "friend of friends" who worked with me to write the first edition of *The Blessing*. He was someone who lived out the Blessing so wisely and well with his own family first and then with others. It amazes me, as I write this, that it has been close to three years since Gary went to be with the Lord. You'll still hear some of his insights and stories in this book, and you'll hear from another author in this edition as well.

Kari Trent Stageberg is a new name on the cover. She is my and Cindy's oldest daughter. Kari is an amazing writer, wife, sister, daughter, and person. With her name on this book, it launches a new generation of Trents writing and teaching about the Blessing. She also has an incredible heart for those who have missed the Blessing. As part of what we do at StrongFamilies.com, she teaches seminars, trains leaders, and has helped many women who have experienced—or are currently experiencing—abuse regain and reclaim the Blessing in their lives.

Kari runs StrongFamilies.com with me and is outstanding at

helping people take information and turn it into action. Because there have been so many people asking us, "How do I do this?" she's written a whole new section of this book (part 3) and created content online at TheBlessing.com that will give you ideas on how to apply the Blessing to specific areas of your life. Look for her words here, in future books, on our podcast, and online at our website to find support and materials to both help you heal and live out the Blessing.

I'm so grateful for two other crucial teammates at Strong Families for their help with this new edition. Dr. Tony Wheeler leads our Institute for the Blessing at StrongFamilies.com. Kari and I are honored to have Tony's amazing insights into helping people put down their facades and self-protection so they can embrace the freedom and life Jesus offers us—freeing them to bless! Tony and I are working on a book right now that numerous people have asked us for years to write. It will be called *The Blessing Cry*, and it is filled with hope and help specifically for those who have missed the Blessing. If that's your experience (as it was for both Dr. Wheeler and me), look for help and hope from Dr. Wheeler, along with Kari and myself, right now at TheBlessing.com and soon in that new book.

And special thanks goes out to Brooke Brown as well. Brooke fills out our leadership team at StrongFamilies.com. Brooke is brilliant and as courageous, observant, and caring a person as I have ever met. She won the Walter Cronkite Outstanding Undergraduate Award for Excellence in Journalism for being the top journalism student at Arizona State University the year she graduated. (And she gave the student speaker address at graduation!) Brooke has written her own story in a wonderful book called *The Little Butterfly Girl*, which you can find in our store at StrongFamilies.com, at TheBlessing.com, or at major online bookstores. She is simply outstanding at helping people capture their life stories—as well as capture and share their Blessing stories. On our website, you'll find some of the writing and training videos she's done to help you capture your own Blessing story. You'll also hear from her in this book, in a special chapter on how we can bless others even when we're in pain ourselves.

There are so many others to thank, from the board at our ministry that runs StrongFamilies.com and TheBlessing.com, to the students I get to teach who keep helping us learn new things so that we can better apply our message to a new generation.

But without our wonderful editor and friend Debbie Wickwire's patience and perseverance, and her belief in *The Blessing*'s importance for a new generation, this edition would never have happened. Thank you, Debbie.

May every minute you spend in these pages and in processing what you learn here and in your Blessing Group bring you closer to the source of blessing than ever before. I pray all this for you as you learn to love more like Jesus, and like him, lead and change lives when you do.

—JOHN TRENT, PHD
PRESIDENT, STRONGFAMILIES.COM
GARY D. CHAPMAN CHAIR OF MARRIAGE,
FAMILY MINISTRY, AND THERAPY
MOODY THEOLOGICAL SEMINARY

Part 1

Understanding
the Blessing

Chapter 1

The Importance of Asking Why

Why does that deep ache of loneliness keep showing up in my life—even after my happiest moments or at the end of my biggest accomplishments? Why do I doubt whether I was really loved and cared for growing up, even though I didn't lack for any physical thing? Or perhaps you wonder, Why do I try so hard to experience close, caring relationships and yet so often feel that the very thing I long for stays just out of reach?

Have you ever been haunted by some version of that incredibly difficult question—why?

Simon Sinek is an outstanding speaker and thinker. Take a look at his TED talk on the golden circle. It's a metaphor for what is most important to a leader, a coach, or anyone trying to figure out relationships—or even how to sell things. At the center of his talk, and the circle that he draws, is the word why.[1] Because it's so important.

I believe that is the reason this book has continued to be of help and encouragement to so many people. Because in the incredibly powerful biblical concept of the Blessing comes the answer for so many people about their deepest need from their most important earthly relationships, an answer to their why?

3

The Day I Found My *Why?*
in the Word *Blessing*

It was several years ago that I experienced what was to me a God-inspired, profound discovery in regard to my own *why?* question. For me, it happened in a span of less than twenty-four hours, twelve of which I spent sitting with someone on suicide watch at a psychiatric hospital, where I was an intern.

My shift had ended. I remember walking out of the hospital that evening, wishing I could have been of more help to that very troubled young man and his *why?* I'd given him all the help and encouragement I could, but I didn't have a clear picture to show him. His *why?* had pushed him to the very brink of a life-and-death choice.

Little did I know that when I got home that night and opened my Bible to Genesis 27 I'd run right into the story of another young man like the one I'd been sitting beside all day. Another person who was beyond heartbroken. In fact, we're told, "He cried with an exceedingly great and bitter cry, and said to his father, 'Bless me—me also, O my father!' . . . 'Have you not reserved a blessing for me?' . . . And Esau lifted up his voice and wept" (Gen. 27:34, 36, 38).

I had read about Jacob and Esau probably a hundred times. The story of one brother getting his father's blessing—and of the other being tricked out of it. But all of a sudden, as I sat in my study, it was like Almighty God opened my eyes and the scales fell off. Now I had a name for that incredible longing I'd been listening to, that I'd seen in that hurting young man at the psychiatric hospital.

He had missed the Blessing. Whatever that was.

But without even knowing all that there was to Esau's cry right then, it was like a light turned on in my own mind and

THE IMPORTANCE OF ASKING WHY

heart. That blessing, even though I didn't fully understand it, was something I knew I had longed for all my life with my own father, who had left our home when I was two months old. The story in Genesis 27 gave me the answer to that *why?* I was still struggling with in my own life. It painted a picture of my *why?* and gave me insight that could bring incredible help to many people I'd worked with. Not just at the hospital, but everyday people: friends and relatives. My own wife, who at that time had never gotten the Blessing from her father. And, certainly, those I worked with and counseled.

The thoughts *Why didn't you (or won't you) give me your blessing?* and even *Why is it so important to make sure we give others the Blessing?* sprang to my mind.

That very night, I started digging into Scripture to find the "return address" for Esau's crushing cry of emotional pain and separation—one that so many of us have echoed in our own lives. The first verse I came to that helped explain it to me wasn't far from that Genesis passage. The book of Deuteronomy records a time the Lord called the entire nation of Israel together and set before them something that was nothing less than a life-and-death choice—a choice that is set before us as well.

"I call heaven and earth to witness that I have set before you a choice. Life or death. The blessing or the curse. So choose life. You and your descendants" (Deut. 30:19, author's paraphrase).

That's where I began to see the double-sided choice that the Lord himself had set before his people, just before they headed into the promised land. There was a choice: Life over death. Blessing over curse. One choice, with two parts, that we'll dig into throughout this book.

The Blessing originated in God giving us life and his blessing. But the deeper I dived into Scripture, the more I realized we also have a choice either to bless others or to withhold the Blessing from them! This choice begins with our children and our spouses, and then extends to those around us.

The apostle Peter, one of Jesus' closest friends and disciples, wrote of Christ's suffering and how his love freed us. At one point, he wrote, "Do not repay evil with evil or insult with insult. On the contrary, repay evil with blessing, because to this you were called so that you may inherit a blessing" (1 Peter 3:9 NIV).

In short, to be a person of blessing is our calling.

Listen to the way Eugene Peterson in his eminently readable paraphrase, *The Message*, translates these same verses: "No retaliation. No sharp-tongued sarcasm. Instead, bless—that's your job, to bless. You'll be a blessing and also get a blessing."

Think about that for a moment.

That's your job, to bless.

You may have sworn that it was to be a heavy-equipment operator or homemaker or policewoman or nurse practitioner or computer coder or teacher. No, your primary job is to bless. It's your calling. And in doing so, you'll see the Blessing comes back from God himself and pours out all over you.

Welcome to a book that, amazingly enough, is in its fourth revision and already in the hands of nearly two million people. This book is going to call you, equip you, encourage you, and cheer you on to do your "job"—starting at home with your spouse, your children, and your grandchildren. But then also with those at work. With those you minister to. With those you serve with, go on shifts with, go to church with, deploy overseas with, do life with.

Kari and I get to lay before you and a whole new generation of parents and couples, single parents and grandparents, students and professors, that amazing, life-giving choice. A choice that does not only affect the quality of others' lives but can impact how we do life and even our ultimate end.

Key Benefits to this Edition

Though the core message of this book remains the same, there are three ways this new edition can be of huge help to you in your life and in the lives of those around you.

1. It pulls back the curtain on those huge *why?* questions.

As we've seen, *why?* questions can ruin relationships and make our hearts sick. Why did it hurt and impact my life so much when my father bailed out on our family when I was an infant, even when I knew nothing about him growing up? Why am I so tripped up by a mother who kept her acceptance just out of reach, putting me on track to feel as if I still have to be perfect or overachieve? Why do I struggle, in my heart of hearts, to really believe that a heavenly Father loves and cares for me—even that Jesus' love can really transform and embrace me as it seems to do with others?

In this new edition, Kari and I will explain the whats and hows that can help you experience, give, and live the Blessing. But our biggest prayer for you is that you would be able to begin answering the whys in your own life. We want to give you clarity on why you need to give the Blessing to others, and why it's so transformational to live out the Blessing before a world and culture filled with people who are desperate for rest and peace for their souls.

"Why?" is not a minor question. In fact, we'd say it is more of an *interrobang* question. If you haven't heard that word before, that's certainly understandable. That's because it refers to a key that used to be on typewriters years ago: ‽. While it's been used in several written languages, in English the interrobang is intended to combine the functions of both a question mark and an exclamation point. It signals that the question it's attached to is hugely important, and the symbol is known in printers' and programmers' jargon as a "bang."

We believe it's a huge deal for you to get to the bottom of your *why?* question, so get ready for a bang as you dig into this book.

2. It answers the question "How do I live the Blessing as a lifestyle and not just a one-and-done thing?"

Kari and I, along with our wonderful teammates at StrongFamilies .com, have taught this concept of the Blessing as a lifestyle to thousands of people across the country.[2] Over the past several years many have asked for more specifics on how to go beyond simply giving the Blessing once as a one-and-done kind of thing.

It's certainly better to give or receive the Blessing once instead of never. For example, I sat with my father for eight and a half hours in a small hospice room on the day he died. He was dying of congestive heart and lung failure—a terrible way to die. I held his hand during the tough, horrible coughing parts. I told him I loved him. I got him water. I tried to help him get comfortable as much as I could. I prayed for him—and had him cuss at me for praying for him.

When my father breathed his last at 4:43 p.m. on an incredibly hot August afternoon in Phoenix, like Esau, I lifted up my voice and wept when I knew that—with my father—I would never get his blessing. I would have loved, on that last day with him, even just once before he was gone, to have received his blessing.

I've received many letters and e-mails over the years from people who have had a loved one who, just once, gave them the Blessing. They've shared how incredibly important that one time was to them. That's awesome. I cheer with them. I'm incredibly grateful for whatever it was in that person that caused him or her to wake up and realize how important even *one time* of sharing the Blessing can be in a loved one's life.

But one-and-done was *never* how we were meant to give the Blessing. While getting the Blessing once is much better than just wishing we had the answer to that fill-in-the-blank in our hearts that was left empty, what we're called to is what the apostle Peter revealed: blessing others is our job.

We are called to get to work creating a *culture* of the Blessing in our lives, homes, workplaces, and neighborhoods. In a fallen, angry, incredibly broken world, our job is to be a people of blessing. Talk about standing out! Be a person of blessing.

You may only see someone once—like when you're on the road and that barista in the drive-through hands you your Americano. In this book you'll absolutely learn how to bless people once. However, the Blessing is meant to be a lifestyle practiced with the people we live with, as a clear way to love like Jesus. For it is because of Jesus' love for us that the DNA of the Blessing can be woven into the very fabric of our everyday lives.

3. It helps you dig deeper, process, and experience the concepts of the Blessing.

Processing concepts through self-reflection and journaling helps you understand and internalize information better. That's why this new edition of the book also includes questions at the end of nearly every chapter. They will call you to dig deeper, to consider your own life and experiences as they relate to the Blessing. Look for the "Pictures Your Heart Remembers" sections, and even if you're tempted, don't skip them.

And there's one more major reason this new version of the book can mean so much to you.

It's the difference between celebrating by yourself—or experiencing the multiplied joy of running onto the field to celebrate with your team.

Chapter 2

Celebrating with Your Blessing Team

We've already mentioned that giving the Blessing to others is our God-given "job." We believe this book will challenge, equip, and motivate you to do that well. And we've listed three objectives—from answering those huge whys in our lives, to creating a culture of the Blessing instead of a one-and-done experience, to processing the material in this book at a deeper level—that distinguish this edition of *The Blessing*.

But there's something else that this edition is built around that we believe is incredibly powerful for retaining this concept—seeing it take root in your life and in the lives of those you bless. It has to do with whether you celebrate solo or with your own team.

Celebrating Alone or with Your Blessing Team

Baz Gray is a former British Royal Marine. Simply put, he is as tough as they come. In fact, he became the first person to complete a 745-mile *solo* trek to the South Pole. In conditions that he described as "absolutely horrendous," the unusually heavy snow he faced made this the toughest period of his life. Gray had to eat 10,000 calories each day simply to maintain enough energy to keep going the average of nineteen miles he fought to cover each day. Which meant he was dragging a 187-pound sled all those hundreds of miles, loaded with his food, bedding, and equipment, to reach his goal.

Finally, thirty-nine days after he began, at 19:00 GMT on Sunday, January 6, 2019, he finished what no other individual had done before. And he got to celebrate reaching the South Pole . . . alone.[1] Which doesn't lessen at all what he did. But think of that solo celebration—and of the celebration of having shared those grueling hours with a team who could now celebrate that achievement together. The hugging and high-fiving. The sharing of joys, the lifelong memories of shared experiences in making the trek together.

Let's make it clear that reading this book is nowhere near as hard as trekking across arctic wastelands dragging almost two hundred pounds behind you! But you're starting an important journey. It can be incredibly fulfilling and tremendously worth celebrating to read this book alone. You can still gain so much emotional and relational ground if you decide to skip this chapter and go on to the core content of what the Blessing is and how we can live it out.

But we would ask you to consider something else.

In all the years we've taught and helped others learn about living and giving the Blessing, it is so often the people who share and celebrate *with a group* who turn these concepts into life-changing gifts and realities in their most important relationships. They don't just get to their destination or goals quicker. They do so in a way that changes their lives through the process of being in a community of people. We were made for relationships.

So we set before you a challenge.

You can do this book as a solo trek. But we'd ask that you make this journey with a Blessing Team. That may be a group of people you already know, like a "life group" or small group of friends or family. Or one of our Zoom, Facebook, or online groups who join through TheBlessing.com. It's your choice. But here are some questions and a plan for working through this book with others that we pray you'll take hold of—and end up celebrating with others.

Some Questions and a Plan for Going Through this Book with a Blessing Team

*What do you call your group? A Blessing
Group or Blessing Team?*

The answer is your choice—we have people who call their group a Blessing Group, and others who, for whatever reason, prefer the "team" label and call their group a Blessing Team. We know this may fly in the face of people who demand that we tell them the "right way" to do things! (In our personality system of Lions, Otters, Retrievers, and Beavers, these folks would be beavers—the awesome detail people who actually balance the checkbook and have sock drawers.) So *you* pick the right label for your group. Kari and I will be using both terms throughout this book as we have both groups and teams, and they're all doing it the right way—their way (which the lions just applauded)![2]

Are these virtual or face-to-face groups?

The answer to this is also yes; you can do both. At TheBlessing. com, we are busy registering and helping launch both online Facebook groups and Zoom groups (Zoom being our favorite video-conferencing platform). These are often made up of people who showed up at the website and let us know they wanted to join a group. So we placed them with a "climbing team" and got them started on their work through the book. Many of the people joining a Facebook group are scattered geographically. However, some may be in the same city. We've even had some people find out they were all in the same city—and then they decided to meet face to face! But primarily our Facebook and Zoom groups are virtual groups.

We also have a number of groups—especially groups from churches, men's groups, MOPS groups, women's groups, and even workplace and military teams—who go through this book with others in face-to-face meetings instead of online.

It's totally your choice. You can recruit a group on your own and go through the book together online or in person. Or you can go to TheBlessing.com and get linked up with a group at our "base camp."

Whether it's virtual or face-to-face, we ask that you register your group at *The Blessing* website. We won't spam you—we never have and never will—but we will send you an e-mail welcoming you and your group, letting you know how you can contact us to get answers to questions or for any other help you may need.

Do I have to sign up my group?

No. As we just shared, we'd love for you to do that. We can pray for you. Encourage you. Provide any help or ideas that other groups have found helpful as well. But you can simply use this book and have all you need without ever having to officially sign up. The group questions and resources are here in the book. However, if you do come to TheBlessing.com and sign up, there are a number of additional tools available to help you and your group as well. Your call.

Where do I find a group?

As we've mentioned, you may have a built-in group you want to put together from your workplace, school, community, or church. Or it might be a group of couples or close friends you see on a regular basis. We've had siblings form a group and many others pull together a group from Instagram or their Facebook friends. (In fact, we've heard many times, "I was shocked at how many people wanted to join something like this when I asked them!")

You may decide to ask people in your neighborhood or where your kids go to school to find others who may be looking for ways to love and bless their kids. Believe us—people *want* to have strong marriages and to bless their children. They don't want to be miserable or feel like they're doing poorly in helping their kids head toward a special future. But many just don't know how to do it. Or, again, they may have never had a name to call what we know we need to give to our kids.

Don't assume people won't want to join a group. We hear all the time how surprised people were at the response they got from just asking. And, as mentioned before, you can always go to TheBlessing.com and join a Facebook or Zoom group there.

How many people should I have in my group?

For a Blessing Group we'd suggest four as a minimum, and six to eight people as the maximum. If you sign up for one of our online groups, you'll be working with six to eight people. We know that sounds like a small group, but if you're going to really hear and see each person in the group in the time frame we're suggesting, that number seems to work the best, though it's not set in stone. If you have more than eight people (for instance, if you have five couples and four singles), we would suggest dividing the group size in half.

Are the groups made up of men or women or both?

Many of the groups we've seen jump into *The Blessing* are all moms, like in a MOPS group or some other type of women's group, or all dads or husbands, as in a men's group. Sometimes it's all single men who are serious about doing relationships well, or it's groups of single women sharing where they are in life as well as examining the Blessing.

Keep in mind that in the reality of how God created us, male and female, we do process things differently. It's why many of the groups we've put together are all-male or all-female.

Then again, a number of Blessing Groups are made up of moms *and* dads who are looking for a way to get on the same page together—both in loving each other well and in blessing their children. All this to say, you can absolutely do a group with men and women.

In short, we've pretty much seen it all. From groups of single parents or students to soldiers—marines, airmen, or sailors, both male and female, who decided in the course of a deployment to go through *The Blessing* so that they could bring the Blessing with them when they returned home. We've even been contacted by groups of prisoners who love Jesus and have wanted to learn about how to give and to deal with missing the Blessing—to learn how to "reverse the curse."

The choice is yours—pick whatever might be the most helpful kind of group for you, depending on your life circumstances and desires for what you'd like to accomplish.

What do you do in the group?

We suggest that you read through each chapter of the book *ahead* of your group meeting to discuss that chapter. We also urge each person to go through the Pictures Your Heart Remembers section and process it individually, *if* there's one attached to that chapter. (Note: Not all chapters have group questions or a Pictures Your Heart Remembers section at the end.)

The Pictures section is a way to more personally process what is being shared. It offers a great opportunity to look closely at your own heart and thoughts in addition to the insights you may gain in your time spent answering the group questions.

With the Pictures Your Heart Remembers section, *we strongly recommend* getting a pen and journal or setting up an online journal to capture your notes and thoughts.[3] (You can also use the same journal to write down thoughts or things you hear in your Blessing Group.) We hear all the time from people, many of whom have never done any journaling before, that writing down their thoughts is super helpful both individually and in the group experience.

You have a story. And a voice. Writing down your thoughts can help you focus when you share in your group, instead of trying to remember or pull thoughts out of the air during the group time.

At the end of each chapter you'll find the Blessing Group Questions section. You are not limited to these questions, and you may wish to change a question or phrase it differently. However, while you're free to adapt what's here, most groups have found these questions helpful in setting up the opportunity for each person to share from his or her own experiences.

Who's the group leader?

We suggest that you vote for or assign two leaders in each group who love to serve others. One would be the *chief time clock servant*. This person serves your Blessing Group by kicking off each session with prayer. The chief time clock servant also makes sure only one person at a time talks through his or her thoughts on the group questions. (We'll share the details of who talks when in the suggested meeting outline below.)

Think of this person as the air traffic controller for the group, not the commander in chief. This person honors the group members individually by waving them onto the runway when it's their time to land—giving them a chance to unload and share their thoughts and heart. The chief time clock servant is also the one who directs the next person onto the runway after the previous group member is finished, giving each member a one-minute warning to wrap up their thoughts so the next member is ready for his or her time to share.

The second key servant-leader role in the group is the *chief prayer servant*. This person takes notes and closes your time with a brief prayer that touches on one thing each person in the group has shared. Some groups also have this person send out a brief summary or prayer list after the meeting if that's agreed on by all to be helpful.

Do we have to do the prayer thing?

We get it that many people today are spiritually homeless when it comes to a church or doing much with their faith. But the Blessing is all about getting to know and love Jesus—whose love and blessing we're going to be living out with others. He modeled loving people well—blessing them. He calls us to be people of blessing as our job and as a key part of our purpose. So we certainly love people who don't know Jesus or see much value in prayer. But a Blessing Group is one where people are going to pray, just like Jesus, who took time out to pray to his Father and with the disciples. Prayer is like spiritual gravity. It's a way of connecting and sharing with God. If you haven't done much praying—alone or in a group—it's *not* as hard as you think! Picture one of those really big balls that are super soft. Whoever is praying is picking up the ball and tossing it to the Lord. And then it gets tossed back, and then we toss it to the Lord. It's like being in a conversation with someone.

Even if this spiritual side of things is a little uncomfortable, we ask that you choose to be uncomfortable for a time. Our prayer is that you'll become more spiritually comfortable in a safe place where people aren't going to grade you on your prayers. Just be glad there are people around you who are tossing the ball back and forth with the Lord—praying for you and one another.

What's the time frame of the group?

We suggest a one-hour meeting for your group. You can change this (increasing or decreasing the time) as needed, but this is why we've suggested you limit your group size. While nearly all of us are crazy busy, most everyone can carve out an hour to work toward building better, stronger relationships.

As we shared at the beginning of this section, though it's possible to do fewer chapters, we suggest going through the entire book—all twenty-one chapters. Amazingly enough, some groups have ended up having even more meetings!

We even had one group of firefighters go through this book and break almost every suggestion above! They picked only ten chapters, met in thirty-minute time blocks, and made other adjustments that fit a model they knew worked at their firehouse. And what happened in their homes and even around the station was tremendous.

Again, it's not that structure doesn't matter. But it's like your grandmother's recipe that creates a great dish even though it's not done with exact measurements. Feel free to go by the book, or make changes that work best for your group. But for the sake of planning, let's go back to the issue of structure.

Suggested Outline for Meeting
One Hour for Each Chapter

Your first meeting (live, via Facebook, Zoom, and so on)

For your group's first meeting we suggest that you don't try to get through the first chapter. Instead, ask the group members to share some of their personal stories. They can answer questions about

- where they are from,
- what their family background was like,
- why they are doing this study,
- how they heard about *The Blessing*,
- what they hope to get out of their time working through the book with others,
- what they are excited about with this group, and
- what they are a little scared about.

These and similar questions will help everyone get to know one another better. After this first meeting you'll be working through the book chapter by chapter.

Remaining weekly meetings

Your one-hour meetings can be broken down as follows:

- Two minutes for the chief time clock servant to open in prayer and welcome everyone.
- Ten minutes total for each person to share his or her thoughts about the questions at the end of the week's chapter. The first seven minutes are for the person's thoughts, followed by three minutes of others asking questions or sharing thoughts about what they have heard. (The chief time clock servant should give a one-minute warning before closing this person's time in prayer.) The goal isn't to correct the sharer but for the other group members to help clarify, encourage, or perhaps offer some insight from their perspective. Not everyone has to participate, and it's okay if no one responds. But it is important that everyone has a turn and a chance to talk through and work through the questions with the group.
- Two minutes for the chief prayer servant—or someone else

in the group—to pray for the person and what he or she just shared.

- Ten minutes for the next person in the group to share, repeating the pattern above.
- Two minutes for prayer for that person.
- And so on through your group.

This assumes five people each have twelve minutes total for an hour meeting. If there are more than five people, then you'll need to add twelve minutes for each extra person to have time to share.

Having a great group experience is not rocket science. It just takes some wonderful people who have an unwavering conviction that they want to become people of blessing, for their families and future.

If you're an Otter personality (fun-loving, relational, party-waiting-to-happen person), the outline above will be more than enough to get you started. But if you're a Beaver personality, there's never enough detail. Whichever personality you might have, feel free to simply get going with your group, or log onto TheBlessing. com to access more information and suggestions and watch the videos we have for you there.

It's really just reading, sharing, praying, encouraging, and then inviting the next person to do the same as you work through the book together. You'll find it's such a blessing to help others in your group figure out how to receive, give, and live the Blessing. Everyone has something to offer to the group that is unique. Maybe you're great at engaging people you don't know. Maybe you're great at listening, praying, encouraging others, keeping record of things, illustrating the "whys" of problems, or being a role model in a certain area of life.

There's no doubt you will gain much in your own life by going through this material. But we know you'll also gain a ton of encouragement and strength of heart by helping others see their families, marriages, kids, or teams grow closer, stronger, and more loving because you prayed or encouraged them into a new way of loving like Jesus.

We thank you in advance for what you can mean in the lives of others in your group. Now it's time to get started. We're praying for you and your Blessing Group or Team to have a great experience!

Chapter 3

The Lifelong Search for the Blessing

All of us long to be accepted by others. While we may say out loud, "I don't care what other people think about me," on the inside we all yearn for intimacy and affection. This yearning is especially true in our relationships with our parents. Gaining or missing out on parental approval has a tremendous effect on us, even if it has been years since we have had any contact with them. In fact, what happens in our relationship with our parents can greatly affect all our present and future relationships. While this may sound like an exaggeration, our offices have been filled with people struggling with this very issue, people just like Brian and Nancy.

The Crushing of Brian's Dream

"Please say that you love me, *please!*" Brian's words trailed off into tears as he leaned over the now-still form of his father. It was late at night in a large metropolitan hospital. Only the cold, white walls and the humming of a heart monitor kept Brian company. His tears revealed a deep inner pain and sensitivity that had tormented him for years. The emotional wounds now seemed beyond repair.

Brian had flown nearly halfway across the country to be at his father's side in one last attempt to reconcile years of misunderstanding and resentment. All his life, Brian had been searching for his father's acceptance and approval, but they always seemed just out of reach.

Brian's father, a career marine officer, wanted nothing more than for his son to follow in his footsteps. With that in mind, he took every opportunity to instill in Brian the discipline and the backbone he felt Brian would need as a marine.

Words of affection or tenderness were forbidden in their home. It was almost as if Brian's father thought a display of warmth might crack the tough exterior he was trying to create in his son. He drove Brian to participate in sports and to take elective classes that would best equip him to be an officer. But Brian's only praise for scoring a touchdown or doing well in a class was a lecture on how he could and should have done even better.

After graduating from high school, Brian did enlist in the Marine Corps. It was the happiest day of his father's life. However, the joy was short-lived. Cited for attitude problems and disrespect for orders, Brian was soon on report. After weeks of such reports (one for a vicious fight with his drill instructor), Brian was dishonorably discharged from the service as incorrigible.

The news of Brian's dismissal from the marines dealt a death blow to his relationship with his father. Brian was no longer welcome in his father's home, and for years there was no contact between them.

During those years, Brian struggled with feelings of inferiority and lacked self-confidence. Even though he was above average in intelligence, he worked at various jobs far below his abilities. Three times he got engaged—only to break the engagements just weeks before the weddings. He just couldn't believe another person could really love him.

Brian didn't know that he was experiencing common symptoms of growing up without the family blessing. He knew something was wrong, though, and that sense of something missing finally led him to seek professional help.

I began counseling with Brian after he had broken his third engagement. As he peeled away the layers of his past, Brian began to see both his need for his family's blessing and his responsibility for dealing honestly with his parents. That is when the call came from his mother. His father was dying from a heart attack.

Brian flew immediately to his hometown to see his father. During the entire journey he was filled with hope that now, at long last, they could talk and reconcile their relationship. "I'm sure he'll listen to me. I've learned *so* much. I know things are going to change between us." Brian repeated these phrases over and over to himself as he sat on the plane.

But it was not to be.

Brian's father slipped into a coma a few hours before Brian made it to the hospital. The words that Brian longed to hear for the first time—words of love and acceptance—would never be spoken. Four hours after Brian arrived, his father died without regaining consciousness.

"Dad, please wake up!" Brian's heartbreaking sobs echoed down the hospital corridor. His cries spoke of an incredible sense of loss—not only the physical loss of his father but also the emotional sense of losing any chance of his father's blessing.

Nancy Relives a Painful Past

Nancy's loss was a different sort, but the hurt and pain she received from missing out on the Blessing stung her just as deeply and caused problems not only with her parents but with her husband and children as well.

Nancy grew up in an affluent suburb outside a major city. Her mother loved to socialize with other women at the club and at frequent civic activities. In fact, with a marriage that was less than fulfilling, Nancy's mother placed paramount importance on these social gatherings.

When Nancy was very young, her mother would dress her up in elegant clothes (the kind you had to sit still in, not play in) and take her and her older sister to the club. But as Nancy grew older, this practice began to change.

Unlike her mother and older sister, Nancy was not petite. In fact, she was quite sturdy and big-boned. Nor was Nancy a model of tranquility. She was a tomboy who loved outdoor games, swinging on fences, and animals of all kinds.

As you might imagine, such behavior from a daughter who was being groomed to be a debutante caused real problems. Nancy's mother tried desperately to mend her daughter's erring ways. Nancy was constantly scolded for being "awkward" and "clumsy." During shopping sprees, she was often subject to verbal barbs designed to motivate her to lose weight.

"All the really nice clothes are two sizes too small for you. They're your *sister's* size," her mother would taunt. Nancy was finally put on a strict diet to try to make her physically presentable to others.

Nancy tried hard to stick to her diet and be all her mother wanted. However, more and more often, Nancy's mother and sister would go to social events and leave Nancy at home. Soon all invitations to join these functions stopped. "After all," her mother told her, "you don't want to be embarrassed in front of all the other children because of the way you look, do you?"

When Nancy first came in for counseling, she was in her

thirties, married, and the mother of two children. For years she had struggled with her weight and with feelings of inferiority. Her marriage had been a constant struggle as well.

Nancy's husband loved her and was deeply committed to her, but her inability to feel acceptable left her constantly insecure and defensive. As a result of this hypersensitivity, Nancy felt threatened every time she and her husband began to draw close. Invariably, some small thing her husband did would set her off, and her marriage was back at arm's length.

Frankly, because of her lack of acceptance in the past, being at arm's length was the only place Nancy felt comfortable in any relationship. Her marriage was certainly of concern to her. Yet where Nancy struggled most was with her children, one in particular.

Nancy had two daughters. The older girl was big boned and looked very much like Nancy, but the younger daughter was a beautiful, petite child. What was causing Nancy incredible pain were the relationships between her mother and her children. For once again, her mother catered to the "pretty" daughter while Nancy's older daughter was left out and ignored. Old wounds that Nancy thought were hidden in her past were now being relived through watching her own children. The heartache and loneliness her older daughter was feeling echoed Nancy's unhappiness.

In spite of herself, Nancy found her attitude toward her smaller, daintier daughter changing. The slightest misbehavior from this child would bring an explosion of anger. Bitterness and resentment began to replace genuine affection.

In her heart of hearts, Nancy was also angry at God. In spite of her prayers, she felt he had changed neither her relationship with her mother nor her present circumstances. She felt doomed to repeat her own painful past through her daughters. As a result of this barrage of feelings, she stopped going to Bible study, calling Christian friends, and even praying to God.

Nancy's relationship with her husband, her children, and God had all been affected by missing out on the Blessing that she had tried for years to grasp but had never quite been able to reach.

Our Need for Acceptance

For Brian and for Nancy, the absence of parental acceptance held serious consequences. In Brian's case, it kept him from getting close enough to another person to become genuinely committed. In Nancy's, the inability to feel acceptable as a person was destroying her most important relationships. Without realizing it, Brian and Nancy were searching for the same thing—their family's blessing.

Brian and Nancy typify all people who, for one reason or another, miss out on the Blessing. For years after they had moved away from homes *physically*, they still remained chained to the past *emotionally*. Their lack of parental approval in the past kept them from feeling genuinely accepted by others in the present. In Nancy's case, her mother's withheld approval even kept her from believing that her heavenly Father truly accepted her.

Some people are driven toward workaholism as they search for the blessing they never received at home. Always hungry for acceptance and approval, they never feel satisfied that they are measuring up. Others get mired in withdrawal and apathy as they give up hope of ever truly being blessed. Unfortunately, this withdrawal can become so severe that it can lead to chronic depression and even suicide. For almost all children who miss out on their parents' blessing, at some level this lack of acceptance sets off a lifelong search.

The search for the Blessing is not just a modern-day phenomenon. It is actually centuries old. In fact, we can find a graphic picture of a person who missed out on his family's blessing in the

Old Testament. Let's look now at a confused and angry man named Esau—the one who started my own adventure in learning about the Blessing. In so doing we will learn more about the Blessing and what it can mean to grow up with or without it.

Pictures Your Heart Remembers

In this chapter you read a story about Brian and Nancy. Where did your story begin?

Here's an important exercise. Think back to when you were ten years old (that's roughly when you were in the fifth grade). Now picture that you are standing outside your home. What did the house look like? Who, if you could look inside the windows, would be inside? Would there be someone, if they saw you through the window back then, who would wave at you, excited to see you? Was there someone who would turn away if they caught sight of you? We all start somewhere.

Now think through some of those same feelings and emotions, but this time, picture Jesus standing right next to you. Do you remember if Jesus was a part of your life at ten years old? If he would have been there in the way you know him now, what would that have meant to you? As you stand outside your home looking in, what's one thing you feel like Jesus would say to you?

Blessing Group Questions

1. When you read about the story of someone who missed the Blessing, does it bring back a picture of your own story?
2. From what you know in your heart as you begin this study of the Blessing, would you say you got the Blessing growing up?

3. If you feel as though you didn't get the Blessing growing up, what makes you feel that way?

4. What is more powerful: fear of loss or desire for gain? (Are people more motivated by the harm they can do or experience, or by the possibility to gain something they don't have?)

5. Share a "picture" with the group of your home growing up, what it was like as you stood outside and looked in. You can take this directly from the Pictures Your Heart Remembers section above.

Chapter 4

"Bless Me—Me Also, O My Father!"

Esau was beside himself. *Could this really be happening?* he may have thought. Perhaps his mind went right back to the events of that day. Just hours before, his father, Isaac, had called him to his side and made a special request. If Esau, the older son, would go and bring in fresh game for a savory meal, Isaac's long-awaited blessing would be given to him.

What was this blessing that Esau had waited for over the years? For sons or daughters in biblical times, receiving their father's blessing was a momentous event. At a specific point in their lives they could expect to feel a loving parent's touch and to hear words of encouragement, love, and acceptance—words that gave them a tremendous sense of being highly valued and that even pictured a special future for them.

We will see that some aspects of this Old Testament blessing were unique to that time. However, the *relationship elements* of this blessing are still applicable today. And although in Old Testament times the blessing was primarily reserved for only one son and one special occasion, parents today can decide to build these elements of blessing into all their children's lives daily.

Esau's family, of course, had followed their culture's custom of waiting until a specific day to give the firstborn son a blessing, and the long-awaited day had come at last. Esau's time of blessing was supposed to begin as soon as he could catch and prepare the special meal.

With all the skill and abilities of an experienced hunter, Esau had gone about his work quickly and efficiently. In almost no time he had whipped up a delicious stew as only one familiar with the art of cooking in the field could do.

Esau had done just as he was told. Why, then, was Isaac acting so strangely? Esau had just entered his father's tent and greeted him:

> "Let my father arise and eat of his son's game, that your soul may bless me." And his father Isaac said to him, "Who are you?" So he said, "I am your son, your firstborn, Esau."
>
> Then Isaac trembled exceedingly, and said, "Who? Where is the one who hunted game and brought it to me? I ate all of it before you came, and I have blessed him—and indeed he shall be blessed."
>
> When Esau heard the words of his father, he cried with an exceedingly great and bitter cry, and said to his father, *"Bless me—me also, O my father!"* (Gen. 27:31–34, italics added)

Little did Esau know that when his aged and nearly blind father called him to his side, another had been listening. Rebekah, the mother of Esau and his twin brother, Jacob, had also been in the tent. As soon as Esau went out into the fields to hunt fresh game, she had run to her favorite son, Jacob, with a cunning plan.

If they hurried, they could kill a young kid from the flock and prepare a savory meal. What's more, they could dress Jacob in his brother's clothing and put animal skins on him to simulate Esau's rough and hairy arms, hands, and neck.

Putting on Esau's clothes did not present a problem, but one thing they couldn't counterfeit was Esau's voice. That almost blew the whistle on them (v. 22). But even though Isaac was a little skeptical, their plan worked just as they had hoped it would. We read in Genesis 27:22–23, "So Jacob went near to Isaac his father. . . . And he did not recognize him, because his hands were hairy like his brother Esau's hands; so he blessed him." The blessing meant for the older son went to the younger.

Jacob should not have had to trick his way into receiving the blessing. God himself had told Isaac, regarding his twin sons, that the "older shall serve the younger" (Gen. 25:23). Yet Esau had grown up expecting the blessing to be his. No wonder he was devastated when he came back from hunting to find that an even more cunning hunter had stolen into his father's tent and taken what he thought would be his.

Was Esau crying over losing his inheritance? Absolutely not. As we will see later, the oldest son's inheritance was something that came with his birthright and entitled him to a double share in his father's wealth. Yet years before, Esau had already *sold* his birthright to his brother for a pot of red stew (Gen. 25:29–34).

No, Esau wasn't lamenting the fact that he lost the cattle and sheep—he had already despised that gift. What ripped at his heart was something much more personal: his father's blessing. In Old Testament times a father's blessing was irretrievable once it was given, so now Isaac's blessing was forever outside Esau's reach.

Filled with hurt, he cried out a *second* time, "'Do you have only one blessing, my father? Bless me—me also, O my father.' So Esau lifted his voice and wept" (Gen. 27:38 NASB). In response to his pitiful cries, Esau did receive a blessing of sorts from his father (vv. 39–40), but it was not the words of high value and acceptance that he had longed to hear.

Can you feel the anguish in Esau's cry, "Bless me—me also, O my father"? This same painful cry and unfulfilled longing is being echoed today by many people who are searching for their family's blessing, men and women whose parents, for whatever reason, have failed to bless them with words of love and acceptance. People just like Brian and Nancy. People with whom you rub shoulders every day. Perhaps even you.

The Importance of the Blessing

The hunger for genuine acceptance was a common denominator in Brian's, Nancy's, and Esau's lives—a need that goes unmet in thousands of lives today. The family blessing provides that much-needed sense of personal acceptance. The Blessing also plays a part in protecting and even freeing people to develop intimate relationships. Perhaps most important, it lays the foundation for a genuine and fulfilling relationship with God that can survive even the rocky teen years, when many young people pull away from faith.

This is especially important today, in a culture that offers many forms of counterfeit blessing to young people. Cult and gang leaders have mastered the elements of the Blessing that we will describe in the pages that follow. Providing a sense of family and offering (at least initially) the promise of personal attention, affection, and affirmation is an important drawing card for many of these groups. And our celebrity-saturated media falsely promises fulfillment and validation through money, fame, sex, and success.

Children who grow up without a sense of parental acceptance are especially susceptible to being drawn in by these counterfeit blessings. In fact, thousands are fooled every year, beckoned like hungry children to an imaginary dinner. But though the aroma of blessing may draw them to the table, after eating they are left hungrier than before.

If you are a parent, learning about the family blessing can help you provide your child(ren) with a protective tool. The best defense against imaginary acceptance is genuine acceptance. By providing genuine acceptance and affirmation at home, you can greatly reduce the likelihood that a child will seek those things in a gang hangout, a cult compound, or an immoral relationship.

Genuine acceptance radiates from the concept of the Blessing. However, the Blessing is not just an important tool for parents to use. The Blessing is also of critical importance for anyone who desires to draw close to another person in an intimate relationship. One of the most familiar verses in the Bible is Genesis 2:24: "For this reason a man shall leave his father and his mother, and be joined to his wife" (NASB).

Many books and other resources talk about the need to cleave—or attach firmly—to our spouses. However, very few talk about the tremendous need people also have to "leave" home. Perhaps this is because people have thought of leaving home as simply moving away physically.

In reality, leaving home has always meant much more than putting physical distance between our parents and ourselves. In the Old Testament, for example, the farthest most people would actually move away from their parents was across the campfire and into another tent! Leaving home carries with it not only the idea of physical separation but also of *emotional* separation.

The terrible fact is that most people who have missed out on their parents' blessing have great difficulty leaving home in this emotional sense. It may have been years since they have seen their parents, but unmet needs for personal acceptance can keep them emotionally chained to their parents, unable to genuinely cleave to another person in a lasting relationship.

This happened to both Brian and Nancy, and it's an important reason many couples never get off the ground in terms of marital intimacy. You or a loved one may be facing this problem. Understanding the concept of the Blessing is crucial to defeating the problem and freeing people to build healthy relationships.

A Journey of Hope and Healing

In a world awash with insecurity and in search of acceptance, we need biblical anchors to hold on to—anchors like the Blessing.

The search for acceptance that Brian and Nancy went through and so many others undertake often leads people to accept a cure that is worse than the problem itself. (Many addictions, for instance, have their roots in the deep loneliness of growing up without a parent's blessing.) In contrast, God's Word and his principles offer a dependable blueprint for constructing or reconstructing truly healthy relationships.

In the pages that follow you will discover more about the Blessing. You will explore the five crucial elements that make up the Blessing—and make it so powerful. You will also have a chance to look back and evaluate whether you received the Blessing as a child, how this childhood experience affects you and your family today, and how—if you missed out on the Blessing—you can find healing.

Most important, if you are a parent, you will discover how to make sure your children—toddlers to teens, and even those who are grown—receive the Blessing from you. In the process, you will be exposed to God's spiritual family blessing that is offered to each of his children.

If you are a teacher, discovering the Blessing can help you better understand your students. If you counsel others, it can provide a helpful framework for understanding many problems and offering practical solutions. If you are involved in ministering to others, it can help you understand this crucial need every person has and provide some resources for meeting that need.

Our prayer is, in the following pages, you will take the time and have the courage to journey into the past, a journey that can lead to hope and healing. Even more, we pray that you will be willing to look honestly at the present and apply what you discover.

These pages may end your lifelong search for acceptance or begin a new relationship with your children, your spouse, your parents, or a close friend. Our deepest desire is that this book will enrich your relationship with your heavenly Father as you learn more about the source of blessing that he is to each believer. All this as we take our first look at the life-changing concept called the Blessing.

Pictures Your Heart Remembers

Imagine that you're an Academy Award–winning film director with an unlimited budget, and you can have any of your favorite actors or actresses to be in your next film. Think about making a modern-day version of Jacob and Esau. What would the story look like if one of the characters knew their father liked a brother or sister best? Or that their mother liked him or a sibling best? And what could happen that would make him feel as though he'd been cut out from their father's (or mother's) blessing? What would the ending be like?

Now that you have your script, what would happen if you could help a family like this change the ending of their story? Maybe not that day, when the blessing was lost, but on another day. What would that look like to you? Take some time to pencil in your thoughts. And if you do produce an Academy Award–winning movie with this story, Kari and I want to come to the premiere!

Blessing Group Questions

1. Do people today really work as hard at getting the blessing from a parent as they did in this biblical story?

2. Did there seem to be favoritism in your family growing up? What did that mean in your family? What did that do to your heart or to thoughts about your future?

3. The father in this story wasn't following God's specific instruction to bless Jacob. In your home, growing up, do you feel as though your parents were really trying to follow after the Lord? Or were they just doing what they felt in their hearts?

4. You can hear Esau's heart breaking in that terrible cry, "Bless me—me also, O my father!" Has there been a time when you've felt that? Cried that way? What happened? Was anyone there to comfort you or to walk through that time with you?

5. Why do you think people minimize getting the Blessing—or making sure that it's something they give to a child, spouse, or loved one? If it is really as big a deal as Esau's experience reflects, why does it seem so easy for some people to just ignore or deny it?

Chapter 5

A Life-and-Death Choice

When I (John) was young, my grandparents came to live with us for several years to help out with three very rambunctious boys. My grandfather was a wonderful man but a stern disciplinarian. He had rules for everything, with swats to go along with all his rules. And there was one ironclad rule that we hated because it carried two automatic swats: "Be home before the streetlight comes on."

There was no grading on the curve in my home. And while spanking may be controversial in many homes, there was no discussion when my grandfather moved in. With the streetlight planted right in our yard, all he had to do was look out the kitchen window and see if we had made it home in time. And one night my twin brother, Jeff, and I didn't.

Never one to delay punishment, I shuffled down the hallway to Grandfather's room and received my two swats. But little did I know that I was moments away from gaining one of the most significant blessings in my life.

After my spanking, my grandmother told me to go back down the hall and call my grandfather for dinner. I didn't feel much like being polite to him at the time, but I didn't want to risk another spanking either. So off I went to his room.

While many children grow up with open access to their elders' rooms, we didn't. We were to knock on Grandfather's door, ask for permission to enter, and always call him "Grandfather" or "sir" when we addressed him.

I meant to knock on the door, but then I noticed it was already slightly ajar. That's when I broke the rule and gently pushed it open to look inside.

What I saw shocked me. My grandfather, a man who rarely showed any emotion, was sitting on the end of the bed, crying. I stood at the door in confusion. I had *never* seen him cry, and I didn't know what to do.

Suddenly he looked up and saw me, and I froze where I was. *I hope catching him crying isn't a sixty-swat offense!* I thought to myself.

Yet my grandfather simply said to me, his voice full of emotion, "Come here, John."

When I reached him, he reached out and hugged me closely. Then, in tears, he told me how much he loved me and how deeply it hurt him to have to spank me. "John," he said, seating me on the bed next to him and putting his big arms around me, "I want more than anything in life for you and your brothers to grow up to become godly young men. I hope that you know how much I love you and how proud I am of you."

I can't explain it, but when I left his room that night, I was a different person because of my grandfather's blessing. As I look back today, I see that evening provided me with a meaningful rite of passage from childhood to young adulthood. For years afterward, recalling that clear picture of my grandfather's blessing helped point me toward a more positive future and shape my attitudes and actions.

A few months later my grandfather died instantly and unexpectedly of a cerebral aneurysm. I know now that the Lord allowed me, for that one and only time, to hear and receive the Blessing from him. While I would never receive the Blessing from my own father, I did receive it that day from my grandfather.

Why the Blessing Matters

Just what is this blessing that seems to be so important? Does it really apply to us today, or was it just for Old Testament times? What are the elements of which it consists? How can I know whether I have received it or if my children are experiencing it now?

These questions commonly surface when Kari and I introduce people to the Blessing. In answering them, we will discover five powerful relationship elements that the Old Testament blessing contains. The presence or absence of these elements can help us determine whether our home is—or our parents' home was—a place of blessing.

A study of the Blessing always begins in the context of parental acceptance. However, in studying the Blessing in the Scriptures, we found that its principles can be used in any intimate relationship.

Husbands can apply these principles in blessing their wives, and wives their husbands.

Friendships can be deepened and strengthened by including each element of the Blessing.

These key ingredients, when applied in a church family, can bring warmth, healing, and hope to our brothers and sisters in Christ, many who never received an earthly blessing from their parents. As we will see in a later chapter, they are the very relationship elements God uses in blessing his children.

Perhaps the best place to begin our look at the benefits of giving or gaining the Blessing is to dig into the biblical ideas behind *blessing*—and the clear choice inherent in the word.

The Blessing and the Choice

Perhaps one of the clearest ways to begin to understand what the Blessing means is to look at an amazing choice God once laid before his people—the same choice that I believe is put in front of each of us today, a choice that is literally a matter of life and death. It's found in an amazing passage in the book of Deuteronomy, in the words that God spoke to Joshua:

> I call heaven and earth to witness against you today, that I have set before you life and death, the blessing and the curse. So choose life in order that you may live, you and your descendants. (Deut. 30:19 NASB)

The context in which these words were spoken can help us understand this idea of a choice. Joshua was the new leader of God's people. They had traveled all the way from Egypt and were finally ready to take their first steps into the promised land. Almighty God laid before them a path that he wanted them to follow—one that began with a crucial choice or, actually, two choices.

The first choice set before his people: life or death.

The second: blessing or curse.

Let's define our terms so we really understand how important these choices were to the Israelites and how they can affect our relationship with God and others today.

A Matter of Life and Death

The Hebrew word translated *life* in this passage carries with it the idea of movement.[1] In other words, things that are alive are things that are moving. Specifically, they're moving toward someone or something. So the first choice we have is to move toward God and toward others. When we do that, we add life to our relationships.

Think about a couple you know who have a great marriage. Almost always you will notice that they *take steps* to move toward each other—not just physically but emotionally. They choose to do things together. They choose to walk together toward a goal or interest or area they like.

Choosing life, then, means getting busy in moving toward the Lord or others. But there's the other side of this choice in the Deuteronomy passage as well. We can also choose death.

Interestingly, the word translated *death* also carries with it the concept of movement—in fact, its literal meaning is "to step away."[2] The idea is that death is stepping away from others, from life, from what we have built or shared with others.

Let's go back to our example of the couple. As a marriage counselor, time and again I've seen one spouse (or both) take a *step away* from the other when challenges come up. When they do this, something starts dying in their relationship. The more they move away from each other, the more problematic their marriage becomes.

So that's the life-or-death choice when it comes to relationships. At any given juncture we make the choice to move toward the other person, choosing life in that relationship, or to step away, choosing death.

To Bless or to Curse

To understand the second choice set before God's people in Joshua's time and in ours today—the blessing and the curse—let's take another look at the Hebrew words. For they also imply two very different paths we can choose to take with the Lord and with others.

The first idea contained in the Hebrew word for *bless* is that of "bowing the knee."[3] (Genesis 24:11 actually uses this word to describe a camel who must bend its knees so its master can get on.) Bowing before someone is a graphic picture of valuing that person.

Most Americans have never actually seen one person bow before another. But in biblical times (and in many cultures today), you bowed before someone of great value—a king, a queen, a prophet, someone considered important and of high worth. When you bless someone, in other words, you are really saying, "I choose to treat you as someone incredibly valuable in my life." Of course, when we say, "Bless the Lord!" we're saying that as well: "Lord, you are so incredibly valuable, you're worthy of our 'bowing the knee' before you."

Along with this first picture comes a second biblical word picture. The word for *bless* (and a similar word, for *honor*) also carries the idea of adding weight or value to someone.[4] Literally, it's a picture of adding coins to a scale. In biblical times, you didn't just hand someone a coin with a specific denomination stamped on it as we do today. In Old Testament times, a coin might carry an inscription or even a picture of a ruler or someone of great value. But the way you determined how much it was worth was to put it on a scale. The greater the weight, the higher the value.

Let's put those two pictures together now to gain a sharper focus on what it means to bless someone. You are basically saying, "You are of such great value to me, I choose to add to your life." And as you'll soon see, there are five specific actions you can take (the five elements of the Blessing) to do just that for another person.

But what about the opposite choice—the curse? In understanding the word picture behind this word, I think you'll see it's a choice that many continue to make today. It's not just a Stephen King scenario, an occult choice that belongs in horror movies. Any of us can make the choice to curse others instead of blessing them.

We do that when we subtract the things that would add life for the other person.

The word for *curse* in this passage literally means a "trickle" or "muddy stream" caused by a dam or obstruction upstream.[5] For Joshua's people, living in desert lands, cutting off water meant cutting off life itself. So do you get the terrible word picture here? When we curse someone, we are choosing to "dam up the stream" on life-giving actions and words that could flow down to that person.

Think of a desert dweller in biblical times who walks for miles to find a life-giving stream, only to get there and find a muddy trickle because someone dammed up the stream. But now picture someone choosing to break down the dam—choosing to add what was missing, bringing life where there had been death.

A beautiful example of this is found in John 4, when Jesus sat down with the woman at the well. We'll look at the story in detail in a later chapter, but let's take a quick peek now. This woman was more or less an outcast in her town—married five times, now living out of wedlock with a sixth man. She came to draw water in the heat of the day, when no one else was around, probably avoiding the other women in the village. And she's a Samaritan, looked down on by all Jews. So many aspects of her life acted to dam up the flow of blessing in her life—by that definition, she's cursed.

But do you remember what Jesus offered this woman? He offered her "living water" (John 4:10–15). And that's because God is the one who can break down all the things in our lives that curse us, slowing the flow of what we need to a trickle. It is he who blesses us with a flow of living water.

In Deuteronomy 23:5, God put it this way: "The LORD your God would not listen to Balaam [someone hired by the Hebrews' enemies to curse them], but the LORD your God turned the curse into a blessing for you, because the LORD your God loves you."

That's God's choice, of course, but the choice to bless or curse others is ours as well. We are told in the book of Proverbs that "death and life are in the power of the tongue" (Prov. 18:21). So it is with the blessing, and so it is in a terribly negative way when we choose the curse.

It's our choice then—yours and mine.

Will we choose life and move toward others, or choose death and step away?

Will we choose to bless our loved ones and the Lord by bowing our knee and weighing our scales in their favor—opening our lives to God's blessing in the process? Or will we choose to curse them by blocking the flow of good things in our own lives and others'?

If you are ready to choose life and blessing, let's be even more specific about those five elements of the Blessing that biblical parents gave and that children today—children of all ages—long for as well.

Pictures Your Heart Remembers

Think back in your life story. Whether you were young or older, who was someone who unexpectedly gave you the Blessing at a time and place and with words that meant a great deal to you? It could be someone you were related to or even a casual acquaintance. Again, what was meaningful to you about that experience? (Remember the unexpected way John received his grandfather's blessing in this chapter.)

Now think back in your life story again. Was there a time, when you were young or even as an adult, where someone cursed you? What impact did that person's words have on you and your life? Did they change how you viewed yourself, the Lord, or others? Take a few moments with the Lord to let him "reverse the curse."

No matter what was spoken over you, *he* gets to determine who you are. And to *him* you are everything. You are valuable enough to die for, valuable enough to fight for. You are his son, his daughter, his beloved. Write down some truths about who he says you are. If you are struggling to find some, start with Psalm 103.

Blessing Group Questions

As you start your group time, have somebody read Deuteronomy 30:19. If possible, read it in the New American Standard version. (If you don't have a Bible, a great place to go is www.BlueLetterBible. org. You can type in verses there and even pick what version of the Bible you'd like to read it in.) Let's go through the choice with two parts that was set before God's people in this verse.

1. Life = movement. How does God get us moving toward him, and others, when his life invades us?
2. Death = stepping away. Was there a time when someone very important to you "stepped away" from you? Not necessarily in death, but did this person choose to step away from you relationally?
3. Blessing = bowing the knee and giving someone a coin, because they are so valuable. Imagine someone handing you a Blessing Coin—who is the first person who comes to mind? What was it like to feel that someone saw great value in you and chose to add to your life?
4. Curse = to dam up the stream. What is so difficult about being in a place where you are cut off from "living water"? Have you had someone curse you? What did that do to your heart, mind, dreams, relationship, and so on? What did that do to you physically?

5. When we choose life in Jesus (who *is* life), he gets us moving toward others and blessing them. Take time in your group to do something incredibly powerful: declare or "plant a flag in the ground" on this day and say, "Lord, give me the strength and wisdom to step toward, not away, to value and to add, not subtract."

Part 2

The Five Elements
of the Blessing

Chapter 6

Our First Look at the Five Elements of the Blessing

What exactly does it mean to give a blessing? What actions and attitudes combine to make this biblical tool so uniquely effective?

The Blessing as described in Scripture always included five elements:

1. Appropriate meaningful touch
2. A spoken or written message
3. Attaching high value to the one being blessed
4. Picturing a special future for him or her
5. An active, genuine commitment to fulfill the Blessing

Let's take a quick look at each of these before exploring them all in greater depth. And know this. By giving and modeling these five elements, you are laying the foundation for a relationally intelligent child, one who can connect with others and God because at least one person was crazy about him or her.

Appropriate Meaningful Touch

Appropriate meaningful touch was an essential element in bestowing the Blessing in Old Testament homes. So it was with Isaac when he went to bless his son. We read in Genesis 27:26 that Isaac said, "Come near now and kiss me, my son." This incident was not an isolated one. Each time a blessing was given in the Scriptures, an appropriate meaningful touch provided a caring background to the words that would be spoken. Kissing, hugging, or the laying on of hands were all a part of bestowing a blessing.

Appropriate meaningful touch has many beneficial effects. As we will see in the next chapter, the act of touch is key in communicating warmth, personal acceptance, affirmation, even physical health. For any person who wishes to bless a child, spouse, or friend, touch is an integral part of that blessing.

A Spoken or Written Message

The second element of the Blessing involves a spoken or written message—one that is actually put into words. In many homes today such words of love and acceptance are seldom received. Parents in these homes assume that simply being present communicates a blessing—a tragic misconception. A blessing fulfills its purpose only when it is actually verbalized—spoken in person, written down, or preferably both.

For a child in search of the Blessing, silence mostly communicates confusion. Children who are left to fill in the blanks when it comes to what their parents think about them will often fail the test when it comes to feeling valuable and secure. Spoken or written words at least give the child an indication that he or she is worthy of some attention. I learned this lesson on the football field.

When I began playing football in high school, one particular coach thought I was filled with raw talent (emphasis on *raw*!). He was constantly chewing me out, and he even took extra time after practice to point out mistakes I was making.

After I missed an important block in practice one day (a frequent occurrence), this coach stood one inch from my face mask and chewed me out six ways from Sunday. When he finally finished, he had me go over to the sidelines with the other players who were not a part of the scrimmage.

Standing next to me was a third-string player who rarely got into the game. I can remember leaning over to him and saying, "Boy, I wish he would get off my case."

"Don't say that," my teammate replied. "At least he's talking to you. If he ever *stops* talking to you, that means he's given up on you."

Many adults we see in counseling interpret their parents' silence in exactly that same way. They feel as though they were third-string children to their parents. Their parents may have provided a roof over their heads (or even a Porsche to drive), but without actual words of blessing, they were left unsure of how much they were valued and accepted.

Abraham spoke his blessing to his son Isaac. Isaac spoke a blessing to his son Jacob. Jacob gave a verbal blessing to each of his twelve sons and to two of his grandchildren. When God blessed us with the gift of his Son, it was his *Word* that "became flesh and dwelt among us" (John 1:14). God has always been a God of words.

"But I don't yell at my children or cut them down like some parents," some may say. Unfortunately, the lack of negative words will not necessarily translate into a verbal blessing. We will see this lack illustrated through several painful examples in a later chapter.

To see the Blessing bloom and grow in the life of a child, spouse, or friend, we need to verbalize our message. Good intentions aside, good *words*—spoken, written, and preferably both—are necessary to communicate genuine acceptance.

Attaching High Value

Appropriate meaningful touch and a spoken (or written) message—these first two elements lead up to the content of the words themselves. To convey the Blessing, the words must attach high value to the person being blessed.

In blessing Jacob (thinking it was Esau), Isaac said, "Surely, the smell of my son is like the smell of a field which the LORD has blessed. . . . Let peoples serve you, and nations bow down to you" (Gen. 27:27, 29).

That pictures a very valuable person! Not just anybody merits having nations bow down to him! And while we might think that calling a person a field would be criticizing him, that is not the case. A *blessed* field was one where there was tremendous growth and life and reward. Just ask a farm kid what a record crop, all ready to harvest, means to his or her parents. That's the picture Isaac gives his son.

As you may have noticed, Isaac used a word picture (the field) to describe how valuable his son was to him. Word pictures are a powerful way of communicating acceptance. Later we will look at the use of these word pictures and learn how to use them in giving a blessing. In the Old Testament they were a key to communicating to a child, spouse, or friend a message of high value—the third element of the family blessing.

Picturing a Special Future

A fourth element of the Blessing is the way it pictures a special future for the person being blessed. Isaac said to his son Jacob, "May God give you of the dew of heaven, of the fatness of the earth. . . . Let peoples serve you, and nations bow down to you" (Gen. 27:28–29).

The blessing was a unique, powerful opportunity for a parent, grandparent, or loved one to speak about the potential of another and how that person could indeed experience a special future. Isaac believed that of his son when he blessed him. We should communicate to our children or loved ones the same idea—that we see something special God has placed in their future.

One distinction should be made between Isaac's blessing and the act of picturing a special future for a person today. Because of Isaac's unique position as a patriarch (God's appointed leader and a father of the nation of Israel), his words to Jacob carried with them the weight of biblical prophecy. We cannot predict another person's future with such biblical accuracy today. But we can help those we are blessing see a future that is full of light and opportunity. We can let them know we believe they can build an outstanding life and future with the strengths and abilities God has given them.

As we will see in a later chapter, our Lord himself speaks quite eloquently about our future in the Bible. In fact, he goes to great lengths to assure us of our present relationship with him and of the ocean full of blessings in store for us as his children.

We need to picture just such a special future for our children if we are serious about giving them our blessing. With this fourth element of the Blessing, a child can gain a sense of security in the present and grow in confidence to serve God and others in the future.

An Active, Genuine Commitment

The last element of the Blessing concerns the responsibility that goes with giving the Blessing. For the patriarchs, not only their words but God himself stood behind the blessing they bestowed on their children. Several times God spoke directly through the angel of the Lord to the patriarchs, confirming his active, genuine commitment to their family line.

Parents today, in particular, need to rely on the Lord to give them the strength and staying power to confirm their children's blessing by expressing such an active, genuine commitment. They, too, have God's Word through the Scriptures as a guide, plus the power of the indwelling Holy Spirit.

Why is active, genuine commitment so important when it comes to bestowing the Blessing? Words alone cannot communicate the Blessing; they need to be backed with a willingness to do everything possible to help the one blessed be successful. We can tell a child, "You have the talent to be a very good pianist." But if we neglect to provide a piano for that child to practice on, our lack of commitment has undermined our message.

When it comes to spending time together or helping develop a certain skill, some children hear, "Wait until the weekend." Then it becomes "Wait until *another* weekend" so many times that they no longer believe the words of blessing.

The fifth element of the Blessing, an active, genuine commitment, is crucial to communicating the Blessing in our homes.

At Home with the Family Blessing

That's a brief overview of the five elements of the Blessing that can become a life-changing part of how we *do* family. Provide the five basic ingredients of the Blessing—appropriate meaningful touch, a spoken (or written) message, attaching high value to the one being blessed, picturing a special future for him or her, and confirming the Blessing by an active, genuine commitment—and personal acceptance can thrive in a home.

Our aim now is to become very practical as we look more closely at each of the five key elements of the Blessing. For each element you will be prompted to look back at the path you walked with your own parents and ask, "Did I receive this element of the Blessing?" Then a little later you will be prompted to consider the path you are walking with your child today and ask, "Am I giving this element of the Blessing to my child?" Both questions, as we go through each of these five elements, can provide a powerful, thought-provoking look at where you have been, where you are today, and where you can go as you accept the challenge of making the Blessing part of your family life.

If you are a little unclear right now as to why these five elements are so significant, get ready for the light to be turned up brighter on this biblical path . . . starting with our look at each child's need for appropriate meaningful touch.

Chapter 7

The First Element: Appropriate Meaningful Touch

Isabel was a sensitive young woman—and a seriously ill one, suffering greatly in the diabetic/medical-surgical unit. She was in so much pain that she cried regularly to the nursing staff, pleading for more frequent painkiller injections. Yet the medicine therapy she was on and her own physical condition precluded her from receiving the shots when she wanted them. The risk for further infection and internal bleeding was simply too great. Finally, after Isabel had badgered the nurses on every shift, the senior nurse in charge went to talk to her.

Nurse Ida Heath was a thirty-year veteran of the wards and a reserved, capable teacher. She explained to Isabel, logically and practically, the potential dangers of giving her injections whenever she asked for them. She also assured Isabel that the nurses were trying to protect her, not harm her, by limiting her injections. Isabel listened intently and even nodded, understanding.

Her mission accomplished, Nurse Heath was preparing to

leave when Isabel stopped her. "If I can't have my shot . . . *can you give me a hug?*"

Not thinking she had heard right, the nurse asked, "Excuse me?"

Isabel repeated, "Could you give me a hug for the pain . . . *please?*"

Caught off guard, the stately nurse said, "Well, okay," and put an arm around Isabel's shoulder. But then, it was as if God spoke to her and said, "For goodness' sake, Ida, that's not what she asked for!" So Nurse Heath put both arms around Isabel and gave her a big hug.

Isabel burst into tears.

"All this time I thought the nurses hated me. I'm just hurting so badly. Whenever I need a pain shot, can I call you and get a hug instead?"

Nurse Heath assured Isabel she could get her hug whenever she needed it. She even wrote it down on her medical Kardex, in the medication section: "Pain hugs for Isabel, upon request."

Isabel died a few months later at the age of thirty-four. But before her death, whenever she was admitted to a different ward in the hospital or when the nights became too long, she would call Nurse Heath for her pain hug.

A hug can't wipe away all our pain, but it can help. And while appropriate meaningful touch can't chase away all our fears and insecurities, it can help with many of them.

A little four-year-old girl became frightened late one night during a thunderstorm. After one particularly loud clap of thunder, she jumped up from her bed, ran down the hall, and burst into her parents' room. Jumping right in the middle of the bed, she sought out her parents' arms for comfort and assurance.

"Don't worry, honey," her father said, trying to calm her fears. "The Lord will protect you." The little girl snuggled closer to her father and said, "I know that, Daddy, but right now I need someone with skin on!"

The honesty of some children! This little one did not doubt her heavenly Father's ability to protect her, but she was also aware that he had given her an earthly father she could run to, someone whom God had entrusted with a special gift that could bring her comfort, security, and personal acceptance—the blessing of appropriate meaningful touch.

This little girl was fortunate. Her father was willing to share this important aspect of the Blessing with his daughter. Not all children are as fortunate. Even in caring homes, most parents, particularly fathers, will stop touching their children once they reach the grade-school years.[1] When they do that, an important part of their blessing stops as well.

Holding and hugging a four-year-old is permissible in most homes. But what about the need a fourteen-year-old has to be meaningfully touched by his mother or father (even if the teenager outwardly cringes every time she or he is hugged)? What about a thirty-four-year-old—or a spouse or close friend?

We all need appropriate meaningful touch and suffer when we are deprived of it. However, children are particularly affected by the absence of touch. Sometimes it can so affect a child that he or she spends a lifetime reaching out for arms that will never embrace him or her.

"I wish . . . I wish . . ." Lisa had slumped down in her chair, hugging herself and rocking back and forth as she repeated these words. Lisa was a new adolescent patient in the psychiatric ward where I was an intern. Whenever she felt afraid or sad, she would wrap her arms around herself and rock back and forth.

We found that Lisa had behaved this way since she was seven years old. That was when her mother abandoned her at an orphanage.

Lisa was trying to escape her hurt and pain by *holding herself.* She had no one else to hold her; all she had was the wish that her

THE FIRST ELEMENT: APPROPRIATE MEANINGFUL TOUCH

mother would return. She needed appropriate meaningful touch so much that she would wrap her arms around herself and try to hug away the hurt.

The Blessing: Appropriate Meaningful Touch

In the Scriptures, touch played an important part in the bestowal of the family blessing. When Isaac blessed Jacob, an embrace and a kiss were involved. We read, "Then his father Isaac said to him, 'Please come close and kiss me, my son'" (Gen. 27:26 NASB).

The Hebrew word for "come close" is very descriptive. It is used of armies drawn together in battle. It is even used to picture the overlapping scales on a crocodile's skin.[2] It may have been a while since you last saw a battle or a crocodile, but these word pictures still call up in our minds a picture of a very close connection.

Isaac wasn't asking his son to give him an "Aunt Ethel hug." (Remember Aunt Ethel—the one who pinched your cheek, then bent over and repeatedly patted you on the back when she hugged you?) Free from the current taboos our culture sets on a man embracing his son, Isaac was calling Jacob close to give him a bear hug.

For fathers in North America, there is a strong correlation between the age of a son and whether his father will touch him.[3] Yet Isaac's grown son was at least *forty years old* when he said, "Come close and kiss me, my son."[4]

Children of all ages need appropriate meaningful touch, particularly from a father. Studies have showed that mothers touch their children in more nurturing ways and fathers in more playful ways. But when the children were interviewed, they perceived their fathers' touch as more nurturing—perhaps because it didn't happen as often.[5]

61

As we have seen with Lisa, our need for appropriate meaningful touch does not go away when we enter grade school. Isaac didn't set up barriers around the need to be touched. He was a model that parents, husbands and wives, and even friends at church need to follow in giving the Blessing.

I deeply appreciate my mother's commitment to meaningfully touch us when we were children even though I did not always value it at the time.

As a single parent, Mom had to work full-time to support three hungry, healthy boys. In the morning she would get us all up and get herself ready. Then we would all pile in the car so she could take us off to school and herself to work. While her taxi service saved us the long walk, there was one thing about it that my twin brother and I hated. Before we were allowed to get out of the car, we had to give Mom a hug.

As you can imagine, hugging your mom in front of all your school friends was not top on the list of two aspiring football players. In fact, each year we would make our mother drop us farther and farther from school—just in case someone saw us hugging her. But she never stopped. Her pattern of hugging us was absolutely dependable, even when we would respond with "Oh, Mom!" or "I can't stand it!" I can remember only one time when it didn't happen, and it got me in major trouble.

On that particular morning, we were all in a rush to get the day launched. We were eager to get to school to shoot some hoops before the morning bell, and Mom had a major presentation at work. Distracted by her busy day, she let us all out of the car without forcing us to give her a hug.

As she drove away, Jeff and I just looked at each other. She hadn't even *mentioned* hugging us—and I instantly thought the worst.

"She must know something," I told Jeff. "I *know* she knows something!"

Unfortunately, at the time there were a number of things she could have found out that could have resulted in our being grounded until we were in our midthirties.

All day we brooded over what our mother might have discovered that made her so angry she had chosen not to hug us. Finally the day was over, and we all sat around the dinner table. Dinnertime at our house was normally filled with enthusiastic conversation, but that night there was dead silence as we waited for the storm to break. While Jeff could have waited all night, the quiet quickly got to me. I broke down and blurted out, "Okay, Mom. We're sorry. I can't believe you found out, but we are *really* sorry."

I wasn't ready for the confused look that came across my mother's face.

"What are you talking about, John?" she asked.

"Well, this morning," I told her. "When we got out of the car . . . you know . . . you didn't hug us!"

Laughing, she said, "Oh, I'm sorry. I guess I was so busy thinking about the presentation I had to make, I just forgot." Then her smile vanished. "But what was it you were confessing to?"

As Jeff glared at me, I realized I had just gotten us both in big trouble—all because I had missed the hug I always hated.

Though I could always count on my mother's touch, the opposite was true of my father. With him, I could rely on touch being off-limits. When my brothers and I finally began a relationship with him after nearly fifteen years of his absence, it was obvious that appropriate meaningful touch wasn't something he was comfortable with.

During my easily embarrassed teenage years, that was all right with me. But as the years went on, I found myself wishing for at least one hug from my father. At my wedding. Or when our daughter Kari was born. Or when Laura, our second "gift" and blessing, arrived. Or at Christmastime. Or anytime.

I did hold his hand on a few occasions—when he was so seriously ill he couldn't object. And each of those times stands out like a beacon—a memory of closeness that was pushed away from me anytime he had the strength.

Another Touching Scene

In the Scriptures, we find another clear example of including appropriate meaningful touch in bestowing the Blessing. This time the blessing involved a grandfather who wanted to make sure his grandchildren received this special gift of personal experience. Let's look in on the "touching" scene:

> Joseph said to his father, "They are my sons, whom God has given me in this place." And he said, "Please bring them to me, and I will bless them." Now the eyes of Israel were dim with age, so that he could not see. Then Joseph brought them near him, and he kissed them and embraced them. . . .
>
> Then Israel stretched out his right hand and laid it on Ephraim's head . . . and his left hand on Manasseh's head. (Gen. 48:9–10, 14)

Jacob (whose name had been changed to Israel) not only kissed his grandchildren and held them close, but he also placed his hands on each grandson's head.[6] This practice of laying on of hands was an important part of many of the religious rituals for the biblical patriarchs.

There are at least two important reasons why placing our hands on someone as a part of the Blessing is so special. First, there is a symbolic meaning attached to touching, and second, there are tremendous physical benefits to the laying on of hands.

The Symbolic Meaning
Pictured by Touching

In the Old Testament, the symbolic picture of the laying on of hands was important. This touch presented a graphic picture of transferring power or blessing from one person to another.[7]

For example, in the book of Leviticus, Aaron was instructed to use this practice in his priestly duties. On the Day of Atonement, he was to place his hands on the head of a goat that was then sent into the wilderness. This picture is of Aaron symbolically transferring the sins of Israel onto that animal. (It is also a prophetic picture of how Christ, like that spotless animal, would take on our sins at the cross.) In another example, Elijah passed along his role as God's prophet to Elisha by the laying on of hands.

Even today the symbolic meaning of touch is powerful. While we may not be consciously aware of it, the way we touch can carry tremendous symbolic meaning.

A young woman holding hands with a new boyfriend can signal "I'm taken" to other would-be suitors. Two businesspeople shaking hands can signify that an important deal has been completed. A minister at a wedding says to a couple, "If you then have freely and lawfully chosen one another as husband and wife, please *join hands* as you repeat these vows."

There are many times when we don't need to say a word to someone to say we love them. Just an act of touch can break through or break down a barrier. I saw this in a story on the network television program *20/20* when it chronicled the story of two Vietnamese children, presumed orphans, who had been evacuated when Saigon fell in 1975. Shelling from the advancing North Vietnamese army had separated this five-year-old boy and four-year-old girl from their parents, and everyone assumed the parents were dead. Actually the children's mother and father were alive, desperately searching for them. But nobody knew that, so the children were taken to the United States as orphans.

They grew up in loving American homes, with caring adoptive parents. The boy joined the United States Army and became a second lieutenant. His sister married and became the mother of three children. They kept in touch over the years, and in high school they began the painstaking research that eventually led them to discover their parents were alive after all.

Decades after the war, with relationships beginning to soften between Vietnam and the United States, the two children were finally granted visas to return and be reunited with their parents and the brothers and sisters they had never seen. Cameramen for *20/20* accompanied them, and the emotion captured by the cameramen was incredible.

Half a world separated this family—along with a terrible war, more than twenty years, and now even language. Yet they still had one thing in common. When they saw each other for the first time, they ran and fell into each other's arms with sobs, hugs, and kisses that said, in a language they all understood, "We love you. . . . We missed you. . . . We're so glad you're home."

They may have needed a translator to talk with each other in *words*, but as they sat and held hands, they clearly communicated the warmth and love that even a war couldn't kill.

The Physical Power of Touch

While important symbolism accompanies our touch, it is not the only reason God made it a part of the Blessing. Appropriate meaningful touch also communicates blessing on a very basic, physical level.

For one thing, over one-third of our five million touch receptors are centered in our hands![8]

Interestingly enough, the act of laying on of hands, associated with the biblical blessing, has more recently become the focus of a great deal of secular interest and research. Dr. Dolores Krieger, a professor of nursing at New York University, has done numerous studies on the effects of laying on of hands. What she found is that both the toucher and the one being touched receive a psychological benefit from this practice.[9]

How is that possible? Inside our bodies is hemoglobin, the pigment of the red blood cells, which carries oxygen to the tissues. Repeatedly, Dr. Krieger has found that hemoglobin levels in *both* people's bloodstreams go up during the act of laying on of hands. As hemoglobin levels are invigorated, body tissues receive more oxygen. This increase of oxygen energizes a person and can even aid in the regenerative process if he or she is ill.

We are sure that Ephraim and Manasseh were not thinking, *Wow, our hemoglobin levels are going up!* when their grandfather laid his hands on them. However, one of the things that certainly stayed with them as they looked back on their day of blessing was the old patriarch's gentle touch.

Hugs and kisses were also a part of appropriate meaningful touching pictured in the Scriptures. Let's look further at the physical benefits of touching and the deep emotional needs that can be met by this first element of the family blessing.

How would you like to lower your husband's or wife's blood pressure? Protect your grade-school child from being involved in an immoral relationship later in life? Even add up to two years to your own life? (Almost sounds like an insurance commercial, doesn't it?) Actually, these are all findings in studies on the incredible power to bless found in appropriate meaningful touching.

More Reasons Why Appropriate Meaningful Touch Blesses Us Physically

Every day, researchers are discovering more and more information about the importance of touch. If we are serious about being a source of blessing to others, we must consider putting these important points into practice. As we saw in the studies of the laying on of hands, a number of physical changes take place when we reach out and touch.

A study at UCLA found, for example, that men and women need eight to ten meaningful touches a day just to maintain emotional and physical health. Gary shared this information once at a marriage seminar. And as he was talking, he noticed a man in the second row reach over and begin patting his wife on the shoulder and counting, "One, two, three . . ." That is *not* what the study meant by meaningful touch.[10]

The UCLA researchers defined meaningful touch as a gentle touch, stroke, kiss, or hug given by significant people in our lives (a husband or wife, parent, close friend, and so on). They even estimated that if some type-A, driven men would hug their wives several times each day, they could increase their life spans by almost two years (not to mention the way it would improve their marriages)!

Obviously, we can physically bless those around us (and even ourselves) with appropriate meaningful touch. But touching does much more than that.

Do you have a newborn in your home? Newborns make tremendous gains if provided with appropriate meaningful touch—and may be at risk if they aren't.

Researchers at the University of Miami Medical School's Touch Research Institute began giving premature babies forty-five minutes of massage each day. Within ten days, the massaged babies showed

47 percent greater weight gain than those children who were not regularly touched.[11] A second study showed that actual bone growth of young children who had been deprived of parental touching was half that of children who received adequate physical attention.[12]

And in groundbreaking studies, Dr. Schanberg and Dr. Butler at Duke University Medical School found that without maternal touch, rat pups do not produce a type of protein crucial to their growth and development. When these rat pups were separated and unable to feel their mother's touch, they responded by slowly shutting down production of an enzyme crucial to the development of major organs. As soon as the pups were reunited with their mother, however, enzyme production returned to normal.[13]

Even the smallest act of touch can help a child who is unable to move. One group of physically handicapped children were placed on a smooth surface (like smooth Naugahyde) and a second group on a highly textured surface (like a rubber floor mat). EMG studies showed marked differences between the two groups, including increases in muscle tone simply from placing children on a textured surface.[14]

You can't get away from it. Overwhelming evidence shows that physical touch benefits and blesses children (and animals). But how about adults?

Are your parents getting up in years? Appropriate meaningful touch can be an important part of maintaining health and positive attitude in older persons. In a practice that has become commonplace now, residents in nursing homes were brought together with pets from a neighboring animal shelter. At first it was thought to be just a good recreational activity. Upon further study, more significant results began to surface. Those residents who had a pet to touch and hold not only lived longer than those without a pet; they also had a more positive attitude about life![15]

Elderly patients with more serious problems have also demonstrated a number of tremendous benefits from regular, appropriate meaningful touch. For those suffering with dementia, a regimen of regular meaningful touch significantly increased their nutritional intake, helping them gain needed weight.[16] In addition, with Alzheimer's patients, physical touch decreased strange movements and repetitive mannerisms such as picking up objects again and again.[17]

But perhaps the most powerful data to come out of research on aging concerns the ways touch may actually help preserve a healthy person's brain as it ages. Robert M. Stapolsky of Stanford University found that even a small amount of extra physical stimulation soon after birth made a lasting effect on rats' brains. Appropriate meaningful touch in infancy caused the rats' brains to put a brake on the development of glucocorticoids, stress hormones that are "a disaster to have in the bloodstream." As a result, when these rats became old, they didn't lose any of the 10 to 20 percent of memory-critical gray matter that older rats, monkeys, and humans normally tend to lose.[18]

While appropriate meaningful touch may not be the "fountain of youth," it certainly does provide a clear stream of physical benefits for young and old alike. And what's more, people who regularly give and receive meaningful touch consistently feel better about themselves and have higher self-worth.[19]

Appropriate Meaningful Touch
Blesses Our Relationships

An interesting study done at Purdue University demonstrates how important touch is in determining how we view someone else. Librarians at the school were asked by researchers to alternately touch and not touch the hands of students as they handed back their library cards. The experimenters then interviewed the students. Do you know what they found? You guessed it. Those who had been touched reported far greater positive feelings about both the library and the librarian than those who were not touched.[20]

A doctor I know, a noted neurosurgeon, did his own study on the effects of brief times of touch. With half his patients in the hospital, he would sit on their beds and touch them on the arm or leg when he came in to see how they were doing. With his remaining patients, he would simply stand near the bed to conduct his interview of how they were feeling.

Before the patients went home from the hospital, the nurses gave each patient a short questionnaire evaluating the treatment they received. They were especially asked to comment on the amount of time they felt the doctor had spent with them. While in actuality he had spent the same amount of time in each patient's room, those people he had come near and touched felt he had been in their room nearly twice as long as those he had not touched.

Other studies have shown similar results in very different circumstances. For example, airline passengers who were touched "accidentally" by flight attendants on a long-distance flight rated those attendants as more qualified, the airline as more professional, and the plane trip *safer* than those who were not touched.[21]

Come on, Trent, you may be thinking. *Do you really mean that a touch lasting a few seconds or less can help me build better relationships?* Actually, we hope you can touch your loved ones much more than that, but even small acts of touch can indeed leave a lasting impression.

Touching a child on the shoulder when he or she walks in front of you, holding hands with your spouse while you wait in line, stopping for a moment to ruffle someone's hair—all these small acts can change how you are viewed by others and even how they view themselves. A ten-minute bear hug is not the only way to give another person the Blessing. At times, the *smallest* act of touch can be a vehicle to communicating love and personal acceptance.

A freelance reporter from the *New York Times* once interviewed movie icon Marilyn Monroe. The reporter was aware of Marilyn's painful past and the fact that during her early years Marilyn had been shuffled from one foster home to another. The reporter asked Marilyn, "Did you ever feel loved by any of the foster families with whom you lived?"

"Once," Marilyn replied, "when I was about seven or eight. The woman I was living with was putting on makeup, and I was watching her. She was in a happy mood, so she reached over and patted my cheeks with her rouge puff. . . . For that moment, I felt loved by her."[22]

Marilyn Monroe had tears in her eyes when she remembered this event. Why? The touch lasted only a few seconds, and it happened years before. It was even done in a casual, playful way, not in an attempt to communicate great warmth or meaning. But as small an act as it was, it was like pouring buckets of love and security on the parched life of a little girl starved for affection.

Parents, in particular, need to know that neglecting to meaningfully touch their children starves them of genuine acceptance—so much so that it can drive them into the arms of someone else who is all too willing to touch them. Analyzing why some young people are drawn to cults, one author writes, "Cults and related movements offer a new family. They provide the follower with new people to worry about him, to offer him advice, to cry with him, and importantly, to hold him and touch him. Those can be unbeatable attractions."[23]

They certainly can, especially if appropriate meaningful touch has not been a part of the blessing a child receives. Even if a child is not lured into a cult to make up for years of touch deprivation, he or she can be drawn into the arms of an immoral relationship.

Women who repeatedly have unwanted pregnancies have told researchers that their sexual activity is merely a way of satisfying yearnings to be touched and held. Dr. Marc Hollender, a noted psychiatrist, interviewed scores of women who have had three or more unwanted pregnancies. Overwhelmingly, these women said that they were "consciously aware that sexual activity was a price to be paid for being cuddled and held." Touching before intercourse was more pleasurable than intercourse itself, "which was merely something to be tolerated."[24]

Touch from both a mother and father is important. If you are a single parent, your choice to provide appropriate touch is hugely important as well. Appropriate meaningful touching can protect a child from looking to meet this need in all the wrong places.

If we ignore the physical and emotional needs our children, spouse, or close friends have for appropriate meaningful touch, we deny them an important part of the Blessing. What's more, we shatter a biblical guideline that our Lord Jesus himself set in blessing others.

Jesus and the Blessing of Appropriate Meaningful Touch

Jesus was a model of someone who communicated the Blessing to others. In fact, his blessing of children in the Gospels parallels the important elements of the family blessing, including appropriate meaningful touch. Let's look at Mark's account of that blessing.

Then they brought little children to Him, that He might touch them; but the disciples rebuked those who brought them. But when Jesus saw it, He was greatly displeased and said to them, "Let the little children come to Me, and do not forbid them;

THE FIVE ELEMENTS OF THE BLESSING

> for of such is the kingdom of God. . . ." And He took them up
> in His arms, laid His hands on them, and blessed them. (Mark
> 10:13–14, 16)

Appropriate meaningful touching was certainly a part of
Christ's blessing as Mark described it. Mobbed by onlookers and
protected by his disciples, Jesus could have easily waved to the
children from a distance or just ignored them altogether. But he
did neither. Jesus would not even settle for the politicians' "chuck
under the chin" routine; he "took them up in His arms, laid His
hands on them, and blessed them."

In this moment, Jesus was not simply communicating a spiritual lesson to the crowds. He could have done that by simply placing
one child in the center of the group as he did on another occasion
(Matt. 18:2). Here, Jesus was demonstrating his knowledge of the
genuine importance of touch to a child.

For children, things become real when they are touched. Have you
ever been to Disneyland and seen the look on little ones' faces when
they come face to face with a person dressed like Goofy or Donald
Duck? Even if they are initially fearful, soon they will want to reach
out and touch the Disney character. This same principle allows
children to stand in line for hours to see Santa Claus—the same
children who normally can't stand still for five minutes.

Jesus was a master of communicating love and personal acceptance. He did so when he blessed and held these little children. But
another time his sensitivity to the importance of touch played itself
out more dramatically, when Jesus chose to touch a man who was
barred by law from ever touching anyone again:

> And a leper came to Jesus, beseeching Him and falling on his
> knees before Him, and saying, "If You are willing, You can make
> me clean."

Moved with compassion, *Jesus stretched out His hand and touched him*, and said to him, "I am willing; be cleansed." Immediately the leprosy left him and he was cleansed. (Mark 1:40–42 NASB, italics added)

In Jesus' day, to touch a leper was unthinkable. Fear banished them from society, and people would not get within a stone's throw of them. In fact, they would throw stones at them if they did come close.[25] A parallel passage in Luke tells us that this man was "covered with leprosy." With their open sores covered by dirty bandages, lepers were the last people anyone would want to touch. Yet the first thing Christ did when he met this man, even before he spoke to him, was to reach out his hand and *touch* him.

Can you imagine what that scene must have looked like? Think how this man must have longed for someone to touch him, not throw stones at him to drive him away. And remember, Jesus could have healed him first and then touched him. But recognizing his deepest need, Jesus stretched out his hand even before he spoke words of physical and spiritual healing.

I know of one person who could understand the pain of not being touched. Her name was Dorothy, and she spent years of her life longing for meaningful touch.

I learned about Dorothy through a speech teacher at a large university, a man in his early sixties who is an outstanding Christian. For nearly twenty-five years, this man had been a source of encouragement to students inside and outside of class. Many young men and women have trusted Christ as their Savior through his quiet modeling of godly principles. However, what changed Dorothy's life was neither his ability to communicate nor his stirring class lectures, but one act of touch.

During the first day of an introductory speech class, this teacher was going around the room, having the students introduce themselves. Each student was to respond to the questions "What do I like about myself?" and "What don't I like about myself?"

Nearly hiding at the back of the room was Dorothy. Her long red hair hung down around her face, almost obscuring it from view. When it was Dorothy's turn to introduce herself, there was only silence in the room. Thinking perhaps she had not heard the question, the teacher moved his chair over near hers and gently repeated the question. Again, there was only silence.

Finally, with a deep sigh, Dorothy sat up in her chair, pulled back her hair, and in the process revealed her face. Covering nearly all of one side of her face was a large, irregularly shaped birthmark—nearly as red as her hair.

"That," she said, "should show you what I don't like about myself."

Moved with compassion, this godly professor did something he had never done before in a classroom. Prompted by God's Spirit, he gently touched her birthmark and said, "That's okay. God and I still think you're beautiful."

Dorothy cried uncontrollably for almost twenty minutes. Soon other students had gathered around her and were offering their comfort as well. When she finally could talk, dabbing the tears from her eyes, she said to the professor, "I've wanted so much for someone to say what you said. Why couldn't my parents do that? My mother won't even touch my face."

Dorothy, just like the leper in Christ's time, had a layer of inner pain trapped beneath the outward scars. This one act of appropriate meaningful touching began to heal years of heartache and loneliness for Dorothy and opened the door that drew her to the Savior.

We know that for many people, appropriate meaningful touch simply wasn't a natural part of growing up. For me (John), growing up in Arizona, the cultural norm was, "It's okay to hug your horse, but not your kids!"

Wherever you live across the United States, you may not come from a warm, affectionate background. Sociologist Sidney Jourand studied the touch behavior of pairs of people in coffee shops around the world. The difference between cultures was staggering. In San Juan, Puerto Rico, people touched on average 180 times per hour. In Paris, France, it was 110 times per hour. In Gainesville, Florida, 2 times per hour. And in London, England, 0 times per hour.[26]

We Americans aren't known as a country of huggers, and with all the media reports of child abuse and sexual misconduct, we have backed away from touch even more. We need to realize, however, that avoiding healthy, appropriate meaningful touch sacrifices physical and emotional health in our lives and the lives of our loved ones.

If we want to be people who give the Blessing to others, one thing is clear. Just like Isaac, Jacob, Jesus, and even the professor, we must include appropriate meaningful touch in our contacts with loved ones. This element of the Blessing can lay the groundwork for the second key aspect of the Blessing—a message that is put into words.

Pictures Your Heart Remembers

Make sure you think through both sides of this issue of appropriate meaningful touch for yourself. Write down a picture of touch that you carry that's encouraging to you, and then a picture you carry that may be painful or challenging.

If you find that there is still a lot of pain in the *hard* pictures, continue to press forward. Let the Lord into that pain, and ask him to help the wounds begin to heal and to give you a *new* picture of the healing power of touch.

Blessing Group Questions

1. What's a memory that you have of appropriate meaningful touch?
2. Think about a time in your life, in history, or in sports where you saw an act of appropriate meaningful touch stand out? (E.g., think about Pee Wee Reese of the Dodgers walking over to second base and putting his arm around Jackie Robinson.)
3. What are some examples where Jesus used touch to heal, bless, encourage, and so on?
4. What are some ways that you have seen the power of touch be used to heal? What are some ways that you've seen the power of touch cause harm?
5. Is this element a personal struggle for you? Is it hard for you to show appropriate meaningful touch to others in your life? Why or why not?
6. Is there an act of touch that you have received, or missed, that you feel is blocking you from blessing others?

Chapter 8

The Second Element: A Spoken or Written Message

Words have incredible power to build us up or tear us down emotionally. This is particularly true when it comes to giving or gaining family approval. Many people can clearly remember words of praise their parents spoke years ago. Others can remember negative words they heard—and what their parents were wearing when they spoke them!

We should not be surprised, then, that the family blessing hinges on being a *verbalized* message. Abraham *spoke* a blessing to Isaac. Isaac *spoke* it to his son Jacob. Jacob *spoke* it to each of his twelve sons and to two of his grandchildren. Esau was so excited when he was called in to receive his blessing because, after years of waiting, he would finally *hear* the blessing. Later, the apostle Paul wrote eloquent words of blessing to growing churches all over the Roman Empire.

In the Scriptures, a blessing is not a blessing unless it is put into words and actually communicated.

The Power of Words

If you are a parent, your children desperately need to receive *words* of blessing from you. If you are married, your wife or husband needs to receive *words* of love and acceptance on a regular basis. This very week with a friend, a coworker, or someone at your church, you will rub shoulders with someone who needs to receive *words* of encouragement.

Throughout the Scriptures, we find a keen recognition of the power and importance of words. In the very beginning, God spoke and the world came into being (Gen. 1:3). When he sent us his Son to communicate his love and complete his plan of salvation, it was his *Word* that "became flesh and dwelt among us" (John 1:14). God has always been a God who communicates his blessing through words.

In the book of James three word pictures grab our attention and point out the power and importance of words. All three illustrate the ability the tongue (the primary conveyer of words) has to build up or break down relationships, the ability to bless or to curse.

First, the tongue is pictured as a "bit" used to direct a horse (James 3:3). If you control a horse's mouth by means of a small bit, the entire animal will move in the direction you choose. (We have ridden a few horses that seem to be exceptions, but the general rule is certainly true.) The second picture illustrates this same principle in a different way. Here a "small rudder" is used to turn a great ship (3:4). These analogies point out the way words can direct and control a person or a relationship.

Parents, spouses, or friends can use this power of the tongue for good. They can steer a child away from trouble or provide guidance to a friend who is making an important decision. They can minister words of encouragement or lift up words of praise. But this power can also be misused, sometimes with tragic results.

That is what the third word picture shows us. It illustrates all too clearly that words can burn deeply into a person's life, often setting the course that person's future will take. Listen to the awesome power a verbalized message can have: "The tongue is a small part of the body, and yet it boasts of great things. See how great a forest is set aflame by such a small fire! And the tongue is a fire, the very world of iniquity . . . and sets on fire the *course of our life*" (James 3:5–6 NASB, italics added).

Just like a forest fire, what we say to others can burn deeply into their hearts. In fact, I once saw a living picture of the darkness that can result from fiery words.

I first met Lynda on a blistering summer's day in Arizona. The temperature outside was over 105 degrees, and most people wore shorts or cool cotton clothing—but not Lynda. A tall, attractive twenty-year-old, she had on a heavy, long-sleeved *black* dress. In Arizona, people avoid wearing black during the summer because it soaks up the already scorching heat. Yet in talking with her in counseling over several weeks, I found out that summer or winter, day or night, black was the only color Lynda would wear.

Lynda grew up with a cruel, abusive father who was addicted to alcohol and horror movies. As early as age five, Lynda was forced to stay in the family room and watch gruesome films. Her father would laugh hysterically when she cried in fear. As the years passed, he continued exposing her to other aspects of the occult. He finally died when Lynda was in high school, and the horror stopped . . . in part.

As Lynda and I talked, I realized it wasn't the pictures of terror that had covered Lynda's heart with such darkness. They were terrible without question. But it was her father's *words* that had done the most damage to her. For of all the hurtful things he did, what haunted her most was his favorite nickname for her. It came right out of his horror films: "demon daughter." That nickname burned its way into her heart and even affected the way she dressed on a searing summer day.

In the Scriptures there is tremendous power in a name. Before Moses went to Egypt to confront Pharaoh, he asked to know God's name. God changed Abram's name to Abraham, "father of many nations." Jesus changed Simon's name to Peter, a "rock." But leave it to an angry, evil father to change Lynda's name to one that represented darkness and death.

Thankfully, the ending to Lynda's story is one of great hope, not hurt. Through counseling and a loving church, she came to know Christ personally and traded in her old nickname for a new one: "child of God." As Jesus promised in the book of Revelation, "I will write on him [believers] the name of My God. . . . My *new* name" (3:12, italics added). God's love broke through to Lynda's heart in a dramatic way. Today, Lynda is married to a devoted Christian man, wears a radiant smile, and has a wardrobe full of beautiful, pastel-colored clothes.

Perhaps you still stumble over hurtful words your parents, spouse, or a close friend once conveyed to you (or negative words you have communicated to yourself), words that come to memory time and again and point you in a direction in life you don't want to go. If so, don't lose hope. As you learn more about the Blessing, you can begin to receive and give words that can lead to a new course of life.

Each of us should be keenly aware of the power of our words. We should also be aware of how powerful the *absence* of such words can be.

Today's Most Common Choice: "I'll Tell Them Tomorrow"

In homes like Lynda's, negative words can shatter children emotionally rather than shape them positively. But that is not the most common choice of parents. Most parents genuinely love their children and want the best for them. However, when it comes to sharing words of love and acceptance—words of blessing—they are up against an even more formidable foe than the temptation to communicate negative words.

A thief is loose in many homes today who masquerades as *fulfillment, accomplishment,* and *success.* This thief steals the precious gift of genuine acceptance from our children and leaves confusion and emptiness in its place. The villain's real name is *overactivity,* and it can keep parents so busy that the Blessing is never shared, even with parents who dearly love their children; as one woman said, "Who has the time to stop and *tell* them?"

In many homes today both parents are working overtime, and a family night makes an appearance about as often as Halley's Comet. The result is, instead of Dad and Mom taking the time to communicate words of blessing, a babysitter named *silence* is left to mold a child's self-perception. Life is so hectic that, for many parents, that "just right" time to share a verbal blessing never quite comes around. What is the result?

A father tries to corner his son to communicate "how he feels about him" before he goes away to college, but now his son is too busy to listen.

A mother tries to communicate words of blessing to her daughter in the bride's room just before the wedding, but the photographer has to take her away to get that perfect shot.

Words of blessing should start in the delivery room and continue throughout life. Yet the "lack of time" and the thief's motto, "I'll have time to tell them tomorrow," rob the children of a needed blessing today.

"Oh, it's not that big a deal," you may say. "They know I love them and that they're special without my having to say it." Really? We wish that explanation worked with many of the people we counsel. To them, their parents' silence has communicated something far different from love and acceptance.

Let's look at what commonly happens in homes where words of blessing are withheld. What we will see is that silence *does* communicate a message. Like an eloquent speech, it, too, can set a course for a person's life—but it's not the path most parents would like their children to take.

What Happens When We Withhold Words of Blessing

Both people and relationships suffer in the absence of words of love, encouragement, and support—words of blessing. Take marriage, for example.

Dr. Howard Hendricks, who was a noted Christian educator, liked to tell the story of a couple who had been married more than twenty years, but whose problems had become so acute they were now considering a divorce. Dr. Hendricks asked the husband, "When was the last time you told your wife you loved her?" The man glared at him, crossed his arms, and said, "I told my wife I loved her on our wedding day, and it stands until I revoke it!"

Take a guess what was destroying that marriage. When words of blessing are withheld in a marriage, unmet needs for security and acceptance act like sulfuric acid and eat away at a relationship.

Not only marriages, but individuals—and particularly children—suffer from the lack of a verbal blessing. Without words of love, acceptance, and encouragement, children often grow up traveling one of two roads that lead to unhealthy extremes.

The Road of Overachievement

Dan grew up in a home where nothing positive was ever said. In fact, little of *anything* was ever said. His parents seemed too busy with their careers or too preoccupied with constantly remodeling the house to do much talking. There came, however, an exception to the general rule of verbal indifference when Dan was just a boy.

At the end of one semester in grade school, Dan received an excellent report card with nearly all As. For the first time in his memory, his parents openly praised him. At last, he felt like somebody.

Like a starving man who stumbles across a loaf of bread, Dan thought he had learned the key to hearing words of acceptance: overachieve. To him, it was worth the hours spent inside studying (with the neighbor kids playing right outside his window) just to hear a few words of affirmation at the end of each semester.

This working to overachieve lasted right through college and beyond, taking his motivation to "show them I'm somebody" right into the marketplace. He quickly found a job and became a *perfect* junior executive—which translated means he was a committed workaholic, always driven to achieve more and more, regardless of the personal or relationship costs.

Why the intense drive and the insatiable need to achieve? Just look back at Dan's home, where words of blessing were given only for spectacular achievement. Dan would never admit it (though inside he always knew), but pulling into his parents' driveway in a new car said he was still somebody—didn't it? Getting that corner office would show them—wouldn't it?

Dan had fallen into the trap many men and women do who never received the Blessing. Like Moses' fading glory, Dan's accomplishments could not provide his missing sense of personal acceptance—at least not for long. Dan was forever having to make one more deal, sell one more product, attend one more motivational seminar. Unsaid words of love and acceptance in his early life made him a driven man.

Dan finally did come to grips with missing out on the Blessing and learned to find a little more balance in his life. Until then, however, his search for personal acceptance kept him on the barren road to workaholism and overachievement.

The Road of Withdrawal

Dan's type of drivenness is one common response to missing out on words of blessing. But many people head in the opposite direction. Convinced they can do nothing to hear words of love and acceptance, they give up and travel down the road of apathy, depression, and withdrawal—where a terrifying, yet beckoning, cliff awaits.

A classic example of a child who took this road is found in a film that circulated a few decades ago. As the movie begins, we see several children waiting for their school bus. The sun is out on a cold January morning. Snow covers the rural countryside like a beautiful white blanket.

All bundled up for winter weather, a few of the children are making snowballs and throwing them at a fence. Others laugh and talk and stomp their feet to stay warm. All except Cliff.

Standing by himself at the edge of the group, Cliff stares down at the ground. In the next few moments, you almost get the feeling that Cliff is invisible. Several other children run right by him in excited conversation; others crowd around him when the bus finally comes. But Cliff never looks up, and the other children never speak to him or acknowledge his existence.

Children rush to get on the school bus first. Glad to be in out of the cold, the children happily take their seats—that is, all except

Cliff. The last one on the bus, he wearily mounts the steps as if climbing each one requires a monumental effort. He stops briefly and looks up expectantly into the faces of the other children, but no one beckons him to join them. Heaving a sigh, he slumps into a seat behind the driver.

There is a whoosh of compressed air from the bus's hydraulic system. The door slams shut. With one look behind him to make sure everything is in order, the driver pulls slowly away from the curb and onto the country lane.

They have traveled only a few miles when suddenly Cliff drops his books and staggers to his feet. Standing next to the bus driver, steadying himself on a metal pole, the boy has a wild and distant look in his eyes. Shocked by Cliff's sudden ill appearance, the bus driver asks, "Are you all right? Are you sick or something? Kid, what's the matter?" Cliff never answers, and half out of frustration, half out of concern, the bus driver pulls over to the side of the road and opens the door.

Cliff begins to walk down the steps of the bus, then pitches forward and crumples into the snow. The opening scene ends with the driver standing over Cliff's prone body, trying to figure out what has happened. As the camera pulls away, we hear an ambulance siren begin to whine in the distance, but somehow you know its coming will be too late.

This scene is from the hard-to-find but excellent educational film *A Cipher in the Snow*, a film that is designed for teachers but speaks to anyone concerned about giving the Blessing to others. It is based on a true story of a young boy who actually died on the way to school one day and the resulting confusion over the reasons.

Medical records indicated no history of problems in either Cliff or his family. Even the autopsy shed no light on his death. Only after an interested teacher looked into his school and family background were the reasons for his death discovered.

This teacher found that Cliff's life had been systematically erased like a blackboard. In his first few years at school, he had done well, up until problems began at home. His parents' marriage had disintegrated, and a new, preoccupied stepfather never had time or interest to fill any of the missing gaps. Resentful of any attention his new wife gave Cliff, the stepfather would limit their time together. His mother loved Cliff dearly, but soon she was either too busy or too intimidated by her new husband to give the boy any attention at all. Like someone pushed away from a seat near the fireplace, Cliff was now left with only the cold ache of indifference.

As a reaction to his homelife, Cliff's schoolwork began to suffer. Homework assignments were turned in late or not at all. Tired of his apparent apathy, his teachers gave up on him and left him to work alone. Cliff also began to withdraw from the other children at school, and he lost the few friends he once had. He would not begin a conversation, and soon other children wouldn't bother to try. Slowly but surely, he retreated into a world of silence.

In only a few months everything and everyone of value to Cliff had either been lost or taken from him. With no place of shelter and no words of encouragement, he felt like a cipher—an empty zero. This sensitive child was unable to stand the pain for long.

Cliff was not killed by an infirmity or a wound. He was killed by the lack of spoken love and acceptance. Cliff withstood the painful silence as long as he could. Ultimately, however, the lack of a spoken blessing from family and friends acted like a deadly cancer. After months of pursuing its course, it finally ate away his will to live. He died a cipher in the snow, believing he was totally alone and unwanted.

Words Matter

Are words or their absence *really* that powerful? Solomon thought so. His words are like ice water in our faces, shocking us into reality: "Death and life are in the power of the tongue" (Prov. 18:21).

If we struggle with communicating words of love and acceptance to our families or friends, another proverb should encourage us. Again, it is Solomon writing: "Do not withhold good from those to whom it is due, when it is in the power of your hand to do so. Do not say . . . 'Go, and come back, and tomorrow I will give it,' when you have it with you" (Prov. 3:27–28).

If we can open our mouths to talk, we have the ability to communicate the Blessing through spoken words. As we will see, writing out words of blessing can be equally powerful, especially when spoken words aren't possible. In fact, written words of blessing have their own special advantage in that they can be composed more carefully and deliberately and can be kept and reread.

Why Is It So Hard to Express Words of Blessing?

The damage of withholding words of blessing should be obvious in the examples of Lynda, Dan, and Cliff. But if words of love and acceptance are so important, why are they offered so infrequently? Here are a few reasons we have gathered from people we have counseled:

- "I don't want to inflate my child's ego."
- "I'm afraid if I praise them, they'll take advantage of me and won't finish their work."

- "Communication is too much like work. I work all day, then she expects me to work all night talking to her."
- "I just don't know what to say."
- "They know I love them without my having to say it."
- "If I get started, I'll have to make a habit of it."

Then there's our personal favorite:

- "Telling children their good points is like putting on perfume. A little is okay, but put on too much, and it stinks."

As far as we are concerned, it's that statement that stinks. And none of those explanations come anywhere close to the real reason many people hesitate to bless their children or others with words of love and acceptance.

The real reason most people withhold this part of the Blessing is that their parents never gave it to them.

The Danger of Family Rules

Both praise and criticism seem to trickle down through generations. That means if you never heard words of love and acceptance, you can expect to struggle with sharing them yourself. Why? It's as if your family had a rule that loving words were best left unsaid, and you may find it very difficult to break this rule.

Every family operates by certain rules, spoken or unspoken, that prescribe "the way our family does things." Some families have a rule that "people who know anything about anything" open Christmas presents on Christmas *morning*. Other families follow the rule that "truly civilized people" open Christmas presents on Christmas *Eve*. (Cindy just groaned when we wrote this!) Conflicting family rules often meet in a marriage. Many an argument has gone fifteen rounds to see whose family rule will win out in a new marriage.

Families set all kinds of rules: what we will eat in this family and what we won't eat. What television programs we can watch and which are dull or off-limits. What is safe to talk about and what subjects should never be brought up. Whom we invite over to the house and who doesn't get an invitation.

In some cases family rules can be very helpful. For example, families can adopt biblical rules like not letting the sun go down on anger and being kind one to another. Another way of setting positive family rules is by using contracts that can help build communication and encourage children.[1] These types of family guidelines can be safely passed down generation after generation.

But not all family rules are worth retaining. In fact, some can devastate a family. Like words cast in steel, a destructive family rule can hammer away at a family from parent to son or daughter. The process will continue from generation to generation until at last someone breaks this painful pattern—someone like Claire.

When Claire was growing up, a simple plaque hung in the family room. The plaque had belonged to Claire's grandfather and had become a kind of unspoken family motto. The plaque was not impressive looking, and it carried only two hand-painted words: *Stand Up*. Just two words—yet these two words had written volumes of hurt into three generations of Claire's family.

The words had originally been part of a longer sentence, a motto that went something like this: "Don't take anything off anyone. Stand up and fight." This may have been a helpful frontier slogan, but it did nothing but damage personal relationships in Claire's family.

Just look at Claire's father, who had been infected with the never-give-an-inch attitude of *his* father. "I'm sorry" or "You're right" were not in the vocabulary of someone who based his life on the words *stand up and fight*. Also absent were any words that were not useful in a fight—words such as *I love you*. *Will you forgive me?* and *You're important to me*. While following this never-give-an-inch family rule pushed Claire's father ahead in business, it pushed him back into a corner with his wife and children.

Claire's mother and father fought constantly, each an expert on the other's faults, neither willing to give an inch in an argument. When each of Claire's four brothers and sisters grew old enough to dislike taking orders from their father, they joined the battle too. Soon there were seven people under the same roof following the family rule of Stand Up and Fight and its corollary principles, Fight for My Rights and Death Before Saying I'm Sorry. This situation persisted until Claire became a Christian.

Claire went away to a Life camp and trusted Christ as her Lord and Savior. The first thing she noticed when she came back home was that plaque: Stand Up. She thought about how Jesus had laid down his life and how tired she was of following this family rule. Little by little and at the painful cost of constant ridicule from her brothers and sisters, Claire began to break several family rules.

Right in the middle of a fight, for instance, Claire would say, "I'm sorry; you're right. Would you forgive me?" and end the argument. She even began saying, "Love you, Mom; love you, Dad" and then giving her parents a hug as she left for school.

Claire's father had never gotten the Blessing from his parents, only a plaque that almost destroyed his marriage and family. But over the next two years, he received the Blessing from Claire. Appropriate meaningful touch, words of high value, the picture of a future filled with hope, and the commitment to love him no matter the cost—all these were relationship tools that chipped away at the existing family structure.

Family rules die hard, but they can be broken. Claire's younger sister was so taken with Claire's changed life that she also trusted Christ. Soon Claire's older brother followed, and the plaque on the wall was beginning to shake. Last Christmas, as a baby Christian, her father took down the plaque.

What a testimony to God's power to break even the most difficult family rule. And what a help to Claire's family to have a new family rule to follow. They are now free to speak up and share words of blessing with each other—because of one child's courage to go to battle with a hurtful rule and dare to speak words of blessing.

Putting Words of Blessing into Practice

We put words of blessing into practice in our homes and relationships by deciding to speak up rather than clam up. Good intentions aside, good words are needed to bestow the Blessing on a child, spouse, or friend.

Note that we are not simply saying, "*Talk more* to your children or others." While talking is normally a good idea, sometimes if you don't know how to communicate in a positive way, you can say less by saying more. As we will see in the next chapter, it is not just *any* words but words of high value that attach themselves to a person and communicate the Blessing. These are the kinds of words you often hear in the final hours before a family reunion ends.

Almost all of us have had the opportunity to attend a family reunion. A common phenomenon at these gatherings is that during the first two days, everyone is busy talking up a storm about this recipe, that football team, this book they've read, or that movie to attend. But something happens the last afternoon of the reunion. Suddenly, with only an hour left before family members say their goodbyes, meaningful words will begin to be spoken.

A brother will say in private to his sister, "I know things will work out in your marriage. I'll be praying for you." An aunt will say to her niece, "You've always made me proud. I know school is hard, but I also know you can do it. I believe in you." Or a daughter will say to a parent, "Look around you, Mom. We didn't turn out half bad, did we? We have you and Dad to thank."

So often, we seem to need the pressure of time before we say things closest to our hearts. But when it comes to your children, your spouse, your close friends, even your parents, it may be later than you think. In some relationships, it is already late afternoon in your opportunity to talk to those you love.

In 1985, a tragic plane crash in Japan took the lives of more than five hundred people. The four people who survived the crash told authorities and reporters the story of their doomed flight. For the last thirty-four minutes, the plane flew erratically, without a rear tail stabilizer to control their descent, and this half hour was a time of panic and horror for all on board. Some passengers cried in fear. Others took the time to don life jackets. But one middle-aged Japanese man, Hirotsugu Kawaguchi, took his last few moments to write a note to his family. Rescuers at the wreckage site found the note on his body, and it finally made its way to his wife and three children.

Listen to the last words of this man who deeply loved his family. They picture his desire for his wife and children to have a special future, even now that they would be physically separated in this life.

I'm very sad, but I'm sure I won't make it. The plane is rolling around and descending rapidly. There was something like an explosion that has triggered smoke. . . . Ysuyoshi [his oldest son], I'm counting on you. You and the other children be good to each other, and work hard. Remember to help your mother. . . . Keiko [his wife], please take good care of yourself and the children. To think our dinner last night was our last. I am grateful for the truly happy life I have enjoyed.[2]

Hirotsugu Kawaguchi died when the plane crashed. His wife and children no longer have him to hold and love. But they do have his final words to them, words that pictured his hopes for their future, words that will echo in their lives in a positive way in the years to come.

Ask any family who has watched a son or daughter go off to war. We hang on to words from them. We long to get our words of love and prayers for their safety to them. Words carry the Blessing, and in the next chapter, you can learn about the kind of words—words of high value—that can especially bless people.

But don't delay. Time passes so quickly. Please don't let that important person leave your life without receiving the second element of the Blessing—the spoken (or written) word.

Pictures Your Heart Remembers

Kari and I want you to capture some words that, whether they were spoken to you or not, can reflect your strengths. To do this, here is a list:

- Takes charge
- Competitive
- Goal-driven
- Enjoys challenges
- Visionary
- Motivator
- Very verbal

- Optimistic
- Loyal
- Has deep relationships
- Adaptable
- Good listener
- Discerning
- Predictable
- Persistent
- Scheduled

Go through that list and circle the terms that sound like you. Feel free to add words as well. Whether someone has spoken them over you or not, read them to your group, and know that Almighty God is speaking them over you.

Blessing Group Questions

1. Was there a time in your life where you missed the opportunity to hear a spoken message? Or to give one?
2. Can you overbless people with your words?
3. Did your family have a spoken or unspoken rule about using verbal words to encourage?
4. The key passage we saw about the Blessing said it was choosing life over death. We are also told in Scripture that life and death are in the power of the tongue. How easy is it for you to speak life into someone?
5. How easy is it for you to say words that would cause someone to step away?
6. Are there some words, spoken or unspoken, that you feel are blocking you from blessing others?

Chapter 9

The Third Element:
Attaching High Value

Hannah's parents had tried unsuccessfully for years to have children. Perhaps that is one reason why their joy was unbounded when they learned that they were expecting their first child. Everything seemed fine during the pregnancy and delivery . . . until they saw the doctor's reaction. When Hannah was given to them for the first time, they saw that her left arm had never developed below the elbow.

There were tears in the delivery room and deep concern as test after test was performed on Hannah. As doctors and specialists sought to determine the extent of her physical problems, Hannah's parents wondered how to handle the anxious questions from relatives and friends.

Two days later the doctors told Hannah's parents some encouraging news. In all their tests, they had not detected any other problems. With the exception of her left arm, Hannah appeared to be a normal, healthy baby girl.

After the doctors had gone, Hannah's parents bowed together in prayer. They thanked God that their daughter had no other serious problems. But they prayed something else that would prove to be of tremendous benefit to their daughter. In that hospital room, with Hannah nestled in her mother's arms, her parents prayed that their love for her would make up for any physical disabilities she possessed. They decided that morning that they would encourage Hannah to become all that God would have her be, in spite of the problems they and Hannah would have to face along the way.

Years have gone by since Hannah's parents prayed for her in that hospital room, and their prayer has been answered in many ways. Hannah went through high school with honors and attended a major university. Even today, something special about Hannah draws your attention away from her empty sleeve, particularly when you listen to her play a beautiful melody on the piano— with only one hand.

Hannah has faced tremendous obstacles in her life: the stares, giggles, and tactless questions from her peers in grade school; the fears and uncomfortable feelings of whether to go to a dance in junior high; the questions and worry that perhaps she would never date in high school or college—just to name a few. However, despite the real struggles of being born with a handicap, Hannah received a precious and powerful gift from her parents: the security of knowing she was highly valued and unconditionally accepted.

"My parents didn't try to hide from me the fact that I was different," Hannah told us. "They have been very realistic with me. But I always knew, and they have told me over and over that I am their 'greatest claim to fame.' Whether I was trying out for softball or my dad was teaching me how to drive, they have been my biggest fans. They have prayed for me and thought the best, even when I've pouted and gotten angry at God because of my handicap. Without question, my parents deserve a lot of credit for helping me accomplish the things I have."

They certainly do deserve credit for deciding, in spite of a physical loss, to value their daughter as whole and complete. Hannah's parents are realists. They have never sugarcoated the very real problem their daughter has faced. But all her life, they have communicated the Blessing to her by showering her with appropriate meaningful touch and words of high value and unconditional acceptance.

Words of High Value

What do we mean by "high value"? Let's look at the word *value* to see the part it plays in the Blessing.

To value something means to attach great importance to it. This is at the very heart of the concept of blessing. As you saw in chapter 6, the root word for *blessing* carries the dual meaning of "bow the knee" and to "add value." In relationship to God the word came to mean "to adore with bended knees."[1] Bowing before someone is a graphic picture of valuing that person.

Notice the important principle here: anytime we bless someone, we are attaching high value to him or her. Let's illustrate this by an example Gary liked to share when his children were young.

In my life, I want God to be of utmost value to me. He is my best friend and the source of my life. If I were to chart this on a 1-to-10 scale, I would value the Lord at a 10, of highest value. Right beneath my relationship with the Lord would come my relationship with Norma, my wife. Humanly speaking, she is my best friend, and I love and value her right beneath my love for the Lord—maybe a 9.5. Then come my children. I love each of them dearly, and while neither they nor Norma are aware that I love them at different levels, I would value them at about a 9.4, right behind Norma. I do not love them less, but in attaching value to them, they come right behind my relationship with my Lord and with my wife.

Emotionally there are times with the kids when my feelings might drop to a 6.4 or even a 4.2—particularly if we are camping in our mini mobile home and it has been raining all week. But, because I want to love and value them at a 9.4, I continually try to push their value back where it belongs. The same thing is true with Norma. I don't want to hurt or devalue her in any way. That is why, if I do offend her, I immediately decide to raise her value to just beneath where I value the Lord.

How does the idea of choosing to raise a person's value—even in challenging circumstances—apply to the Blessing?

It bears repeating that when we bless someone, we are deciding—choosing—to hold on to the fact that he or she is of high value. That is what the psalmist was telling us in Psalm 103:1 when he said, "Bless the LORD, O my soul; and all that is within me, bless His holy name!" When we "bless the Lord," we are actually recognizing God's intrinsic worth and attaching high value to him. We are saying that he is worthy of our bowing the knee to him.[2]

In the Scriptures we are often called on to bless or value the Lord, but the Scriptures also give many examples of humans blessing other humans (Deut. 33:1–2; Josh. 14:13; 2 Sam. 6:18; and others). When they did so, each was attaching high value to the person he was blessing, recognizing him or her as a very special individual.

This is exactly what the patriarchs in the Old Testament were doing when they extended the family blessing to their children—attaching high value to them. We do the same when we bless our children, spouses, or friends. This concept of valuing another person is so important that we believe it can be found at the heart of every healthy relationship. Every person needs the Blessing to feel truly loved and secure about himself or herself.

Words of High Value in Old Testament Homes

In the Old Testament, shining threads of love and value run through the fabric of a blessing. Remember Isaac's word picture, "Surely, the smell of my son is like the smell of a field which the LORD has blessed" (Gen. 27:27)? But Jacob understood exactly what his father meant by that. So can you if you remember driving through the country when hay or wheat has been harvested recently. Particularly with the morning dew on the ground, or after a rain shower, the smell of a newly cut field is as fresh and refreshing as a mountain spring.

Isaac also pictured his son as someone whom other people, including his own family, should greatly respect. "Let peoples serve you," he said, "and nations bow down to you" (v. 29).

In the United States today, no premium is placed on physically bowing before dignitaries. About the only people who know how to bow anymore are actors and orchestra conductors. Most of us would have to practice for hours to properly bow if we were going to meet a visiting king or queen. In Isaac's day, however, bowing was a mark of respect and honor, something that was expected in the presence of an important person.

We can't miss the idea in these two pictures of praise that Isaac thought his son was very valuable, someone who had great worth. This message is exactly what modern-day children need to hear from their parents. It's what Hannah heard from her parents, the message that caused her life to blossom and grow in spite of her physical deformity.

The Key to Communicating Value

Telling children they are valuable can be difficult for many parents, especially if the parents never heard such words when they were young. Besides, as we saw in a previous chapter, that just-right time to say such important words can get crowded out by the urgent demands of a busy schedule.

Some children do hear the obligatory "I love you" during holidays or at the airport, but it seems stiff and out of place.

Other children (like Dan in chapter 8) may hear an occasional word of praise, but only if they perform well on a task. When words of value are only linked to a child's efforts to obtain a blessing, the child retains a nagging uncertainty about whether he or she ever really received it. If his or her performance ever drops even a small amount, that child may ask and ask again, "Am I loved for who I am or only for what I can do?"

We need to find a better way to communicate a message of high value and acceptance, a way to express a person's valuable qualities and character traits apart from his or her performance. Hidden inside the family blessing is a key to communicating such feelings to our children, spouses, friends, or church families, a key that we can perfect with only a little practice and that even gets around the walls a defensive adult or child can set up. This key is found in the way word pictures are used throughout the Scriptures. In fact, word pictures are so powerful that we wrote an entire book about them called *The Language of Love*. You can find more help on word pictures or learn more about the book at EncouragingWords.com.

The Power of a Picture

We may not be aware of it, but we use word pictures all the time. Let me give you one example that I (John) remember vividly.

I was at lunch some time ago with a close friend in Dallas, Texas. We were eating at a quaint little basement restaurant where you walk down a steep flight of steps to reach the front door. The hostess seated us, and from our table we had a view of the stairs leading down to the restaurant.

While we waited for our meal, we noticed at the top of the stairs a little girl of about two. She was holding the hand of someone we could not completely see. In fact, all we could see were two huge tennis shoes and a massive hand that totally engulfed the little girl's. As these two came down the stairs, we were able to see more and more of this very large man helping his little daughter down the steps.

When they reached the foot of the stairs and the door to the restaurant opened, in walked a football player for the Dallas Cowboys. At six feet four and 265 pounds, this huge defensive tackle took up nearly the whole doorway. As he and his daughter walked by our table (the ground shaking and plates rattling as he passed), my friend leaned over to me and said, "Boy, what a moose!"

Calling this man a moose is using a word picture. Hall of Fame tackle Randy White does not have antlers and fur, and while he is very large as far as human beings go, he does not outweigh even a baby moose. Yet when my friend pictured him as a moose (out of his hearing, of course), I instantly understood: a very large individual was walking by our table!

Most of us do this all the time. We use word pictures to convey an emotional feeling apart from the literal meaning of the words. For instance, we may take a much-needed vacation "once in a blue moon," especially if we are busy. If we find something to be extremely easy or simple, we might refer to it as "a piece of cake." We even tell our boss that we "feel under the weather" if we've come down with a cold. Obviously these word pictures do not refer to the fact that the moon is currently blue or that our task involves a literal piece of cake or that we are trapped underneath the weather.

Positive or negative, word pictures are a useful communication tool because they are vivid and easy for most people to understand. They have an emotional impact that ordinary words may lack. That's why word pictures are so effective in giving a blessing.

We can see this clearly in the blessing Jacob used with three of his sons. Each is a beautiful example of how this communication tool can be used to attach high value to a child.

Jacob picked a different word picture for each of his sons to bestow the blessing on them. We read, "And this is what their father said to them when he blessed them. He blessed them, every one with the blessing appropriate to him" (Gen. 49:28 NASB).

"Judah is a lion's [cub] . . . and as a lion, who dares rouse him up?" (Gen. 49:9 NASB).

Judah was depicted as a lion's cub. In the Scriptures a lion portrayed strength, and the lion was also a symbol of royalty in the ancient Near East.[3] Judah's leadership qualities and strength of character were illustrated by this picture.

"Naphtali is a doe let loose, he gives beautiful words" (Gen. 49:21 NASB).

Jacob pictured Naphtali as a doe. The grace and beauty of this gentle animal were used to show the artistic qualities this son possessed. He was the one who spoke and wrote beautiful words.

"Joseph is a fruitful bough, a fruitful bough by a spring" (Gen. 49:22 NASB).

Joseph was described as a fruitful bough by a spring. This word picture illustrated how Joseph's unfailing trust in the Lord allowed him to provide a place of refuge for his family. Jacob's word picture carries a similar message to one used first of Jesus in Psalm 1:3: "He will be like a tree firmly planted by streams of water, which yields its fruit in its season and its leaf does not wither; and in whatever he does, he prospers" (NASB).

Each of Jacob's sons was an individual, and each of them received a blessing that depicted his value to his father in the form of a word picture he could remember always. It's an example we would do well to follow when we give the Blessing. But before we rush off to call our child or spouse a lion, doe, or fruitful bough, we need to learn a little more about word pictures.

To do so, let's turn to a book in the Old Testament that is filled with them. While this book pictures a marriage relationship, the same principles can be used in giving children—or anyone else—the Blessing. Let's look in on how this couple communicated words of love, acceptance, and praise. In doing so, we will discover four keys to communicating high value.

Word Pictures: Four Keys to Communicating High Value

In the Song of Solomon, God's picture of an ideal courtship and marriage, a loving couple praise each other using word pictures more than eighty times in eight short chapters. That's a lot! But they had a lot they wanted to communicate about how highly they valued each other and their relationship.

Let's begin our examination of how they used these descriptive words with each other by looking in on their wedding night. Not often is someone's wedding night written up for posterity, but this one is worth remembering. It is a vivid record of a loving, godly relationship.[4]

Seven times (the biblical number of perfection) Solomon praised his bride, who was altogether beautiful to him. He began his praise of her by saying, "Behold, you are fair, my love! Behold, you are fair! You have dove's eyes behind your veil" (Song 4:1).

Key 1: Use an Everyday Object

What Solomon did with this word picture (and what wise parents do in blessing their children) was use an everyday object to capture a character trait or physical attribute of his beloved. In this case, he pictured her eyes as those of a dove. The gentle, shy, and tender nature of these creatures would be familiar to his bride. By picturing this familiar animal, Solomon was able to communicate far more meaning than he could by using words. (Words themselves are often one-dimensional, but a word picture can be multidimensional.) An added feature is that each time she saw a dove thereafter, she would be reminded of how her husband viewed her and valued her.

The parents of one young woman we know shared a similar kind of familiar word picture in blessing their daughter. Emma was born in late December, near Christmas Day. As she grew older, her parents would repeatedly say to her, "Just remember, you're God's special Christmas gift to us, a gift of great price because you're so special to us." As an illustration of their feelings, each Christmas a small package would appear next to the Christmas tree, addressed from Jesus to Emma's parents. Each year Emma would be given the honor of opening this package, which always contained her baby picture and a reminder that she was her parents' Christmas gift. Last we heard, this had been going on for more than thirty-five years and not just at Christmas.

Listen to Emma's thoughts about how this word picture has ministered to her:

There have been many times when I haven't felt very special. I can remember one time in particular. It was my thirtieth birthday, and I was struggling with growing older. When I was at my lowest point, I received a package in the mail from my parents. In the package was a brightly wrapped box, and inside was my baby picture and a note from my parents. I've always known I was special to them. But I *needed* to know I was special that day. It wasn't even Christmas, but reading again that I was their special "Christmas gift" and very special to them—even on my thirtieth birthday—filled my heart with love and warmth.

Key 2: Match the Emotional Meaning of the Trait You Are Praising with the Object You've Picked

Over and over Solomon used everyday objects that captured the emotional meaning behind the trait he wanted to praise. These objects may not be familiar to us, but they were familiar to his bride. Take, for example, his praise for his beloved just a few verses later. He looked at his bride and said, "Your neck is like the tower of David, built for an armory, on which hang a thousand bucklers, all shields of mighty men" (4:4).

Was Solomon trying to end his marriage before it began? Certainly not. Let's look at just how meaningful this analogy would have been to an insecure, blushing bride on her wedding night.

High above the old city of Jerusalem stood the Tower of David. A farmer working outside the city walls could look up from his work and see this imposing structure. What would impress him— even more than the height of this tower—was what hung from it.

Hanging on the tower during times of peace were the war shields of David's "mighty men"—King David's greatest warriors and the leaders of his armies. The sun shining off their shields would be a reassuring sight for one outside the protection of the city walls. By the same token, if that farmer looked up and saw that the shields of the mighty men had been taken off the tower, he would know it was time to hightail it inside the city walls! Danger was in the land.

Solomon comparing his bride's neck to David's tower now begins to make a little more sense. In Old Testament times a person's neck stood for his or her appearance *and* attitude. That is why the Lord would call a disobedient Israel a "stiff-necked people" (Ex. 33:5). For Solomon, the peace and security represented in David's tower provided a powerful illustration to express his love for his bride. He was praising the way she carried herself—with serenity and security.[5]

Let's look at a modern-day example to reinforce what we have discovered about this kind of word picture, something that took place in my home.

For the first four years of her life, Kari had our undivided attention. So it's understandable that there were adjustments for all of us when a precious baby named Laura came home with Cindy from the hospital.

While there were times when Kari felt envious of all the attention the new baby demanded, she still tried her best to be the perfect big sister. She would run to get a diaper for Mommy or tiptoe down the hall on those rare occasions when the baby was napping. Or she would simply sit next to Cindy when she was feeding the baby, stroking Laura's little head or holding her dainty little fingers.

Cindy noticed and appreciated our older daughter's efforts, and she wanted to find a creative way to communicate high value to Kari. She looked around for an object that would represent some of the same qualities she saw in Kari. She found it one day while they were watching television.

While feeding the baby that day, Cindy and Kari enjoyed a

National Geographic afternoon special about eagles in Alaska. The breathtaking footage included a long scene where a beautiful mother eagle helped feed, protect, and shelter her young. There was the picture that Cindy had been looking for. On a trip by a local toy store, she bought a small, inexpensive stuffed eagle and waited for a quiet time to talk with Kari.

"Sweetheart," she said, "do you remember watching that television program about the eagles?"

Instantly Kari recalled many of the details and talked about how much she liked the program.

"Well, honey, I want you to know that you remind me of that mommy eagle. You've helped take such good care of your little sister since she's come home—even when it hasn't been easy—and I want you to know how proud I am of you."

For days Kari carried that stuffed eagle around with her, never letting it out of her arms. It was the first thing I saw when I got home that night and the only stuffed animal she allowed to sleep with her at bedtime.

By using an object familiar to Kari to praise her, Cindy wisely communicated more than a simple compliment. She gave our daughter a living—or at least a stuffed—illustration of one way she was so valuable to her mother.

Key 3: Use Word Pictures to Unravel Defenses

Solomon took advantage of a third aspect of word pictures: the ability to get around the defenses of people who, for one reason or another, have a hard time hearing. This quality is something that a parent, spouse, or friend can use today. Whether we are dealing with defensive people or those who battle with insecurity, using a word picture can help us get around their resistance and communicate high value to them.

Let's look first at how a word picture can encourage an insecure person. We can see this with Solomon's bride herself, known in Song of Solomon as the Shulamite woman.

Like most young women who would unexpectedly meet a dashing young king, the Shulamite woman was insecure about her appearance. When she first met Solomon she said, "Do not look upon me, because I am dark, because the sun has tanned me" (Song 1:6). But after she had been around Solomon for only a short time, she called herself "the rose of Sharon, and the lily of the valleys" (2:1). That is quite a change of perspective! How did it happen?

It happened because Solomon's word pictures made their way around his bride's defenses. If Solomon had simply said, "You're cute," her insecurity could have thrown up a dozen reasons why this matter-of-fact statement could not be true: "Maybe his eyesight is bad." "I bet he's been hunting for three months, and I'm the first woman he's seen." "Maybe my father paid him to say that." These same kinds of reasons are used by insecure people today to ward off any compliments they hear about themselves. But word pictures have the ability to capture people's attention in spite of their defenses.

How do we know word pictures really got through to Solomon's bride in their marriage? Just look at how her attitude changed over the course of their married life.

During their courtship, she viewed their relationship with a certain insecurity and possessiveness. These feelings are evident in the way she talked about their relationship: *"My beloved is mine, and I am his"* (2:16, italics added).

As their story continued after the wedding—and as she grew more secure in his love—watch the subtle but powerful change in how she viewed their relationship. Once they were married, she told the ladies of the court, *"I am my beloved's, and my beloved is mine"* (6:3, italics added). This statement shows a little more security.

Then, as their story draws to a close, she even said, *"I am my beloved's, and his desire is toward me"* (7:10, italics added). This final statement shows a lot more security than her view of their relationship just before their wedding night.

Why? The major reason is the way word pictures of praise and great value have brought security to an insecure woman's heart. Repeatedly (more than fifty times), Solomon expressed his high value for his bride by using word pictures, and his words gradually transformed her view of herself and their relationship.

Most people will listen to a message more intently when it comes packaged in a word picture. That is one reason Jesus used word pictures to communicate both praise and condemnation through his teachings and his parables. He would talk about being the Good Shepherd who watched over the flock, the Bread of Life that would provide spiritual nourishment. By speaking in word pictures, he was able to penetrate the walls of insecurity and mistrust these people had put up, because stories and images hold a key to our hearts that simple words do not.

Jesus' extended object lessons kept his audience's attention even when some, like the Pharisees, did not really hear what he was saying. That is another advantage of word pictures. They are not just effective in getting through to an insecure person. They can also be immensely helpful in getting around the defenses of someone who, for some reason, just does not want to listen.

Gary once counseled a young couple who had been having heated arguments for a long period of time. Things had become so strained between Bill and Barb that they had even considered separating. They were angry and defensive when they walked into the office and they sat with their arms crossed, looking straight ahead. Their nonverbals were saying, "You just try and say something to change my mind. I'm walking out of this marriage."

Bill was a rugged outdoorsman who had moved his family outside the city limits so he would be close to the hunting and fishing he loved. He didn't mind the thirty-five-mile drive to work each day as long as he could live in the wilderness. At first, his wife had enjoyed joining him on his backpacking trips. But now she stayed home with their two young children, and he did all his camping alone.

Barb was a petite city girl who enjoyed socializing. With the move out of town, she was now an hour from her closest friend. The only socializing she did during the day was with two toddlers. While Barb loved her children deeply, being isolated from her friend and having a husband who hunted or fished every spare minute was leading her to become bitter and resentful.

After listening to Bill and Barb talk for more than an hour about how insensitive the other person was, Gary shared with them this word picture that opened their eyes to a completely new way of viewing each other.

"Let me close our time together by telling you two a word picture that came to my mind as I listened to you talk. Bill, I could see you as a picture, hanging on a wall, of a mighty stag with a huge rack of antlers. You are standing proudly near a mountain stream, looking over the forest, with your doe and newborn fawns in the background. The square frame around the picture is heavy and made out of antique wood.

"Barb, I see you as a painting of a delicate, beautiful wildflower with dazzling colors and fine brushstrokes. Your picture has a lovely oval mat, and the frame is narrow and classy looking, with white glossy paint.

"Both of you are beautiful pictures even though you look so different. However, you're not seeing the beauty in the other person's picture. In fact, each of you keeps trying to repaint the other picture to make it look more like your own. This week I'd like you to put down your brushes and look for the beauty that is already in the other person's painting. And let's get back together next week and talk about it."

What a difference a week can make. That one word picture

communicated volumes to this couple. Instead of trying to change each other into their own image, they actually began appreciating each other—and rediscovering the attraction that had drawn them together in the first place. Instead of dishonoring each other in anger, they began to be more patient with each other and to honor the uniqueness of the person they married. All because a word picture managed to circumvent their defenses and speak to their hearts.

Key 4: Use Word Pictures to Point Out a Person's Potential

A fourth reason for using word pictures is to illustrate the undeveloped traits of a person—qualities they may not acknowledge or even be aware of. Jesus did this in changing Simon's name to Peter, which literally means "rock" in Greek. Peter certainly didn't act like a rock of strength and stability when he tried to talk Jesus out of going to the cross, when he went to sleep in the garden, or when he denied Jesus three times. But Jesus knew Peter's heart and understood what he could become. After the resurrection, Peter did become the rock Jesus had pictured him to be.

In a modern-day instance, I (John) saw this happen with a young lady in my home church. This young woman's husband had divorced her to pursue an immoral relationship. Left with two young children under three and no marketable skills or workforce experience, she faced one struggle after another. But six years after her husband left, she was back on her feet, with a good job that allowed her to spend time with her children and still provide for their basic financial needs.

When we asked her what helped her most during those early, difficult years, she said, "The Lord was certainly the greatest source of help to us when Jack first left; but from a human perspective, I would have to point to my father. Every time I wanted to quit school or just give up, he would say to me, 'You'll make it, Jenny.

You're my Rock of Gibraltar. I know you'll make it.' I didn't feel like a rock at the time. My whole world seemed to be caving in. But it helped me so much to know that he pictured me this way. It gave me the hope that maybe I could make it."

Multiplying the Message

To review, we have discovered four keys to using word pictures in communicating words of high value:

1. Use an everyday object.
2. Match the emotional meaning of the trait you are praising with the object you've picked.
3. Use word pictures to unravel defenses.
4. Use word pictures to point out a person's potential.

Here's one last example of how powerful a word picture can be in blessing a person. It's an example I look at every day.

One afternoon when our daughters were young, I took them outside to play. I was heading out of town the next day for a seminar, so I wanted us to have some time together before I left.

At one point, Laura (our youngest) walked up and handed me a clothespin. The metal was rusted and the wood water-soaked and starting to splinter. I was looking at it when Cindy called us in to dinner.

As I walked inside, I stopped at the door and handed Cindy the clothespin.

"What's this?" she said.

"It's you," I said.

"Meaning . . . ?" Cindy said quizzically.

"Meaning . . . just pretend this is a solid-gold clothespin.

Sweetheart, you do such a great job of holding everything together when I have to go on a trip. You're like a solid-gold clothespin."

Cindy smiled, we all trooped in to dinner, and I left on my trip the next morning. When I came home, I learned something dramatic had happened—to the clothespin, that is. Cindy had painted it white, drawn a small red heart on it, and glued a magnet to the back. Today, years later, it's still on our refrigerator, right where *really important* things go.

To everyone else, that painted clothespin may look like a cute knickknack from a craft store or even something one of the kids made. But to Cindy it says, "I'm a clothespin. I do a great job of holding everything together for my family."

A very well-known saying tells us that one picture is worth a thousand words. When we link a word picture with a message of high value, we multiply our message a thousand times. That is the amazing power of the third element of the Blessing.

Pictures Your Heart Remembers

Think about a map.

It's so easy to believe we don't have high value. It's as if we've been handed a map, and it looks like the destination is way out in the desert or leads into a dark, secluded cul-de-sac. But take some time right now to read this verse:

> "For I know the plans I have for you," declares the LORD, plans
> for welfare and not for evil, to give you a future and a hope.
> (Jer. 29:11 ESV)

Think about how God's reality, Jesus' love, and his Word can reroute you to a place of worth and value.

Blessing Group Questions

1. I (John) carry a letter with me that my great-uncle Max gave me years ago. It's handwritten, and it says at the end, "You are my son." My uncle Max chose to call me his son. What is something you've kept, or remember being given, that had words that attached high value to you? (This could be anything from a diploma with your name on it to a personal note—anything in writing that is a picture of high value to you.)

2. How does using the first element of the Blessing, appropriate meaningful touch, communicate our attaching high value to someone?

3. If you have children or a spouse, how easy is it for you to come up with a word picture to help them "get the picture" that they're of high value to you?

4. In Matthew 10, we're told that the Lord knows even when a sparrow falls to the ground, and that he looks at us as having great value. Is there something that blocks you from feeling like you have great value in God's eyes?

5. If you were to write a letter/e-mail/Instagram post that attaches high value and send it to a loved one—what would it say?

Chapter 10

The Fourth Element: Picturing a Special Future

"How could anyone as dumb and ugly as you have such a good-looking child?" Mark's mother was grinning as she cuddled her grandson in her arms. To most observers, her words might have been brushed aside as a bad joke, but they brought instant tears to Mark's eyes.

"Stop it!" Mark said emphatically. "That's all I've ever heard from you. It's taken me years to believe I'm not ugly and dumb. Why do you think I haven't been home in so long? I don't ever want you to call me dumb again."

Mark's mother sat in stunned silence. Tears came to her eyes. She really had meant her words as a joke. But for the first time, one of her children had had the courage to confront her. For years, without realizing the impact of her words, this mother had constantly kidded her children about being stupid, fat, or ugly. After all, she had been kidded unmercifully by *her* mother when she was growing up.

What Kind of Future Do Our Words Picture?

When it comes to predictions about their future, children are literalists—particularly when they hear predictions from their parents, the most important people (from an earthly perspective) in their lives. This is why communicating a special future to a child is such an important part of giving the family blessing. But this element of the Blessing isn't just for children. Feeling and believing that the future is hopeful and something to look forward to can greatly affect anyone's attitude on life. By picturing a special future for our children, spouse, or friends, we are providing them with a clear light for their paths in life.

Have you ever been camping in the woods on a dark night? If you have, you probably remember what it's like to walk away from your campfire into the night. In only a few steps, darkness can seem to swallow you up. Turning around and walking back toward the fire is a great deal more reassuring than groping around in the dark. But if you light a lantern from that fire, you actually will be able to see your way on the dark path.

Words that picture a special future act like a campfire on a dark night. They can draw a person toward the warmth of genuine concern and fulfilled potential. They act like the lantern as well. Instead of leaving us to stumble into a dark unknown, they can illuminate a pathway lined with hope and purpose.

Children (and others) begin to take steps down the positive pathway pictured for them when they hear words like these: "God has given you such a sensitive heart. I wouldn't be surprised if you end up helping a great many people when you get older," or "You are such a good helper. When you grow up and marry someday, you're going to be such a help to your wife (or husband) and family."

Of course, the opposite is true as well. If children hear only words that predict relationship problems or personal inadequacies, they can turn and travel down the hurtful path that has been pictured for them. This can happen if they hear statements like "You'd better hope you can find someone who can take care of you when you're older. You're so irresponsible you'll never be able to do anything for yourself," or "Why bother to study so much? You'll just get married and drop out of school anyway."

Let's look back at Mark's family to see how this happened in his home. Over the years, Mark's mother had repeatedly given her children a negative picture of their future.

"Nobody's going to want to date a fat mess like you!" she would say with a resounding laugh—and her daughter would ache inside.

"You might as well drop geometry now; that's for smart kids," she would remark—and her youngest son would throw down his pencil and quit trying to understand the math problems in front of him, hating himself for giving up.

From the mother's conscious perspective, these were just playful words. But they failed to acknowledge the critical need every child has to have a special future pictured for him or her. The way Mark's mother talked to her children robbed them of a crucial part of the Blessing. The prospect of facing the future as dumb, ugly, or unappealing—even if such words were spoken in jest—eroded each child's self-confidence, and the fallout was devastating.

For Mark's brother and sister, the mother's descriptions became self-fulfilling prophecies. The youngest son dropped out of high school after flunking his junior year. After all, he "never was intelligent" anyway. Mark's older sister neglected her appearance so much that no boys were interested in dating her. After all, she knew she was "ugly" anyway. Mark took just the opposite approach to the negative future pictured for him. He became the family overachiever. His entire lifestyle bordered on extreme workaholism—all in an attempt to try to prove to his mother that her predictions were wrong.

If you add up the incredible costs exacted from the children in this family, you can see how devastating picturing a negative future can be. You can also see why a blessing in the Scriptures puts such a high priority on picturing a special future for each child.

Picturing a Special Future in Patriarchal Homes

In the Old Testament, picturing a special future for children was an important part of the formal family blessing. We can see this by looking at the words Isaac spoke to Jacob:

> Therefore may God give you
> Of the dew of heaven,
> Of the fatness of the earth,
> And plenty of grain and wine.
> Let peoples serve you,
> And nations bow down to you.
> Be master over your brethren,
> And let your mother's sons bow down to you.
> Cursed be everyone who curses you,
> And blessed be those who bless you! (Gen. 27:28–29)

When Isaac spoke these words, much of his son's blessing lay in the future. Jacob was not swamped with people wanting to bow down to him, and he had no land or flocks of his own that God could bless. Yet the picture gave him the security of knowing he had something to look forward to.

One generation later, Jacob's son Judah received a similar picture of a special future: "Judah, you are he whom your brothers shall praise; your hand shall be on the neck of your enemies; your father's children shall bow down before you" (Gen. 49:8). Like father, like son—Jacob passed down this part of the blessing. This blessing pictured a special future that would take years to become reality but offered Judah a special hope as each year unfolded.

As we mentioned in chapter 7, these patriarchs' words had a prophetic nature that is not a part of the Blessing today. We as parents cannot predict our children's futures with biblical accuracy, but we can provide them with the hope and direction that can lead to meaningful goals. As they begin to live up to these goals, they gain added security in an insecure world.

In Orthodox Jewish homes and services, the wish for a special future for each child is constantly present. At the synagogue, the rabbi often says to young boys, "May this little child grow to manhood. Even as he has entered onto the Covenant, so may he enter into the study of Torah, into the wedding-canopy and into a life of good deeds."[1] In the home, family blessings are also interlaced with words that picture a special future.

I (John) saw this aspect of the Blessing clearly in a Jewish home I was invited to visit one Thanksgiving. By the time I arrived, almost forty people were preparing or waiting patiently for a scrumptious dinner. Three generations—grandparents, parents, and their children—had assembled for this special occasion.

When the meal was prepared and before it could be served, the patriarch of the family (the grandfather) gathered all the family together. He had all the men and their sons stand on one side of the living room and all the women and their daughters stand on the other side. He then went around the room, placing his hands on the head of every person and speaking to them. To each man, he said, "May God richly bless you, and may he make thee as Ephraim and Manasseh." And each woman received the words, "May God richly bless you, and may you grow to be like Rebekah and Sarah."

From the oldest grown son to the youngest grandchild, this

time of blessing pictured a special future for each person in the room—even me, a stranger to him. Far from being a meaningless ritual, it provided everyone with a warm wish for a fulfilling life in the years to come.

Bringing Out the Best in Those We Bless

Picturing a special future for a child, spouse, or friend can help bring out the best in his or her life. It gives that person a positive direction to strive toward and surrounds him or her with hope. We can see this very thing in our relationship with the Lord. Listen to the beautiful way the prophet Jeremiah assures us of the special future we have in our relationship with God: "For I know the thoughts that I think toward you, says the Lord, thoughts of peace and not of evil, to give you a future and a hope" (29:11).

Jesus also went to great lengths to assure his insecure disciples that they had a special future with him. During their last Passover meal together, Jesus made sure they knew their future together would not end at his death. "In My Father's house are many mansions," he told them, "if it were not so, I would have told you. I go to prepare a place for you. And if I go and prepare a place for you, I will come again and receive you to Myself; that where I am, there you may be also" (John 14:2–3).

Time and time again in the Bible, God gives us a picture of our special future with him. However, his written Word is not the only way God communicates this message to us. Scattered throughout nature are a number of physical pictures of spiritual truths, pictures that illustrate the importance of providing a special future for the ones we love.

Anyone who has ever watched a caterpillar emerge from its cocoon as a butterfly has seen such a picture. The caterpillar is probably not on anyone's list of the world's "ten most beautiful creatures." Yet a caterpillar has the potential to be transformed into a list-topping, beautiful butterfly. What does this have to do with the Blessing? Words that picture a special future for a child, spouse, or friend can act as agents of this kind of transformation in that individual's life.

Words really do have that kind of transforming power. The apostle Paul certainly thought so.

The actual term for the transformation of a caterpillar to a butterfly is *metamorphosis*, based on a Greek word. Paul used this same Greek word in the book of Romans. He was aware that the world had tremendous power to squeeze and mold the saints in Rome into a godless image. To counter this, he told these young believers, "Be transformed by the renewing of your mind, that you may prove what is that good and acceptable and perfect will of God" (Rom. 12:2).

What does it mean to be "transformed by the renewing of your mind"? One excellent New Testament commentator explains the concept this way: "Since men are transformed by the action of the mind, transformed by what they think, how important to have the organ of thought renewed!"[2] In other words, godly thoughts and thinking patterns have the ability to transform us into godly men or women rather than leaving us to be squeezed into the imperfect mold of the world. Let's see how this works with regard to the Blessing.

Children are filled with the potential to be all God intended them to be. It is as if the Lord places them on our doorstep one day, and we as parents are left as stewards of their abilities. During the years we have children in our homes, the words we speak to them can wrap around them like a cocoon. What we say can shape and develop them in a positive way.

In chapter 9, we saw how this picture of the future helped a child named Hannah. In spite of her physical handicap, Hannah's parents provided emotional support and words of a special future that lay before her. When Hannah emerged from the cocoon of her parents' home and went out into the world, her love for the Lord and other people shone as brightly as the colors on a monarch butterfly's wings.

Sadly, it does not always happen that way. In some homes the words that wrap around developing children actually restrict growth and positive change rather than promote it. This restriction was true in Damion's home.

"You're a bum. You'll always be a bum." Damion's father said these words to him on his way to his college graduation—a ceremony his father did not even attend. This was not the first time, nor would it be the last, that Damion would hear these words. In fact, they were the only comments Damion ever received from his father about his future.

When I (John) saw Damion in counseling, he had just lost an important position in a major insurance company. At first glance, this seemed hard to believe. Damion was extremely intelligent and gifted. He was an eloquent speaker, with that charisma that marks many successful businessmen. However, less than a year after landing his current position, Damion had self-destructed. All the motivation he had shown when seeking the job seemed to evaporate once he was hired. He became irresponsible in handling projects and people, and within six months he was looking for work.

What was it that acted like an anchor in holding Damion back from reaching his God-given potential? Three words: "You're a bum." Repeated over and over in Damion's presence and in his mind—even eight years after his father's death—they had wrapped themselves around him like a restricting cocoon, and he emerged an insecure, irresponsible, defeated, and self-defeating man.

A law of physics says that water cannot rise above its source. A similar principle could be applied to Damion and many people like him. If a parent pictures for a child that his or her value in life is low, that child will find it difficult to rise above these words. One insightful study of fathers and their daughters revealed a direct relationship between the life achievements of the women studied and the level of their father's acceptance of them.[3] Our experience as counselors indicates the same is true for boys. Those who truly desire to give their children the Blessing will provide room for them to grow by encouraging their potential and by picturing a special future for them.

Let's look at another important picture in nature that mirrors what happens when we bless our children with words of a special future. This picture, explained to me by my twin brother, Jeff, a doctor in the field of cancer research, is found in something that happens in every cell in our bodies.[4]

Imagine a typical cell in your body by thinking of a circle. Attached to the outside of this circle are a number of receptor points. We could picture these receptor points as little squares that almost look like gears on a wheel. To make things easier for us to understand, let's picture these receptor sites as little square people.

Floating around near the cell are hormones and enzymes. Think of them as Harry Hormone and Ethyl Enzyme, who would each love to shake hands with (or activate) these little receptor people. And while a great number of these hormones and enzymes have the ability to connect with a receptor site, some have a special ability to stimulate a cell's activity and cause it to work harder.

We can picture this special ability as someone coming up to you and shaking your hand up and down so vigorously that your whole body shakes and you feel energized. In fact, your neighbors start shaking and feel energized too. Such stimulation by hormones and enzymes, which causes the receptor sites to work harder, is called *positive cooperativity*.

But other hormones and enzymes act in a negative way when

they shake hands with a receptor site. This is *negative cooperativity.* Have you ever had your hand squeezed so hard that you almost crumpled over in pain? That's the kind of thing that happens when these hormones and enzymes grab hold of a receptor site. In fact, not only does this one receptor site shut down and stop working because its "hand" is being squeezed, but all the receptor sites around it stop too.

And this applies to the Blessing . . . how?

Words that picture a special future for a child act like positive hormones that attach themselves to a cell. They stimulate all kinds of positive feelings and decisions within a child that can help him or her grow and develop. Words of a special future can inspire a child to work on a particular talent, have the confidence to try out for a school office, or even share his or her faith with other children.

But just like the negative hormones that shut down cell activity, a critical, negative picture of the future can crush or pinch off healthy growth in a child. Emotional, physical, and even spiritual growth in a child can be stunted because of the stifling effect of a negative picture of the future.

The Power of Past Consistency

By now you know how important it is to provide our children with words that point out a special future for them. But words alone may not be enough to get this message across to those we want to bless. Unless our words of a special future are backed up by a consistent track record, the person we are trying to bless may be unwilling or unable to believe what we say.

If we are serious about offering a message of a special future to our children, we need to follow the example the Lord sets. His consistency in the past acts as a solid footing on which words of a special future can stand.

Throughout the Scriptures the basis for believing God's Word in the future lies in his consistency in fulfilling his Word in the past. In Psalm 105:5 we read, "Remember His marvelous works which he has done, His wonders, and the judgments of His mouth." And in Psalm 33:9 the psalmist wrote, "He spoke, and it was done; He commanded, and it stood fast."

Because God has been reliable in the past, his words of a special future for us in the present have credence. The same principle applies to our desire to picture a special future for those we wish to bless. Our credibility in the past—or lack of it—will directly affect how our words are received in the present. Just as it did for Ted.

Ted was a sales manager for a national marketing chain. His job responsibilities meant that he was in town one week and out the next. In an average year (adding in an occasional back-to-back trip and sales conferences and subtracting major holidays), Ted was gone thirty-one weeks. His schedule ate away at the credibility of his statements that his children had a special future.

Ted had two young children at home, and they loved their daddy dearly. All week they would besiege their mother with the question, "Is Daddy coming home today?" When Daddy finally did come home, however, he was so tired from jet lag and his demanding schedule that he had little energy to spend meaningful time with the children.

Ted did a good job of "picturing" a special future for his children. The only problem was that he never followed through on his word. For instance, he would notice his daughter's deep love for animals and tell her, "Samantha, we're going to get a horse for you so you can ride it and take care of it. You might even become a veterinarian someday." To his son, who was very athletic for his age, he would say, "Bobby, you're pro shortstop material. Just give me a little time to rest up; then we'll go down to the park, and I'll hit you some grounders." But in just a few days it would be time for Ted to go back on the road. And somehow there was never enough time to settle all the details of buying a horse for Sam, never a free afternoon to hit grounders to Bobby.

After nine years of being on the road, Ted finally realized that he needed to greatly reduce his traveling schedule if he was ever going to build a secure marriage and family life. He even took a cut in pay to take a position that would enable him to stay at home. One of the first things he did was to surprise his daughter with a new horse—but Samantha wasn't interested in horses anymore. Neither was Bobby interested in going with his father to a pro baseball game. His children had listened to the empty promises of a special future for them for so long that Ted's words carried as much weight as the air used to speak them. They had their friends, their relationship with their mother, a new set of interests, and a deep-set impression that any future they had would not include their father's involvement.

This story has a happy ending, however. Ted truly loved his wife and children, and he persevered in trying to regain the lost ground with his family. As the weeks turned into months, Ted began to build up a track record of honored commitments. It took nearly two years, but he finally built up a *past* with his children that assured them he really did want the best for their futures. Interestingly, Samantha even began to rekindle an interest in animals, and Bobby dug his baseball glove out of the bottom of the closet.

Perhaps your past has been anything but consistent with those you want to bless. Today really *is* the first day of the rest of your life. And by honoring commitments to your children today, you can begin to build the kind of history that words of a special future need to rest on. Remember, there is no such thing as "quality time" that makes up for inconsistency in our relationships. We need to have a track record of daily decisions that demonstrate our commitment to our children, our spouses, or anyone we would bless. Only then will our words of a special future really find their mark.

The Power of Present Commitment

As we have mentioned, if our words of a special future are to take hold and grow, we need to demonstrate commitment in the present. This idea of commitment is so important that we will spend the next chapter examining it in depth. However, one aspect of a present commitment applies directly to picturing a special future. The effectiveness of our predictions depends on the degree of certainty our children have that we will be around long enough to see those predictions come to pass.

Gary's oldest child, Kari (now a mother herself), brought up this subject at the dinner table when she was in grade school.

We were all sitting around the table, enjoying a meal my wife, Norma, had prepared. We were all talking about our day and having a nice conversation when, out of the blue, Kari turned to her mother and said, "Mom, do you think you'll ever divorce Dad?" Everyone got quiet the moment she asked the question, and Norma nearly choked on her dinner. "'Kari!" she said in shock. "'You know that I would never divorce your dad." Then stopping to think about it a little more, Norma added with a twinkle in her eye, "Murder, maybe, but never divorce!" After we stopped laughing, we found out why Kari had asked her question. We were only two months into the school year, and already the parents of two of her classmates had gotten a divorce.

What Gary's daughter was asking that night was the same thing all children ask about their parents—whether out loud or in the silence of their hearts: "Will you be here in the future as I grow up, or will one of you leave me?"

Recently I counseled a husband and wife who were constantly fighting. I had asked the entire family to come in to try to get a better picture of what was happening with the couple. That meant that I had an eleven-year-old boy and a six-year-old girl join us for our counseling session. I began the session by addressing the six-year-old young lady. (Children are *so* honest, even when their parents hesitate to be too specific.)

"What bothers you the most about your parents' arguing?" I asked. Her answer surprised me. What was causing her the greatest pain and insecurity wasn't their loud voices or even what they said. It was this: "Every time my daddy gets mad at my mom, he takes off his wedding ring and throws it away."

Children are incredibly perceptive, and this little girl was no exception. While her father said it was "no big deal," his habit of pulling his wedding ring off his finger and throwing it somewhere in the house sent out a message loud and clear. Every time he "threw away" his wedding ring, this little girl saw her future with her parents (the greatest source of security a child has) go sailing right along with it.

Words of a special future for a child can dissolve into ashes when a husband or wife walks out on a relationship. In a later chapter, we will see just how difficult it is for some children who have lost a parent due to divorce or death to feel blessed (and also how a single parent can help correct this). For those of you who are married, an important part of picturing a special future for your children is keeping your present commitment to your spouse strong and intact.

A Guiding Light to Follow

Thankfully, many people realize the importance of providing their children, spouses, or friends with a picture of a special future. These people use words of blessing to help mold, shape, and guide a person to move into the rich future God has in store for him or her. Even when that person is someone like Maria.

Maria struggled throughout her years in school. If it took her classmates a half hour to do an assignment, you could bet Maria would only be halfway through the same project an hour later. Her parents even received the disturbing news from her teacher that Maria was being placed in the "slow learners" group. But this news did not discourage Maria's parents from picturing a special future for her. While they knew she was struggling in school, they also knew their daughter had many positive characteristics.

Rather than pushing Maria to hurry up or work faster, her parents would praise her for being methodical and for staying with an assignment until she finished it. They also noticed that Maria had an obvious gift for verbally encouraging her younger sisters and the neighbor children and a talent for explaining things to them in a way they could understand. Her parents began to encourage Maria to use her talents by letting her help teach the young children in Sunday school, using her gifts to serve these little ones.

After Sunday school one morning Maria announced to her parents that she wanted to be a teacher when she grew up. Her comments could have been met with a chuckle, a "What'll you want to be next week?" or even the pious words, "Now, Maria, let's be realistic." (The quarter's grades had just come out, and Maria was still at the bottom of her class.)

However, Maria's parents looked beyond her sagging test scores and recognized her God-given talents. Instead of laughing at her, they pointed out these gifts and encouraged her. They said that if she was willing to stay with it, one day she would become a teacher—a future that few "slow learners" would ever dream of picturing for themselves or hear pictured for them by their parents.

Maria continued to struggle through every year of school. Her parents had to pay for tutors in grade school and special reading classes in high school. When Maria decided to go to college, it took her six and a half years to graduate from a four-year program because she could not handle taking a full load of classes. Nonetheless, on a beautiful Saturday afternoon in May, Maria graduated from college with an elementary education teaching degree.

While graduation day meant that many of her classmates were just beginning to look for a job, Maria already had one. She did such a magnificent job of student teaching at an elementary school in a fine school district that the principal asked her to return the next year and take over a first-grade teaching position.

Actually, three people deserved to be honored that graduation day. Maria certainly deserved a great deal of credit for plodding forward day by day to reach her goal of being an elementary school teacher. Yet her parents also deserved high praise for encouraging her to reach her dream. Even more, they deserved acclaim for encouraging their daughter's dream by picturing a special future for her—even when years' worth of school report cards had branded Maria a slow learner.

Are you providing your children, spouse, or intimate friends with a blessing that pictures a special future for them? Did your parents take the time and effort to provide you with the hope of a bright tomorrow as you grew up? Wherever the Blessing is given or received, words that picture a special future are always shared—words that represent the fourth element of the Blessing.

Pictures Your Heart Remembers

Luke was called the disciple of hope because his gospel is so encouraging. Let's change that to talk about the *discipline* of hope. Write down—honestly—some things you have hoped would be part of a special future for you. What are some that have come true? What are some you are still waiting to experience? Next, again being honest, write down some things you've considered to be a picture of your heading toward a special future.

Blessing Group Questions

1. Think back to when you were younger, like in high school or even junior high. Can you think of some words that you may have heard (possibly often) that tied in with your future?

2. What did the important adults in your life predict about you?

3. Think about someone you want to bless—such as your children or spouse. What are some traits you see in their life today that you could see the Lord using when they grow older or in their future? (Such as, "Angel is so sensitive, I wouldn't be surprised if she used that sensitivity someday to care for others as a teacher/ nurse/doctor.")

4. We all have people in our lives who had *great* potential. What is so difficult about trying to bless someone who could have done X and has instead chosen a path that led him or her away from what could have been a special future?

5. Does God ever give up on us? (Read Hebrews 13:5.) What's so encouraging about knowing that even if we haven't quite measured up to what someone else has or has done, God still is moving us forward toward a special future?

Chapter 11

The Fifth Element: An Active, Genuine Commitment

M ost children have at least one subject in school that they particularly dread. Whether it is history, English, or geography, the course represents the worst hour of the school day. For Gary, that subject was geometry. Yet it was a geometry class in high school that taught him the incredible power of an active, genuine commitment—the fifth element of the Blessing.

> Mathematics was always the subject I dreaded the most. In grade school it was my poorest subject, and that continued to be true during my first two years of high school. In fact, when I had to repeat geometry my senior year, I was sure after only a month that I was going to flunk the course. My only solace was the fact that more than half the class was flunking with me. Our teacher would constantly remind us of this fact by arranging our chairs according to our current grade. Those of us who were failing lined the back wall.
>
> One Monday morning, when we dragged ourselves into

the classroom, all that changed. Sitting behind the teacher's desk was a substitute teacher—good news in itself. Then, when we found out that our regular teacher had been reassigned to a different district, we felt like the people in Paris during World War II who had just been liberated! But the fact remained that half of us were still failing the course. And I was still discouraged because I believed I was below average when it came to mathematics.

Then the new teacher said something that literally changed my life. In fact, it motivated me so much that I ended up minoring in mathematics in college. While I didn't realize it at the time, he actually blessed me and the other students in the class. He did this by providing us with a clear picture of active, genuine commitment—the fifth element of the Blessing.

Standing before the class that morning, our new teacher told us, "If anyone fails this class, then I have failed." He made a commitment that morning to do whatever it took to see that we all passed the course. He pledged himself to see that we learned and enjoyed the subject to the best of our abilities. Whether that meant his staying after school to tutor us or even coming in for a special session on the weekend, he dedicated himself to see that each of us made it through the course. Nearly every Saturday morning he would help several of us with our homework, then play a little volleyball with us for fun.

Imagine the turnaround that took place in that class. Where once we had dreaded geometry, now it became something we looked forward to. Even better was what happened the last day of school, when our teacher posted our grades. We all passed, and I received my first A in math!

You should have seen it. We were all jumping around and hugging each other. All because one man committed himself to a struggling bunch of students.

In the school of life, children desperately need adults—preferably parents—who will make the same type of active, genuine commitment that teacher did to Gary. In the areas where they are weak, they need to be encouraged and built up. They need to be appropriately touched or hugged and verbally praised for their strengths. When they are hurting, they need to feel someone's arms around them, giving them assurance and helping them back on their feet. Undeveloped potential needs to be brought out into the open and developed. These actions and attitudes are a part of bestowing the Blessing. And all of them need to be given not just once, but again and again. Which brings us to the fifth element of the Blessing.

Making the Blessing Happen

In the past several chapters we have looked at the first four elements of the Blessing:

1. Appropriate meaningful touch
2. A spoken (or written) message
3. Attaching high value
4. Picturing a special future

These four elements are the building blocks of the Blessing. But the mortar that holds them together is an active, genuine commitment, the fifth element of the Blessing.

Why is an active, genuine commitment such an important part of the Blessing? As we have seen in earlier chapters, words of blessing alone are not enough. They need to be backed by an ongoing dedication to see the Blessing come to pass.

This principle is what the apostle James wanted us to understand in his letter. There we read, "If a brother or sister is naked and destitute of daily food, and one of you says to them, 'Depart in peace, be warmed and filled,' but you do not give them the things which are needed for the body, what does it profit?" (James 2:15–16).

To answer the apostle's question, words without commitment are about as useful as a crooked politician's promises on the eve of Election Day. Giving the Blessing involves action, linked to our words. If we *talk the talk* but then fail to put the elements of the Blessing into practice, we leave our children, spouse, and friends undernourished and ill-clothed in their need for love and acceptance.

The Blessing as found in Scripture offers a strong contrast to speaking empty words to our loved ones. It features several important steps we can take to demonstrate an active, genuine commitment to those we want to bless.

Step 1: Ask the Lord to Confirm the Blessing

When you look at the Blessing in the Old Testament, something that stands out is the way the patriarchs committed their children to the Lord. When Isaac blessed Jacob, we read, "May *God* give you of the dew of heaven, of the fatness of the earth" (Gen. 27:28, italics added). Years later, when Jacob blessed his sons and grandchildren, he began by saying, "The *God* who has been my shepherd all my life to this day . . . bless the lads" (Gen. 48:15–16 NASB, italics added).

One reason these patriarchs called on God to confirm their child's blessing was because they were sure of his commitment to them. We can see this clearly with Isaac and Jacob.

In Genesis 26, Isaac was facing real problems. Living in the desert, he knew that his most precious assets were the wells he dug for fresh water. Twice Isaac had been driven from wells his father had dug. He was then forced to dig a third well to provide water for his flocks and his family. That night, as if to assure Isaac of his

137

future in this land, "The LORD appeared to him . . . and said, 'I am the *God* of your father Abraham; do not fear, for I am with you. I will bless you, and multiply your descendants'" (Gen. 26:24 NASB, italics added).

Isaac had been driven away from two wells that rightfully belonged to him. Hearing his heavenly Father declare his ongoing commitment to Isaac's family must have been like drinking cool, refreshing water on a hot summer's day.

God echoed those words of commitment to Jacob at a difficult time in his own life. Fleeing his brother Esau's anger, Jacob stopped one night to sleep out in the desert. It was there that God spoke to him and said, "I am the LORD God of Abraham your father and the God of Isaac. . . . Behold, I am with you and will keep you wherever you go, and will bring you back to this land; for I will not leave you until I have done what I have spoken to you" (Gen. 28:13, 15).

Isaac and Jacob were sure of their relationships with God. A natural extension of that certainty was to ask the Lord to bless their children through them. This is something we frequently see in churches today.

This past Sunday, in churches all across the country, pastors closed their services with the words "May the Lord bless you and keep you." By linking God's name to the blessing they spoke, these pastors were asking God himself to be the one to confirm it with his power and might—the very thing Isaac and Jacob did with their children.

We see the same idea in the dedication of children at a church. Often the pastor will lay his hands on children and say similar words of blessing, picturing the desire the parents and the entire congregation have in asking God to bless these little ones.

Wise parents will follow this practice in bestowing the Blessing on their children. When they say, "May the Lord bless you," they are first recognizing and acknowledging that any strength they have to bestow the Blessing comes from an all-powerful God. Even the very breath of life they have to speak words of blessing comes from him.

We are all prone to be inconsistent, and we stumble occasionally in providing the elements of the Blessing for our children. In contrast, God remains changeless in his ability to give us strength to love our spouses and children the way we should.

A second important reason to commit our children to the Lord when we bless them is that doing so teaches them that God is personally concerned with their lives and welfare. Stressing that the Lord is interested in their being blessed is like introducing them to someone who can be their best friend, a personal encourager they can draw close to throughout their lives.

Bringing the Lord into our words of blessing provides a sense of security for a child that we, as frail humans, cannot convey. We saw this in the way the children in one family reacted after the unexpected death of their father.

Lindsay and Kelly were still in grade school when their father died of a massive heart attack at the age of forty-one. These children no longer had his arms to comfort them or his encouraging words to bless them. But they did have a certain knowledge that Papa was with the Lord and that Jesus would confirm their blessing. Why such certainty? Because a wise father and mother had reassured them of this fact over and over. Listen to the words of his widow, Lisa, who also drew comfort from her husband's words.

> Before Ray died, he used to gather us all together right before dinner. We would all get in a little circle, holding each other's hands. Then Papa would pray and thank the Lord for our day and for the food. He would end each prayer by squeezing my hand and saying, "Lord Jesus, thank you that you are Lindsay's,

and Kelly's, and Lisa's, and my Shepherd. Thank you that you will never leave us or forsake us. Amen." It's been rough this past year without Ray, but it has helped so much to be able to remind the children that Jesus is still their Shepherd as well as their father's.

Children need the certainty and security that comes from committing them and their blessing to the Lord. That does not mean that we do not participate in the Blessing. Rather, it means that we recognize and acknowledge that only by God's strength and might will we ever be able to sustain our commitment to truly bless our children.

Step 2: Seek the Best Interest of the One Being Blessed

How do we begin committing ourselves to our children's best interests? First, as we have noted throughout the book, we must dedicate our time, energy, and resources to caring for them and spending time with them. However, Jacob observed another important principle in blessing his children. He recognized that every one of his children was unique.

In Genesis 48 and 49, Jacob (now called Israel) pronounced a blessing for each of his twelve sons and two of his grandchildren. After he finished blessing each child, we read, "This is what their father [Jacob] said to them when he blessed them. He blessed them, *every one* with the blessing appropriate to him" (Gen. 49:28 NASB, italics added).

In Hebrew, the end of this very verse reads, "He blessed them, every one with his own blessing." While the elements of the Blessing might remain the same, how they are applied in blessing a child is an individual concern. One daughter might need a dozen hugs and kisses at night before going to bed while her sister does well with two. One son might feel secure with hearing encouraging words only once while his brother may need to hear "You can do it" over and over again in approaching the same activity. Wise parents will realize that each child has his or her own unique set of needs. The book of Proverbs shows us this.

Most of us are familiar with the verse "Train up a child in the way he should go, and when he is old he will not depart from it" (Prov. 22:6). However, another helpful way to view this verse would be to translate it as "Train up a child according to his bent . . ."[1] In training (or blessing) a child, we need to take a personal interest in each child. The better we know our children and their unique set of needs, the better we will be able to give them their own unique blessing.

Please pay close attention to this next statement: physical proximity does not equal personal knowledge. We can spend years under the same roof with our spouses and children and still be intimate strangers. Many people feel as though they know another person's interests and opinions because they took an active interest in their lives in the past. However, people's thoughts, dreams, and desires can change over the years. Doctors tell us that every cell in our body wears out and is replaced by new cells within a few years. We are constantly changing both physically and emotionally.

In our homes we can be close in terms of proximity to one another but far away in terms of understanding another person's real desires, needs, goals, hopes, and fears. However, we can combat this distance by taking the time to observe and understand the unique aspects of those we wish to bless.

Blessing our children involves understanding their unique bents. In addition, it means being willing to do what is best for those children, even if it means having to correct them when they are wrong.

Step 3: Discipline When Appropriate

Discipline may seem the very opposite of blessing another person. But in actuality we bless our children by providing them with appropriate discipline. We see this when we look back at the individual blessings Jacob gave to each of his children.

Genesis 49 records a blessing for each son. We are told this very clearly in verse 28: "He [Jacob] blessed them, every one with the blessing appropriate to him" (NASB). However, at first glance the blessing that Reuben, the oldest son, received looks more like a curse than a blessing. Yet Jacob dealt with each son individually, and in Reuben's case his blessing included discipline as well as praise:

> "Reuben, you are my firstborn;
> My might and the beginning of my strength,
> Preeminent in dignity and preeminent in power.
> Uncontrolled as water, you shall not have preeminence,
> Because you went up to your father's bed;
> Then you defiled it." (Gen. 49:3–4 NASB)

If we look closely at these verses, Jacob balances words of praise with words of correction. Reuben had several positive qualities his father praised (his might, strength, dignity, and power). However, he also had a glaring lack of discipline in his life. His unbridled passions led him to the bed of one of his father's concubines. As a result he was disciplined for his actions.

It should not surprise us that blessing and discipline go hand in hand. If we genuinely love someone, we will not allow that person to stray into sin or be hurt in some way without trying to correct him or her. This lesson was explained by the writer of Hebrews when he said, "MY SON, DO NOT REGARD LIGHTLY THE DISCIPLINE OF THE LORD . . . FOR THOSE WHOM THE LORD LOVES HE DISCIPLINES" (12:5–6 NASB).

God actively deals with our wrong behavior rather than merely ignoring it because he sees us as his beloved children. Parents are naturally more concerned about the behavior of their own offspring than they are about other people's children. Like a loving parent with a highly valued child, God does care about our behavior.

Our sons' and daughters' actions should also concern us if we are going to be a person who truly blesses them. We should not shy away from including loving discipline when it is appropriate and in their best interests.[2]

Initially, discipline can seem painful for both parents and children. Yet taking that risk can help bring out the best in children's lives by training them and guiding them to a place of peace and righteousness (Heb. 12:11). Discipline is an important way of actively committing ourselves to a child's best interest.

We have looked at three ways in which we can demonstrate an active, genuine commitment in blessing others: we can commit them to the Lord, we can seek their best interests, and we can apply appropriate discipline. A fourth way to show an active, genuine commitment is something I have seen modeled all my life.

Step 4: Become a Student of Those You Wish to Bless

Have you ever lost a loved one and then had to pack up that person's possessions for an estate sale or to donate? For years my (John's) precious mother had her nest in a modest condominium in Phoenix, Arizona. It was a small place, easy for her to get around in. After seven major operations due to rheumatoid arthritis, it slowed her down a bit. Yet her home always seemed warm and welcoming, just like she was. All her life, my mother was busy, engaged in helping others, loving beyond words. She was lots of fun to be with and, as she grew older, to visit.

If you had dropped in to Mom's little condo during her last

years, you would have seen something in her home that pictured what it means to be a student of your children. It probably wouldn't have caught your eye right off, though whenever I walked into my mother's home, it flashed at me like a neon light. It was also the thing that was the hardest for me to pack up after she passed away.

It was just a nondescript bookshelf. But it carried extra-special meaning for my two brothers and me.

One rack of the bookshelf was always filled with theology and psychology books. A second shelf overflowed with medical journals and books on genetics. The third shelf seemed even more out of place for a seventy-six-year-old arthritic woman. Lining this shelf were dozens of issues of *Heavy Equipment Digest* and how-to books on driving heavy equipment.

These seemingly unrelated books and magazines might lead a person to think this woman was an eccentric who would read anything or perhaps even had a touch of schizophrenia that caused her to jump from one topic to the next. Neither of these explanations would be close to the truth. This collection was a beautiful picture of the active, genuine commitment our mother made in choosing to give her sons the Blessing.

Over the years my mother collected not only the books I had written but also the books on counseling and theology I had recommended to her. They were in her bookcase because she had taken an interest in my interests. To help her understand my brother Jeff's field of interest and converse with him about it, she read (or tried to read) loads of his medical and genetics articles and books. She even enrolled in a genetics class at the University of Arizona at the age of sixty so she could talk to Jeff about what was important to him. To be truthful, she ended up dropping the course after failing the first two major exams. However, sitting proudly on the shelf with the other highly technical books was the slightly worn textbook she struggled to understand. Each book was a trophy of her willingness to learn and her desire to communicate with my brother in his areas of interest.

But what about the magazines and books on operating road-construction equipment? My older brother, Joe, for years has been a heavy-equipment operator. Because my mother was committed to affirming and being a student of each son, she made a point of learning about his interests too. When she passed away at age seventy-six, she was a current subscriber to *Heavy Equipment Digest* and able to talk to Joe about the latest bulldozer or earth mover.

I doubt if *Heavy Equipment Digest* magazine receives many subscriptions from gray-haired, arthritic grandmothers, but they did from this one. All because she made a commitment to becoming a student of each son and his individual interests.

First Steps Toward Becoming a Student of Your Children

One thing that can greatly help us learn to become students of our children is to be lovingly persistent in communicating with them. Particularly if we have struggled in our relationships with our children or we haven't been close to them in the past, getting them to open up with us can take loving persistence. That doesn't mean badgering them or trying to pry the words out of their mouths. But it does mean consistently setting up times with them when meaningful communication can develop.

Second, realize that any shared activity with our children—from driving them to school or athletic practice to an airplane trip before they put on their headphones—offers tremendous opportunities to learn about them.

And taking the initiative in asking questions can be a third important way to become students of our children. Don't grill your child with questions as if you were giving a test. Just ask some casual questions in an offhanded way, and then really listen to the answers.

Ask Your Children

Possible questions you can ask in those unguarded times at the hamburger place, at the ball game, or while taking a walk:

1. What do you daydream about most often?
2. What would you really enjoy doing when you are a young adult (twenty to thirty)?
3. Of all the people you have studied in the Bible, who would you most like to be like? Why?
4. What do you believe God wants you to do for humankind?
5. What type of boyfriend or girlfriend are you most attracted to, and why?
6. What is the best part of your school day? What is the worst?

Listen with full attention—that is the fourth practical way to get started in becoming a student of those we wish to bless. We actually bless our children by being emotionally present when they talk to us rather than being preoccupied with something else.

Have you ever carried on an entire conversation with a child while absorbed in a television show or reading Facebook posts? "Uh-huh" or "That sounds good, honey" uttered with our eyes glued to a screen does not communicate acceptance to our children, nor does it help us become a student of what they want to share.

One way to remind ourselves to actively listen to our children, spouses, or others is found in the book of Proverbs: "Bright eyes gladden the heart" (15:30 NASB).

My mother was so good at this, saying, "John, look at me," when she spoke to me about something important. Most of us have had the experience of walking into a room and seeing somebody's eyes light up when he or she saw us. That sparkle in another person's eyes communicates to us that the person is really interested in us and in what we have to say.

I once read of an interesting research study based on this very verse. A number of college men were given ten pictures of college-aged women who were more or less equally attractive. Each student was then asked to rate the pictures from "most attractive" to "least attractive."

What these young men did not know was that five of the women had been given an eye-drop solution just before their pictures were taken. This solution dilated the pupils in their eyes—the same thing that happens naturally when we are really glad to see someone. The results of the study were just as we might expect. The girls with the "bright eyes" were chosen hands down as the five most attractive women in the pictures.

Do our eyes light up when we listen to those we wish to bless? Our children or spouses will notice if they do or don't. We can decide to put down the iPhone or turn off the television to talk to our loved ones as we take an active interest in their interests. Active listening is an important part of communicating acceptance and blessing.

Those of us who are parents need to realize that our children are incredibly complicated people. So are our wives or husbands and our friends. If we would begin today to list all their wishes, opinions, goals, and dreams, it would take us a lifetime to complete the task. That is just the right amount of time needed to finish the course titled "Becoming a Student of Your Loved Ones," a class men and women will enroll in if they are serious about bestowing an appropriate blessing to each person in their lives. All it takes to register is a decision to actively commit ourselves to others—and a pair of "bright eyes."

One Final Look at the Cost of Commitment

No doubt about it, commitment is costly. If you are serious about committing yourself to blessing those you love, expect to pay a price. Not necessarily in terms of money—a spouse and even small children are far too wise to be bought off with presents for very long. But you will need to invest time, energy, and effort to see the Blessing become a reality in their lives.

Is the price worth it? The book of Proverbs certainly seems to show us that it is.

The final chapter of Proverbs describes a woman who blesses her family in many ways. She is industrious and loving, has a positive outlook on the future, and is committed to her husband and children. Her words to her family are filled with wisdom and kindness.

Did she just happen to be born this way? Certainly not. Each of these qualities was developed at a price. What is often skipped over when this passage is taught is how often this woman was up at dawn and how hard she worked to bless her family with her actions and words. She used the same kind of energy that gets parents out of bed on the weekend to take their children camping or enables a husband or wife to stay up late to help his or her spouse complete a project.

Was blessing her family really worth all that effort? It was for this woman. Read what her family has to say about her and her decision to make a genuine commitment to them: "Her children rise up and call her blessed; her husband also, and he praises her: 'Many daughters have done well, but you excel them all'" (Prov. 31:28–29).

It takes hard work, wrapped in the words *active, genuine commitment*, to provide the Blessing to another person. It takes time to meaningfully touch and hug our children when they come home from school or before they go to bed. It takes courage to put into a spoken or written message those words of love for our spouses that have been on the tips of our tongues. It takes wisdom and boldness to "bow our knees" and highly value those we love. It takes creativity to picture a future for them filled with hope and with God's best for their lives. But all this effort is worthwhile.

One day, perhaps years later, the blessing that you give will return. Those you bless will rise up and bless you. What's more, you will find that the joy at seeing another person's life bloom and grow because of your commitment to seek their best is a blessing in itself.

Just ask one couple who took the time early on in their only son's life to provide him with the Blessing. When he grew up, he would return words of blessing to them—in a most unusual way.

"Bubs" Roussel was only seventeen on that infamous Sunday morning in 1941 when Pearl Harbor was bombed. Later that day, he told his father and mother the shocking news of the Japanese attack.

Not long afterward, Bubs was called into the army and ended up serving in the Army Air Corps (now called the air force). After special training in communications, he was assigned as a radio operator in a B-29 bomber. The youngest in his crew, Bubs had to grow up fast. In only a few months he found himself stationed on the island of Saipan in the western Pacific.

From this tiny island, B-29s were making bomber runs on Japan. The work was dangerous, even deadly. On the morning of December 13, 1944, eighteen bombers soared out over the Pacific to make a bomb run on factories at Nagoya, Japan. Four of the planes that left Saipan that morning never returned. Bubs's plane was among them.

Official word that Bubs had been killed in action came to his parents from the War Department. They, like so many other family members in those days, received a telegram along with a small white flag, bordered with red and trimmed with blue and gold. The flag had one small gold star in the middle—the symbol of a son who has fallen in battle.

However, Bubs's parents also received something else. Almost a month after his plane went down, a letter came in the mail. Bubs had placed it on his pillow before his last mission:

> Dear Folks,
>
> I have left this with instructions to send it on to you if anything happens to me. I send you my love and blessings. My life has been a full one. I have been loved like very few persons ever. I love you all with the best that is in me. It hasn't been hard for me, knowing you believe in me, trust me, and stand behind me in fair or foul. Knowing this has made me strong.[3]

Would your children be able to write a letter like this to you? They could if they grew up in a home committed to being a source of blessings, a home like the one in which Bubs grew up. The words might be different, but the sentiment would be the same. Giving our children the Blessing is like casting bread upon the waters. In years to come they, too, will rise up and bless us.

Kari's and my prayer for every person who reads this book is that you will become a person of the Blessing. The cost is genuine commitment, but the rewards can last a lifetime and beyond.

For nine chapters we have examined the various elements of the Blessing and looked at homes that bestow that blessing on children. In the next section, we will get really practical with what it looks like to give, live, and create a culture of blessing in your family. Kari will walk you through a wealth of practical ways that you can make the Blessing an ongoing part of your most important relationships, starting now.

Pictures Your Heart Remembers

If you have been blessed by someone (or several someones) in your life who have modeled for you an unchanging, unwavering commitment, then write down why that has been so helpful to you—and give this person a call. If they've since passed away, and if their spouse or child is still living, call them and thank them for that person who demonstrated an active, genuine commitment to you. If you aren't fortunate enough to have someone like that in your life, you *must* read Psalm 103. There are thirteen different traits of our heavenly Father there in the psalm. Read the whole thing, but write down the traits of a loving God that mean the most to you.

Blessing Group Questions

1. You are several weeks into your Blessing Group time. What's something you appreciate about your group already that links with active, genuine commitment?

2. Have you had an experience where you saw someone live out active, genuine commitment to you—even when this person could have bailed or not followed through?

3. When you think about Jesus, do you see him waiting for you, ready to welcome you to himself one day? Or is that kind of image hard for you to bring into focus?

4. In the Bible, the Greek word for forgiveness literally means to "untie the knot." Is there someone or some experience in your life where you still need to untie the knot and forgive? What's forgiveness got to do with truly experiencing a sense of genuine commitment?

5. When those feelings of being alone or unwanted sneak up on you—even if you're in a crowd or have a busy family around you—what is something you've learned that can help you know you're loved, valued, and blessed and especially that Jesus and his love are never going anywhere?

Chapter 12

First Steps: A Written Blessing

The two thin, watermarked sheets of white stationery are now folded down into a small square. I (John) carry them in the safest zippered part of my backpack, which goes with me everywhere. The writing on the paper is starting to fade, and I keep promising myself that I'm going to make a copy of it. But I haven't done it yet—because the paper was his. The writing in black pen was his. The words I had longed to hear all my life were his.

Those two small sheets headed simply by a date: December 1986. They contain some of the most encouraging words I have ever received—a blessing beyond price to me. They came to me unexpectedly. But they are an example of something we are going to challenge you to think about, plan out, and pray over.

You have now spent a number of chapters understanding how important the Blessing can be. You have gained a clear picture of each of its five elements and their impact on a person's life and future. Now it's time for ground school to end and flight school to begin. We believe you are ready to fly solo and soar now. In this chapter Kari and I are going to ask you to take your first step toward the Blessing by first writing out a formal blessing for your child and then sharing it with him or her.

Why Write?

As we have seen in earlier chapters, both the spoken word and the written word are important in giving the Blessing. For several reasons, however, we suggest that you put your words of blessing into written form first, before you share them out loud with your child.

First of all, ideally, your written blessing will also be spoken—we will include ideas for doing that below. But writing your words out first can take away a lot of pressure. You have the opportunity to put the words together at your leisure. You can double-check that you have included all the elements of the Blessing and that your words convey exactly what you want. And if your words have been chosen ahead of time, when you do speak your blessing, you can concentrate on connecting with your child.

Another reason to write out your blessing, though, is that a written blessing can be saved. The words can be read and reread, and the paper it is written on can be tucked away as a keepsake. (Even e-mailed blessings can be stored and reread.) Written blessings can also be sent by letter or e-mail and thus cover great distances. A written blessing has the capacity to bring warmth and light and love to your child again and again throughout his or her life—far beyond the mere ink marks on paper.

That's what the letter I carry in my backpack does for me. But to understand that, you need to hear a little more of the story, and about the man who wrote the letter for me, my uncle Max.

I met Uncle Max when I moved from my home state of Arizona to attend Texas Christian University (home of the mighty Frogs) in the city of Fort Worth. In one of my English composition classes,

I was assigned a topic for a major paper by my professor. The only problem was after he assigned the topic, he told me our library at TCU didn't have what I needed to complete it.

"Do you have a car?" the professor asked. When I replied that I did, he explained that the best place for finding information on my topic was to drive to nearby Dallas and use the library at Southern Methodist University. Apparently, they had a "plethora" of articles and books on the subject.

Not sure exactly what a plethora looked like, I made the drive on a Saturday and parked next to a beautiful redbrick library. (The whole campus at SMU is beautiful.) I walked inside and was headed toward the reference desk when I saw it—a nameplate on a glass door, right next to the reference desk. The nameplate read, "Robert M. Trent, Head Librarian."

The door was almost all the way open, and a man was sitting inside—presumably the head librarian himself. Spontaneously, I thought of something funny to do. I stopped, stuck my head in the door, and said, "Hi, Uncle Bob. I'm your long-lost nephew, John Trent, from Arizona."

It was a totally throwaway line. Sure, we shared the same last name, but I had no reason to believe we were actually related. I was sure he would just look puzzled or slightly annoyed at being interrupted, and either response would have been fine with me. What I wasn't ready for was his next question:

"Are you Joe Trent's boy?"

I was dumbfounded. You see, at that point, I had essentially no relationship with my father. I had met him only once, and not under the most encouraging circumstances. And I knew exactly *none* of my relatives on my father's side of the family. I did know my father was from Indiana, but the possibility that he had relatives in Texas had never crossed my mind. So walking right into the office of my great-uncle—my father's uncle—was a total shock.

I soon learned that he went by Max, not Robert, and he was extremely gracious to invite me into his office for a conversation. After we talked a good while, he picked up the phone and called his wife—my aunt Sally, it turned out. To my surprise, while he was on the phone, he asked Aunt Sally if she had cooked enough to invite me home for dinner, and then he held the phone down and asked me if I would join them. So began a relationship that became one of the most important in all my life.

Uncle Max and Aunt Sally had no kids. They had books. Both held PhDs from Columbia University, and both were head librarians—she at the Dallas Public Library and he at SMU. Over the next twelve years, during my college, seminary, and graduate-school days, they became my Texas family. They would invite me over for holidays if I couldn't go home to Arizona and have me over often for a weekend meal. Uncle Max spent hours talking to me about my father—opening up doors into his life that I had never been aware of and never would have discovered from any conversation I ever had with Dad.

It was Uncle Max, for instance, who told me that my father had been abandoned by *his* father—what a shock that he would grow up and do the same thing to my brothers and me. Uncle Max also told me about my father's war experience and its aftermath—the Bronze and Silver Stars he earned from fighting at Guadalcanal, the wounds that sent him home more dead than alive, the nightmares that drove him to drink. As I learned more about my father's life, I found it harder and harder to hate him. In fact, I owe it all to Uncle Max that I finally met with my father and asked forgiveness for being so angry with him for so long. Not so he would change—he didn't—but so I could "untie the knot" and be free from hating him.

Uncle Max and Aunt Sally helped me a lot during those years, including modeling for me something I had never seen up close—a good marriage. Then came that terrible day when a double-wheeled wrecker hit Aunt Sally, sending her to the hospital in critical condition. Uncle Max and I arrived at almost the same time. On top of her traumatic injuries, she had also suffered a heart attack from all the pain and stress of the accident.

Uncle Max had given me so much in terms of warmth and love and information and understanding. Now I had a chance to give back what I could to him. For four days and nights I stayed with him at Baylor Hospital, praying the whole time. Praying for him. And praying for Aunt Sally, who was his whole life—and who, we had been told, wouldn't make it through the first night.

But she did make it through that first day and night. Then a second. Then a third. And then the doctor came into the waiting room where we were sleeping on the fourth morning. He told us that he had just finished his early morning rounds and that Aunt Sally was going to be all right. In fact, it was miraculous the way she had rallied.

Uncle Max and I hugged and cried, and I prayed and thanked the Lord for his grace in healing Aunt Sally. Then Uncle Max asked me to pray one more time. Actually, first, he asked me to explain to him more clearly just who I had been praying to those four days. And then he wanted me to pray again as he accepted Jesus into his heart so he could thank him for Aunt Sally's healing too.

Four years later Aunt Sally passed away in her sleep. By that time I had moved back to Arizona. But Uncle Max and I stayed close. We talked often, and I would see him whenever I was in Dallas.

Then one day, out of the blue, I got a letter—the same two-page note I still carry in my backpack. "Dear John," it began, "I know it is going to come as a surprise to learn that I have drawn up a living will. . . ."

He went on to detail his last wishes and give me instructions for retrieving his will from the lawyer. That's how I found out Uncle Max was dying of cancer. But then on the second page, in the last paragraph, came those incredible words of blessing—those unexpected words I have treasured and carried with me every day since.

"Thank you, John," he wrote. "You have helped me so much in the past. I am sure you will continue to do so—*because you are my son*. Affectionately, Max."

I carried my biological father's name, but he never chose to call me *son*. Uncle Max did that. And even as he told me he was dying, he chose to give me his blessing. With those words, in some incredible way, I was an emotional orphan no more. I was a chosen son. And I knew it because Uncle Max had made the choice to write out his blessing to me.

That is the choice I would like you to make as well.

What Do I Say?

Keep in mind that there is no wrong way to craft a blessing, and there are lots of creative right ways. And whether it comes out all at once in a rush of words or takes you a few tries and several evenings to outline and polish what you want to say, your child will cherish both what you write and what it represents about your relationship.

How you actually do the writing depends on what you are comfortable with. Some people work best in pencil on a yellow legal pad. Others can't even think without their iPad or laptop. You could even talk into a voice recorder and then transcribe your words.

And what should you say? Your words can be plain or poetic. They just need to carry with them a picture of your blessing that can help your child know that he or she is of high value to you. Here are a couple of examples to inspire you:

A Poetic Blessing

If you lean toward the creative or romantic side, then perhaps you can draw inspiration from this letter of blessing below. It was written by a father to his young daughter and given to her on June 11, 1948, when she was twelve years old. Today, more than fifty years later, it is still very much worth reading. I'll share the letter first; then I'll tell you who wrote it:

Dearest Joanne,

Those beautiful quaking aspens that you've seen in the forest as we have driven along have one purpose in life. I would like to tell you about them because they remind me a lot of Mommy and you kids and me.

Those aspens are born and grown just to protect the spruce tree when it's born. As the spruce tree grows bigger and bigger the aspens gradually grow old and tired and they even die after a while. But the spruce, which has had its tender self protected in its childhood, grows into one of the forest's most wonderful trees.

Now think about Mommy and me as aspens standing there quaking ourselves in the winds that blow, catching the cold snows of life, bearing the hot rays of the sun, all to protect you from those things until you are strong enough and wise enough to do it yourself. We aren't quaking from fear, but from the joy of being able to see your life develop and grow into tall straight men and women.

Just like the spruce, you have almost reached the point where you don't need us as much as you used to. Now you stand, like the young spruce, a pretty, straight young thing whose head is beginning to peep above the protection of Mommy and Daddy's watchfulness. . . .

I am telling you all this because from now on a lot of what you eventually become—a lovely woman, a happy woman and a brilliant, popular woman—depends on you.

You can't go through life being these things and at the same time frowning. You can't achieve these things and be grumpy. You have to grow so that your every deed and look reflect the glory that is now in your heart and soul.

Smile. Think right. Believe in God and His worldwide forest of men and women.

It's up to you.

> I love you,
> Daddy[1]

That's quite a letter, isn't it? In fact, in reflecting on it, his daughter Joanne states, "I still cry every time I read it. He was a master with words. He was a romantic."[2]

And who was Joanne's father? He wasn't a poet, pastor, or teacher. He was a *politician*—Barry Goldwater. In fact, he is usually named as among the most hard-nosed of politicians. When he ran for president in the 1960s, he was demonized and said to be heartless. But that is not the side his daughter saw.

My point here isn't political. It is deeply personal. It's about the words that Goldwater wrote to his young daughter at a turning point in her life. I'm not saying Goldwater knew about the five elements of the Blessing as he wrote them—but reread it and just look at how many elements are there.

He pictures for her a positive future. He praises his daughter in words that demonstrate a genuine commitment. He attaches high value to her even during a difficult period in her life. (For most of us, keeping a good attitude during adolescence is tough.) With the exception of appropriate meaningful touch—which is hard to provide in a letter if he didn't hand it to her or sit next to her while she read it—that letter includes every element of the biblical blessing. No wonder it still means so much to her.

So feel free, in writing your blessing for your child, to be poetic like that hard-nosed politician. But don't worry if you are more the practical, straightforward sort. You don't have to be a poet to give a meaningful blessing—as another letter shows us.

Practical Words of Praise

"Dear Michael," writes an engineer who thought long and hard before writing out a much more practical but just as precious letter to his newborn son:

> As I sit beside you, and read you this letter today, I hope you'll know how much time and thought I've put into each word. After all, it's been nine long months, one week, and two days since we found out you were coming! I want you to know, today and always, that we prayed for you before you were born. That every day you were in Mommy's tummy, we prayed for you. And I want you to know that on this day when they handed you to me, the day of your birth, I had tears in my eyes and had to sit down, I was so filled with joy. We are so grateful to God for you, and so committed to being the best parents we can for you and God. This letter is the first official "birthday blessing" letter that I'm committed to writing you. Each year, as God gives me strength and life, I'll write more about why I love you, why you're so special to me, and why I'm so glad and honored to be your dad.
>
> Your Dad[3]

You would think there wouldn't be very many words to bless a child only a few hours old, but that letter says so much so well. And so will your letter to your child. Whether your child is twelve years or twelve hours old, whether your blessing is handwritten or typed out, whether you can write elegant prose or can barely spell—none of that matters. It's the words that count, and the time is now!

Sharing Your Blessing with Your Child

Once you have written your words of blessing, we encourage you to talk with your spouse (if you're married) and pick a special time and place to share these words with your child. If at all possible, do it face to face. Pick a meaningful time, place, or event—a family affair with lots of friends and relatives, a milestone celebration such as a birth or graduation, or a quiet dinner with just the two of you. Just make sure that it is at a time and place that allows you to be quiet long enough to read or recite the blessing you have written to your son or daughter.

Don't forget to include the element of meaningful, appropriate touch along with your blessing—a hand on the head, an arm around the shoulder, and hopefully a big hug. You might even want to snap a picture of the two of you together or give the child a keepsake copy of your blessing done in a special font, calligraphy, or just your best handwriting.

What if you can't be physically present—if you are deployed overseas, for instance, or divorced and living across the country? If you will be together soon, why not write out your blessing now and wait until you are together to deliver it? But don't wait too long. You can always write out your blessing in your best handwriting or format it on the computer and put it in the mail. You could even do a video of your blessing and e-mail it to your child or do the whole thing via Skype or FaceTime.

Keep in mind that there is no wrong way of giving a child your blessing. Even if you choose to do a special dinner and burn the hamburgers, if it rains on the one night you have counted on a starlit sky, if the dog decides to throw up just before the special event or the camera batteries fail, it doesn't really matter. If you will write down your words and make your plans, I believe you will find that God just works it out!

The fact that your child receives your blessing is far more

important than any challenges you face in delivering it. It is your blessing, prepared just for him or her. And however you choose to deliver it, make sure your child has a copy of your written words. Perhaps he or she will keep it and carry it along to college or out into the world. Perhaps one day it will be tucked into a backpack as well.

Don't Leave the Blessing to Chance

Before you actually get to work on your written blessing, there are a few more things I would urge you to keep in mind. First, don't assume your children will automatically know your heart or "just figure out" what you think about them. *How* you choose to bless a child is not nearly as important as making that choice—being intentional about the blessing.

As I have shared throughout this book, my mother gave me all five elements of the Blessing time and time again. But one very special blessing from her was almost thrown away.

After Mom passed away, my brothers and I were going through her things, trying to sort out what to keep and what to give away. This was very hard for me because I wanted to keep everything. The blue sweater she loved to wear. The little stick she held in her arthritic hands to poke the television channels on the remote (and whack the TV occasionally if someone was sharing an opinion she didn't like). Everything had a meaning and value.

But what almost got thrown out was a small notebook with a scuffed-up cover that we thought was empty. It wasn't. I picked it out of the trash bin at the last minute before it was bagged up and found this on the first page: "A Journal of Rededication to Jesus Christ."

None of us boys had ever seen this journal. Written in my mother's hand, it recorded her thoughts and prayers, dreams and hopes. I would like to share with you the last journal entry before her death. (All spelling, capitals, and quotation marks are as she wrote them.)

> God has granted me yet another new beginning. There have been so many before. My hopes and dreams have been so high . . . but each time I fail. I call another driver STUPID. I make a cutting remark about another. I bring into a place of beauty discordant behavior, and thus foul up again.
>
> But God has poured out blessing on me from the day of my birth. He has allowed me to live, "all the days of my life," at a time of great wonder, and in a State that dazzles the eyes and soul with beauty.
>
> He has brought me a Teacher of his word who is exceptional. He has provided me with an annotated Bible, and so often restored my health.
>
> All these plus 3 miracles of creation who are my sons.
>
> How blessed could one woman be?
>
> Thank you, Lord. How inadequate is language to praise you.

It is painful to me to realize those words were a moment away from being thrown out. How tragic if God hadn't stopped me and allowed me to rescue them from the trash. And how tragic if we keep our words to ourselves, assuming our kids will just somehow "know" that they have our blessing without our written or spoken words to tell them.

Accidentally on Purpose

My wife's father, George, was a hardworking, hard-drinking man, a B-17 bomber pilot in World War II. Raised on a dairy farm in

Wisconsin, he did his pilot training at Arizona's Luke Air Force Base in December, and he swore that if he survived the war, he would come back there to live, where he could wear shorts in the winter.

He did just that. After the war he jumped into construction work in Arizona, got married, and fathered my Cindy. Unfortunately, he started jumping into a bottle as well, and he was an angry drunk. He was also openly hostile against any form of faith—he used to say that the nuns in his Catholic school had "beat all the religion out of" him as a child. When Cindy, his only daughter, was growing up, no one was even allowed to mention Jesus—unless, of course, you wanted to make fun of believers.

Then Cindy came to know Christ, and she began talking to her father about Jesus. He loved to debate and argue, and as a new Christian, Cindy would often get stumped by his questions. But instead of getting angry, she used her inability to respond as motivation to dig deeper into God's Word and find answers for him.

Year after year Cindy kept loving, encouraging, praying for, and otherwise blessing her father, even when he was an angry alcoholic. A turning point came when he faced a drunk-driving conviction. The judge gave him a choice between jail and AA. He chose AA, got into recovery, and mellowed . . . some.

Amazingly, incredibly, George would place his faith in Jesus a year before he passed away. His decision, a direct result of Cindy's prayers and persistence over the years, was certainly a blessing to our family. But it was an accidental meeting that happened a dozen years before he came to faith that blessed Cindy most dramatically . . . and still does today.

It was Christmastime, and we were all at a party at the home of my older brother, Joe. Joe had one of those long, narrow, galley-style kitchens, barely wide enough for two people to walk through side by side. That's why my father-in-law didn't realize he was blocking Cindy's path.

Cindy was helping get platters of food out of the kitchen and onto the serving table in the other room when she walked up behind her father. He was in the middle of an animated conversation with one of our family friends and had no idea Cindy was standing behind him. And he was talking about her, using words she had never heard him use.

Cindy knew her father loved her. But she hadn't heard those words.

She knew her father was proud of her. But she hadn't heard those words either. Not out loud. Not directly.

Now she found herself standing behind her father, a plate of food still in her hands, listening as he went on and on about how proud he was of her. How she was the only one in his whole family (at that point) to graduate from college. What a great teacher she was and what a tremendous mother and wife she was and how she delighted him in so many ways.

Cindy just stood there in shock, listening to her father's words. Words of affirmation and praise and high value that he had never shared with her personally, he was now rattling off to a stranger. And perhaps it was that stranger's look that finally caused him to stop, look behind him, and see Cindy.

I walked into the kitchen at that exact moment—to see a father and daughter hugging each other, crying (yes, even the bomber pilot), and telling each other that they loved each other. Those were words that Cindy had waited for all her life, words she may never have heard had it not happened accidentally. And that is one huge reason why we encourage people to "accidentally on purpose" write out a blessing to share with their children.

A Lifetime of Blessing

Don't wait! Don't leave your blessing to chance! Make an intentional plan to give your son, your daughter—everyone you care about—your blessing. Write it down. Speak the words. Make a memory now and give a keepsake for tomorrow.

But don't stop there.

The kind of planned, formal blessing we have described in this chapter can be wonderful and life-changing, but if you really want your child to thrive, you will not only *give* the Blessing but also *live* it, seeking out ways to include appropriate meaningful touch, spoken and written words, messages of high value and a special future, and evidence of active, genuine commitment in every day you spend together, every moment.

At the breakfast table and over bedtime prayers, some parents memorize a little blessing to say or sing to their children. In the car on the way to school can be the perfect time for an offhand conversation with a teen. While on the soccer field, in the movie theater, at church, at the park, or in the backyard, look for ways to inject little words of blessing in everyday conversation.

Make it a habit, and the blessings will flow through your life—as the pictures in the next chapter show.

Pictures Your Heart Remembers

Who is someone in your life who has been an "Uncle Max," someone who put something down in words? Maybe it's something you've kept and treasured. Or maybe it's something you didn't keep but you'll never forget. Who is somebody who actually took the step to say something that made a huge difference to you?

Pray for the opportunity to be that kind of person for somebody else as well.

Who is someone you can be an Uncle Max to?

Blessing Group Questions

1. In writing a blessing, so many of us think we have to be creative or compose something that would win a major writing award. But, really, even simple words can carry a profound effect. What is holding you back from putting something in writing?
2. Are you struggling with finding the "right time" to bless? Take the pressure off yourself to come up with that perfect time to share your blessing. It could be an opening the Lord provides when you are putting a child to bed. Or on the way to soccer practice. Or while you are making dinner. Take a minute right now to pray for flexibility and timing that will make your blessing most meaningful to its recipient.
3. You've been in your Blessing Group now for several weeks or longer. Write out something that has blessed you that someone in the group has said to you or encouraged you with.
4. Spend the rest of your group time working on your blessings for your kids (or others). Before you leave, take time to read what you have written to the group.

Blessing Activity

Give your child your written blessing sometime this week. Don't forget to share about that experience with your group next week.

Part 3

Living the Blessing

Chapter 13

Your Blessing

Now that you understand what the Blessing is and you've dug deeper into the elements of the Blessing and you've committed to giving the Blessing to your kids and loved ones, it's time to get practical.

Concepts and words hold power, but they mean little if we don't live them out. When we are consistent with living them out, everything changes.

That's why we created this section for this new edition of *The Blessing*. Over the next few chapters, I (Kari) will walk you through the practical side of living the Blessing. As you learned in the last chapter, the Blessing is not a one-time action. It takes genuine commitment to continue to give our blessing to those God has placed in our lives. It's doing small things consistently that will really add up to make your home a place of blessing.[1]

If you're anything like me, it can be hard to keep coming up with new ways to share our blessing. It can also be challenging to know where to start when the Blessing has never before been present in a relationship. We also may need some additional support to bless in relationships where brokenness or hurt currently exists. These chapters are designed to give you ideas that you can apply today as well as help you create your own ideas as you continue to live the Blessing.

While each chapter deals with specific relationships, I'd encourage you to read each chapter, even if you don't currently have that type of relationship in your life. Feel free to substitute in a different relationship if that particular one doesn't apply to you. The stories and processing tools in each chapter can still add value and give you new ideas and practical ways to live the Blessing.

These chapters are designed to be short, to the point, and interactive—so it will feel different from the other sections of the book. We pray that these chapters allow you to put the Blessing into action on a daily basis in your home and in your life.

As you begin to try some of these ideas, or even create your own, we'd love to hear from you—and with your permission, we'd love to share your ideas with our Blessing community:

- E-mail us directly at TheBlessing@StrongFamilies.com.
- Tag us on social media (Facebook: @drjohntrent, Instagram: @strong.families, @karitrentstageberg).

Okay, now for the fun part! In order to truly live out the Blessing, there is one blessing that needs to happen first: yours.

To be fully free to bless, we first need to know—and believe—we are blessed ourselves.

If you've made it this far into the book, you have a good idea of whether you've received the Blessing. Sadly, many of us have not. Even if you did receive the Blessing, you may have realized that you are still struggling with either believing it or living it out. Still others of us are feeling thankful that we received the Blessing and can't wait to share it with others.

No matter where you are, before we ask you to bless others,

we want to take a few minutes to bless each of you and make sure you *know*—and believe—you have the Blessing.

If you are working through this book with a Blessing Group, this is something that we'd like you to do together. When you meet next, make sure to either add some extra time or skip the group questions in order to ensure that each person in your group is given a blessing. You can use the blessings we've provided below or you can create your own.

If you are working through this book on your own, we'd strongly encourage you to get someone to do this with you. Ask your spouse, best friend, pastor, coworker, or someone else you are close to. There is power in having someone you love speak life over you.

If you aren't ready to do that, or if there isn't someone you feel comfortable asking, that's okay. My dad (John) and I will be the ones speaking life over you today.

The purpose of this chapter is not just for you to hear the Blessing from someone else; it's for you to begin to speak words of life and blessing over yourself as well.

Before we jump into your blessing, there are a few things to keep in mind as you read and work through this chapter with your Blessing Group, chosen friend, or on your own:

1. It can be uncomfortable to receive this type of affirmation and blessing, especially if you have never experienced it before. It's okay to feel any emotion that comes up as you read this. We've heard it all—from no emotion at all to anger and disbelief, from tears and pain to laughter and joy. Feel whatever it is you need to feel. But no matter what that emotion is, keep rereading your blessing—out loud—until you "get it" in your heart.
2. If you are struggling with accepting this truth about yourself, one suggestion is to look in the mirror. Literally. Eight years

ago, when I was at my lowest point, I didn't believe a single good thing about me existed. A dear friend of mine had me stand in front of the mirror and repeat truth about who I was and how much God loved me. At the time, I wanted to kick, scream, storm out of the room, and never talk to her again. However, I did it. And it changed my life. To this day, I have truth in the form of verses hanging on my mirror and around my house to remind me to continue to speak blessing over myself.

It's amazing how hard it can be to bless ourselves. We often feel so free, and much more comfortable, doing this for others. But let me tell you, if you don't take the time to make sure that *you* know you are blessed and live from that place yourself, any blessing you share with others will always be a fraction of what it could be.

So here's how this chapter works: pick one or all of the blessings below and follow the process we have laid out for you. We have three categories of blessing for you to choose from:

1. I've never received the Blessing.
2. I need a blessing for this season.
3. I got the Blessing, and I'm ready to bless.

Again, feel free to just read the option that applies to you or even all three!

I've Never Received the Blessing

If you are reading this and you have never received the Blessing, we are going to give you one right now.

If you are doing this with your Blessing Group, pick one person to read the following blessing out loud (or your group can choose to have each person read a line or two). If you are doing this with your spouse, friend, or coworker, get that person to read this out loud. If you are doing this on your own, you guessed it—read it out loud. Know that we (John and Kari) along with the Lord have prayed this over each person who is to pick up and read this book.

If you are the person reading this blessing for someone else, place your hand on the shoulder of the person who is to receive it (the rest of your Blessing Group can do this as well). Read these words, all of which come right out of God's Word and are truths that *He* says about *you*:

- You are chosen.[2]
- You are wanted.[3]
- You are loved.[4]
- You are redeemed.[5]
- He has called you by name—and *you are his*.[6] Part of his family. His son. His daughter. His beloved.[7]
- There is nothing you have done, or ever can do, that will cause him to walk away from you.[8] He will never leave you.[9]
- He has created you with a *great* purpose, on purpose.[10] And he has *great* plans for you: plans for your good—not your destruction. Plans for hope and a special future.[11]
- Every place that is broken, he will redeem and restore.[12] Every place that is rough, he will make smooth.[13] Every place there is doubt, fear, or confusion—be replaced with courage, peace, and wisdom, in the name of Jesus.
- You are not alone. *We* choose you. The Lord chooses you. *You have our blessing.*
- You are blessed. You've been designed to bless. And right now, you are choosing to use your unique God-given strengths to bless others as well.

175

Don't Skip This Step

Now, if you are the one receiving this blessing, it's your turn! Take a moment to read the same blessing out loud, replacing the word *you* with *I*. Reading the blessing out loud and declaring it for yourself are two key parts to moving knowledge from your head to your heart. If you are doing this with your Blessing Group or a friend, have them continue to stand with you and keep their hand on your shoulder in agreement. Read the following truth about who Almighty God says *you* are:

- I am chosen.
- I am wanted.
- I am loved.
- I am redeemed.
- He has called me by name—and *I am his*. Part of his family. His son. His daughter. His beloved.
- There is nothing I have done, or ever can do, that will cause him to walk away from me. He will never leave me.
- He has created me with a *great* purpose, on purpose. He has *great* plans for me: plans for my good—not for my destruction. Plans for hope and a special future.
- Every place that is broken, he will redeem and restore. Every place that is rough, he will make smooth. Every place there is doubt, fear, or confusion—be replaced with courage, peace, and wisdom, in the name of Jesus.
- I am not alone. I am chosen by the Lord, and by _____ _____ _____ (fill in as many names as you can think of here).
- I am blessed. I've been designed to bless. And I choose to use my unique God-given strengths to bless _____ _____ . (fill in names here) as well.

I Need a Blessing for This Season

Even if you've received the Blessing, there are many reasons why you may feel like you need some extra encouragement or a good reminder. Maybe you haven't heard the words in a long time. Or it's been a tough season, one where your circumstances or personal decisions have left you feeling discouraged or full of shame. No matter the reason, we all face times where we just need to hear the Blessing.

If you are doing this with your Blessing Group, pick one person to read the following out loud (or your group can choose to have each person read a line or two). If you are doing this with your spouse or friend, get that person to read this out loud. If you are doing this on your own, you guessed it—read it out loud. Again, know that we (John and Kari) along with the Lord have prayed this over each person who is to pick up and read this book.

If you are the person reading this blessing, place your hand on the shoulder of the person who is to receive it (the rest of your Blessing Group can do this as well). Read these words, all of which come right out of God's Word and are truths that *he* says about *you*:

- You are the Lord's.[14]
- He is proud of you.[15]
- He has designed you specifically as you are[16]—and has *great* plans for you.[17]
- He has created you to be a voice for his love.[18]
- You are able, through him, to love others like Jesus.[19]
- Nothing you've done, or ever will do, can remove his love from you.[20]
- Every place that's dry, be filled with living water.[21] Every place that's weary, be filled with strength.[22] Every hurt or

disappointment, be turned to joy.[23] Every place of shame be covered in grace and be fully whole, in the name of Jesus.

- You are blessed. You are loved. You are chosen. We choose you.
- And you can choose to bless others as well.

Don't Skip This Step

If you are the one receiving this blessing, it's your turn. Take a moment to read the blessing you just received out loud, replacing the word *you* with *I*. As you read it, ask the Lord to give you fresh encouragement and reminders about how much he loves you. Remember, there is power in our words, and saying them ourselves is part of making them our own. The rest of your group can support you and keep their hands on your shoulders in agreement as you read as well:

- I am the Lord's.
- He is proud of me.
- He has designed me specifically as I am—and has *great* plans for me.
- He has created me to be a voice for his love.
- I am able, through him, to love others like Jesus.
- Nothing I've done, or ever will do, can remove his love from me.
- Every place that's dry, be filled with living water. Every place that's weary, be filled with strength. Every hurt or disappointment, be turned to joy. Every place of shame be covered in grace and be fully whole, in the name of Jesus.
- I am blessed. I am loved. I am chosen by the Lord, and by ___
  _____
  _____ (fill in as many names as you can think of here).
- And I choose to bless _____
  _____ (fill in names here).

I Got the Blessing, and
I'm Ready to Bless

If you got the Blessing and you're feeling great about jumping into blessing others, we still have a blessing for you. This blessing comes right out of Psalm 103.

If you are doing this with your Blessing Group, pick one person to read the following out loud (or each person in your group can choose to read a line or two). If you are doing this with your spouse or friend, get that person to read this out loud. If you are doing this on your own, you guessed it—read it out loud. We (John and Kari) along with the Lord have prayed this over each person who is to pick up and read this book—and we know God wants to bless you.

If you are the person reading this blessing, place your hand on the shoulder of the person who is to receive it (the rest of your Blessing Group can do this as well). Read these words, all of which come right out of God's Word and are truths that *he* says about *you*:

- Praise the LORD, my soul; all my inmost being, praise his holy name.
- Praise the LORD, my soul, and forget not all his benefits— who forgives all your sins and heals all your diseases, who redeems your life from the pit and crowns you with love and compassion, who satisfies your desires with good things so that your youth is renewed like the eagle's.
- The LORD works righteousness and justice for all the oppressed.
- He made known his ways to Moses, his deeds to the people of Israel: The LORD is compassionate and gracious, slow to anger, abounding in love.
- He will not always accuse, nor will he harbor his anger

forever; he does not treat us as our sins deserve or repay us according to our iniquities.

- For as high as the heavens are above the earth, so great is his love for those who fear him; as far as the east is from the west, so far has he removed our transgressions from us.
- As a father has compassion on his children, so the LORD has compassion on those who fear him. (Ps. 103:1–13 NIV)

Don't Skip This Step

If this is your blessing, it's time for you to read it out loud. Take a few moments to praise the Lord for all that he has done and continues to do for you:

- Praise the LORD, my soul; all my inmost being, praise his holy name.
- Praise the LORD, my soul, and forget not all his benefits— who forgives all [my] sins, and heals all [my] diseases, who redeems [my] life from the pit and crowns [me] with love and compassion, who satisfies [my] desires with good things so that [my] youth is renewed like the eagle's.
- The LORD works righteousness and justice for all the oppressed.
- He made known his ways to Moses, his deeds to the people of Israel: The LORD is compassionate and gracious, slow to anger, abounding in love.
- He will not always accuse, nor will he harbor his anger forever; he does not treat [me] as [my] sins deserve or repay [me] according to [my] iniquities.
- For as high as the heavens are above the earth, so great is his love for [me] who fear[s] him; as far as the east is from the west, so far has he removed [my] transgressions from [me].
- As a father has compassion on his children, so the LORD has compassion on [me] who fear[s] him.

What's Next?

For some of you, that blessing was the first time you've been told the *truth* about who you are, your value, and the fact that someone—including Jesus—is crazy about you.

If you need to keep rereading any of the blessings above, do it! You can even order a print of any of these blessings at TheBlessing.com/store. Or feel free to rewrite it yourself. Hang it on your mirror. Put it in your car. Place it on your desk. Anytime the Enemy begins to tell you lies about who you are, who you're created to be, or if you really have value, read your blessing out loud.

Whether that was your first blessing or your hundredth, if you feel like you need more breakthrough in believing that you are chosen for a great purpose, dig in and get more help.

Here are a few ways we recommend you do that:

1. Find a great counselor.
2. Take one of our Blessing courses. (We have several, including one on what to do if you didn't get the Blessing.)
3. Get in a Blessing Group, if you aren't already in one, to walk through this book and process with others.
4. Read the book *The Blessing Cry* by Dr. John Trent and Dr. Tony Wheeler.

For many of us it's a combination of these things that brings the breakthrough we need. The goal is to keep moving and, no matter what steps you choose, to take a step toward blessing. It really does start with you.

Okay, before we jump into living out the Blessing starting with our kids and grandkids, take some time to work through the

Pictures My Heart Remembers, Blessing Group Questions, and a new section you will see in each chapter in this part of the book, Making the Blessing a Lifestyle.

Pictures Your Heart Remembers

Take some time to journal about what the blessing you just received means to you.

Let's go a little bit deeper: Was there something that stood out to you? Was there a new truth that you felt impacted by? Was there something in the blessing that was hard for you to believe or receive? Was there something that made you feel "unleashed" to bless others? Was there something that reminded you of how valued and loved you are by the Lord? Was there something in the blessing that "reversed the curse" in an area of your life, or in a belief you've held about yourself?

Blessing Group Questions

1. Which of the three groups did you most identify with ("I never got the Blessing," "I need a blessing for this season," "I got the Blessing, and I'm ready to bless"), and why?
2. Was it hard for you to receive the blessings in this chapter? Why or why not?
3. Is it easier or harder for you to bless yourself than it is to bless others? Why?
4. Do you feel like you need to take more action to really believe the Blessing for yourself? If yes, what action seems the most helpful to you? (Get your group to keep you accountable.)

5. What is one way you can continue to choose to bless yourself as you get ready to bless others?
6. Share the blessing you wrote for yourself in the Making the Blessing a Lifestyle section below with your group.

Blessing Activity

Pick one of the blessings in the chapter (or if you completed the Making the Blessing a Lifestyle section that follows, choose that blessing you wrote on your own).

Write down this blessing (or order the print from our website) and put it in a place where you are going to see it every day.

Every day, for the next thirty days, read it *out loud* to yourself.

Make sure to share this with your Blessing Group to help keep you accountable.

Making the Blessing a Lifestyle

In the next few chapters we are going to walk you through how to create blessings for the people you love most. However, as we've talked about in this chapter, being able to bless others really starts with you. So we are going to spend a few minutes helping *you* create a blessing for yourself.

Now, before you freak out and throw this book aside, stay with us. Not only is this really simple, but if you take the time to write a blessing for yourself, it can provide a lot of healing, affirmation, and hope as well.

First, spend a few minutes filling in your answers to the following questions:

1. If (name of someone who is crazy about you) was sitting here with me, this person would say that I am great at ___ _____.

2. One of my strengths is _____ _____.

3. Some verses that really make me feel loved are _____.

Next, take a few minutes to ask the Lord to share some other ways that he is crazy about you. If you've never done this before, don't worry. There's nothing scary about it. He may give you a Bible verse like those from lines in our blessings above. He may remind you of a story where you lived out your strengths and they were used to help and bless others. He may bring to mind some of your unique gifts and attributes that he's specifically designed you with, or he may give you something else entirely. Just take a few minutes and ask him. Write down what he shares with you.

Finally, take one of the blessings we shared in this chapter and use it as a guide to write your own blessing. You can copy lines directly from those blessings. Make sure to add the additional things you've written down here.

Chapter 14

Blessing Your Kids
and Grandkids

Many of you picked up this book because you want to know how to give your blessing to your kids or grandkids. This chapter will give you many practical ways to do just that.

You may notice that many of these stories are about our family. However, I (Kari) want to be very clear that the reason I chose these stories is *not* because my family is, was, ever has been, or ever will be perfect. We are, quite honestly, very far from it. But these stories are things that I've lived, experienced, and tried. They are also stories that we've shared with others, and we've seen these ideas work for them as well.

As you work through the Making the Blessing a Lifestyle section at the end of this chapter, please know that we would love to hear your ideas. We want to know what worked, and even what didn't work, with your family. And we'd encourage you to share those stories with your Blessing Group and our community online as well.

Blessing Babies

Is it ever too early to start blessing? No! Just as babies can hear their parents' voices when they are still in the womb, these little ones can see, hear, and comprehend even more than we've previously given them credit for.

So what does it look like to bless your baby?

1. Use the right tone.

Your baby may not be able to understand the meaning of your words, but research shows he absolutely understands your tone.[1] While the words may not be as important at this age, it is a *great* time to practice speaking blessings out loud and incorporating them into your daily routine.

2. Turn it into a song.

From YouTube videos to scientific journal articles, we've seen just how responsive babies are to music. Many babies even dance to or babble their own songs before they began speaking words.[2] By making up a blessing song and singing it again and again to your child, you are not only helping your little one learn but giving her something she can participate in even before she says her first words.

3. Write it down.

They may not be able read yet, but they will be able to someday. The blessings you write down for your small children today will not only help you become more comfortable with sharing your blessing but will be something they will get to read with you as they get older. In fact, I (Kari) have a book of blessings that I still keep in my nightstand. The blessings are all from my parents, starting from the day I was born all the way until today. These are letters I go back to again and again on hard days when I need encouragement or a reminder that I have their blessing.

4. Use your smile.

Babies as young as nine hours can already distinguish faces. At eleven hours, they can even tell the difference between their mom and a stranger. It's no surprise then that while it takes babies some time to identify voice tone with corresponding emotions (about five months is when this starts to occur), they prefer to look at smiling faces—even just hours after being born.[3] Studies also show that smiling builds trust, paints a picture of approval and security, and encourages your baby to explore the world around him.

So, to start your child off with a blessing, and to help him feel confident and affirmed even hours after he is born—smile![4]

Blessing Young Kids

What does it look like to bless your younger children?

1. Tell them a story.

I'll never forget being driven to school each morning—not because of the car ride, but because of the stories my dad would tell. Each morning, from our first day of kindergarten through our last day of junior high, my dad would drive my best friend, Brynne, and I to school—and he would give us his blessing in the form of a story.

These stories often centered on our favorite character, Bungee Bear, a super cute bear who had a bungee cord attached to him. Since Bungee Bear lived on a cloud, this bungee cord was especially helpful in ensuring that he would never fall out of his home. But it also kept him tied to something even more important . . . Jesus. Each day, Bungee Bear would face something that we were struggling with—from someone taking our lunch to friends being hurtful. And at the end of each story, as we were pulling into the drop-off zone, my dad would pray a blessing over us. He made sure that we knew—just like Bungee Bear—that our parents and the Lord were crazy about us and weren't going anywhere, no matter how challenging it got.

These Bungee Bear stories became such an important part of our lives that once a year, our dads, Brynne, and I would have a Bungee Bear breakfast. Brynne and I would get dressed up, grab one of our favorite stuffed bears, and go with our dads to a "fancy" restaurant (it was actually a cozy café located at the Scottsdale Airpark where we could watch the planes take off and land). Once we were there, our dads would tell us a Bungee Bear story and give us their blessing. Decades later, Brynne and I *still* remember Bungee Bear and our daily blessings. We've even asked our dads to continue to do grown-up Bungee Bear breakfasts with us (minus the teddy bears).

2. Pick something they love.

No matter what your child loves, there's a way to relate it back to a blessing. Does your child love trains? Cars? Princesses? Bugs? Dinosaurs? Superheroes? Horses? Music? Sports? Art? Whatever it is that has captivated his or her affection, take a few minutes and follow the formula below to come up with a word picture that will help your child "get" your blessing.

Hey [child's name], you really love [interest/thing], don't you? Well, you know how [interest/thing] makes you feel happy, excited, and is something you want around you all the time? That's exactly how I feel about you! In fact, I love you *even more* than you love [interest/thing]. And no matter what you love, or how grown-up you get, I'm always going to love you and be excited about how God has made you. And you know what else? Jesus is *even more* crazy about you than I am!

It's really that easy to help your child get the picture of how much you love them.

3. From potty training to learning to read, plan a date night to celebrate.

Brynne, my best friend I mentioned above, and her husband, John, took potty training their kids to the next level. When their beautiful daughter began the process of potty training, they told her that as soon as she had completed her potty training chart, she would get to have a special date night with her dad. She sailed through her potty training, and on the day of her date with Daddy they pulled out all the stops. They bought her a special dress, complete with "grown-up girl" shoes. Their daughter's favorite babysitter came over and did a special big-girl hairstyle. And John, being a true gentleman, showed up at the front door with a corsage for his daughter. He had also borrowed a special car for the evening, complete with a single flower waiting for her in her car seat.

John took their daughter to her favorite restaurant (where she could have pancakes for dinner), and while they were there, he gave her his blessing. When she got home, more surprises were waiting for her. Both sets of grandparents, several close friends, and Brynne were there in the decorated living room. They each gave her their blessing as well. While that may seem like a lot for a three-year-old, their daughter (now five) still talks about "date night with Daddy." And this is something they've replicated for other big achievements in her life as well.

4. Keep singing.

Just like babies, kids love music too! In fact, I can still sing you the blessing song my parents made up for me when I was young. Each morning when they woke me up for school, they would come in my room singing. The lyrics were:

> Good morning, good morning, how are you today?
> The Lord bless you and keep you throughout the day.
> We love you, we love you, we love you, Kari.

While that may sound super corny, when I was five, my parents saw firsthand how much that song meant to me. They were trying to put me to sleep one night, and I had crawled out of bed for the eighth time. After they had threatened everything except for monsters under the bed to try to get me to go to sleep, my little voice called down the hallway, "Good night, Mom! Good night, Dad! Don't forget to bless me in the morning!"

Even at five years old, I *wanted* my parents' blessing each morning. I longed for it. And your kids do too.

5. Use the Special Plate.

When I was growing up, there was no greater sign of achievement or accomplishment in our house than getting to eat dinner with the Special Plate. The Special Plate has a long history in my family, and it can in yours as well.

The Special Plate first made an appearance the day I was born. Donna, a good friend of our family, showed up at the hospital not with baby clothes, flowers, or balloons but with a box containing a red china plate with the words *You Are Special Today* written across it. She told my parents to use this as a way to bless me as I was growing up. Four years later, when my sister, Laura, was born, Donna showed up with a second *You Are Special Today* plate.

As a kid, there was no higher honor in our home than getting to eat dinner on the Special Plate.

The reality was, we got the Special Plate *a lot*. We got the Special Plate on our first day of school, for doing an extra chore to help at home, for completing a hard homework assignment, for defending a friend who wasn't being treated kindly, for trying our hardest even if we didn't make the team, for making a hard decision, and so on.

While to some it may seem that we overused the Special Plate, it never felt like that. Each time we were the recipient of that beautiful red plate, my mom and dad would tell us that we had their blessing, and that they would always be there as we continued to become the women God had created us to be.

When Joey and I got married, I got a package in the mail from Donna. When I opened it, tears flooded my eyes. Inside was my very own red *You Are Special Today* plate. It's been a blessing to continue to use the Special Plate with Joey and celebrate key moments in our lives and the commitment to help each other grow as well.

If you like the idea of a Special Plate for your family, you can get your very own Special Plate, exactly like the one we have, at this link: https://StrongFamilies.com/living-the-blessing/the-special-plate.

Blessing Older Kids

What does it look like to bless children who are older?

1. Leave a message at their desk.

I used to *love* parent-teacher "back to school" night at the beginning of the school year—not because I wanted my parents to meet my teacher, but because I knew the next day was going to be a *great* day. This was because the night before, while my parents traveled to my different classrooms, they were also leaving a trail of notes for me.

Starting in kindergarten and going through my senior year of high school, my parents would hide encouraging notes for me in places where I would find them throughout the year.

Some were in my pencil box, and others waited in books, my cubby, art supplies, inside my locker, or even taped to my seat for me to find first thing in the morning.

My parents were so devoted to this practice that they actually got in trouble for passing notes during parent-teacher night one year.

I may not have been crazy about going to school the next morning, but I *was crazy* about finding my parents' notes. And the ones that were better hidden always seemed to make an appearance on days when I really needed them.

Notes like these don't need to be long or wordy. In fact, ours were always written on sticky notes. Even a "We are super proud of you—Love, Mom and Dad," or "You are going to change the world with your words" in an English book can add so much life to your child. Really, just a few notes of encouragement for your kids can go a long way.

2. Traveling? Make it special.

Growing up, my dad traveled a lot. But I can honestly tell you that while he was a million-miler with two different airlines, it *never* felt like it.

Whenever my dad went out of town, he took time before and after the trip to make sure we knew that he loved us.

Before he would leave, he would have Laura and I sit down at the kitchen table. He would pull out a placemat with a map of the United States on it. He would ask us where we lived, and we would point to Phoenix on the map. Then he would tell us what city he was flying to and help us find it on the map. He would then walk us through what he was going to do while he was there.

Now, let me pause here. You may think that kids don't really care about what their parents do for work. But you're wrong. To most kids, when their parents travel for work, it's like a black hole. They don't know where their parents are, what they are doing, or if it's really even important. Taking a few minutes to walk your kids through your trip can change that.

For us, when my dad would show us where he was going and briefly describe what he would be doing—we got the picture. We realized the trips were intentional, he was doing something important, and we knew exactly where he would be. It added both peace and security for Laura and me and made us feel like our dad wanted us to be a part of what he was doing when he wasn't at home.

I'm not saying you need to go into great detail about your meetings or get into the technical aspects of your job. But a simple "I'm flying to Omaha, and I have meetings with some important people about our new project all day Tuesday, and I have a big lunch with my boss on Wednesday before I fly home" can be super helpful for your kids. You can even ask your kids to be praying for you and your meetings, projects, presentations, and more as you travel!

When my dad got home, Laura and I would race to the door, because we knew something special was coming . . . we would get a surprise! These surprises were small, inexpensive gifts that my dad would bring home from his trip. Think a rock, postcard, or even sometimes a complimentary lotion from the hotel he had stayed at. While they were small gifts, and often disregarded after a few minutes, they let us know that he had been thinking about us while he was gone. However, there was a catch. Before we got our gifts, he would sit down with us and tell us about his trip. Again, this wasn't a long, detailed list of what he had done. It was an overview so that we knew, again, that he had been gone for a reason and that he had missed us while he was gone.

While that may sound like a lot, the real work came on the longer trips. Whenever my dad was gone for more than three days, or anytime he and my mom were traveling at the same time, Laura and I felt like it was Christmas.

Before they left, they would put out a brown lunch bag, one for each day they were gone, and number them 1, 2, 3, and so on for the total number of days they would be out of town.

Each morning before we got ready for school, Laura and I would race to our paper bag and open it with excitement. Inside would be a short note of encouragement, along with a small present.

Again, these weren't expensive gifts. Sometimes it was a pack of gum or a toy from the dollar store, or sometimes my dad would take a stuffed animal we already had and put it inside the bag with a short note about how he loved us more than we loved that animal.

The gifts weren't important. The important thing was, *each* day he or my mom was gone, we knew beyond a shadow of a doubt that they were thinking about us, missing us, and that they would continue to find ways to give us their blessing—even if they weren't able to be with us.

Okay, so now that you're totally overwhelmed, let's step back. Practically, this does take some planning, time, and effort. But if you travel a lot or even just a few times a year, let me tell you— there is no better way I've found to help your kids *know* you are with them, even when you can't physically be there.

I asked my dad how long planning this took, and he said he spent about five minutes the night before a short trip to tell us where he was going, plus an additional ten to fifteen minutes the night before a long trip to make the bags. In fact, my mom would buy small gifts at the dollar store and keep them in a hidden place in their closet so my dad could grab those when he needed them.

So, next trip, as you pack, add in an extra ten minutes to bless your kids. You'll be glad you did.

3. Play Twenty Questions.

Turn off the iPad or DVD player in the car and play Twenty Questions. While every family has their own rules for Twenty Questions, for ours the game looked something like this:

- My parents would ask us a question. We would answer, and then we'd get to ask them a question.
- This would go on until we reached our destination—which usually involved some type of treat for us: a trip to the park, ice cream, or an hour to play before we had to start on our homework.

Playing Twenty Questions not only taught us how to communicate as a family but also taught us that we could ask our parents questions.

My parents would also end every session by reminding us that they would always want to know more about us—and that they were open to talking with us about any questions we might have.

Creating this type of safe environment for questions and communication early on will make it tremendously easier for your kids to relate to you as they enter the teen and adult years.

It's also a great tip to remember for older kids. We've all had the after-school conversation:

Us: Hey, honey, how was school today?
Them: Fine.
Us: Okay. What did you learn at school today?
Them: Nothing.
Us: Did you do anything fun?

Them: No.

Us: What did you do with your friends?

Them: Nothing.

Anyone else feeling the all-too-real pain of that conversation? The great thing about Twenty Questions is you get to be specific. Let them know that for their answer to count, it can't be one word—it needs to be a full sentence, and they need to ask you a question in return. You can also add in a bribe—think a snack or activity that they enjoy—to get them to participate. That's right, in the Trent household we are not above bribing teenagers to talk to us . . . or do errands with us . . . or choose to continue to drive with us.

Blessing Teens

Here are some thoughts for blessing teenagers in your family.

1. Look at the calendar.

While this is something you can do with your kids at any age, or even with your spouse and friends, there is something about the teenage years that make them heavily schedule driven. And once your teens start driving, it can seem like your entire family is hardly ever in the same place at the same time!

However, you can turn even the craziest schedule into a weekly blessing.

Here's what you do:

- Once a week, sit down as a family and talk about the upcoming week. At our house, this always seems to happen at Sunday dinner, since it's the one time we all end up at home—but you can pick any day that works for your family.

- Once you are together, go around and have each person share any big things that will be going on for him or her this week. Now, you may have to ask your teenager specific questions like "Do you have a test?"—but the goal is to have everyone share at least *one* thing that will be happening in the next seven days.

Here are some ideas if you need help getting teenagers to share: Do they have a sporting event, tryouts, finals, speech debates, a school dance, a big test, a hard conversation, a class they really hate going to, a goal they are trying to reach, something they are nervous or excited about?

Once all the family members have each identified at least one thing happening this week, ask them (or help them figure out) what time that event is going to happen, and on what day.

For example: Maddie has a science test during second period (which is 9:15 a.m.) on Tuesday, and Diego has soccer tryouts after school (which is 3:45 p.m.) on Thursday.

Now, when my parents did this with Laura and me, my dad would set a timer on his watch, and my mom would write it in her Day-Timer.

Today, with iPhones, Apple Watches, Google Home, and Google Calendar, it's even easier. Just tell Siri or Alexa to remind you to "pray for [name] and his or her [test, tryout, conversation, and so forth] at [time] on [day]" right there at the dinner table.

As you add the reminder, tell your kids that you love them, you will be praying for them at that exact moment, and, no matter the outcome, they have your blessing and you will always be crazy about them.

My parents did this with us each week. I cannot tell you the number of times I'd be sitting in class, terrified about the test the teacher was handing out, and my eyes would go to the clock. I'd instantly be reminded that my parents were praying for me at that exact moment and that, no matter what, I was coming home to a mom and dad who were proud of me.

Bonus: When your kids get home that day, *ask them* how their event went. It's a perfect opportunity to talk to them about what happened that day and how they are feeling and to give support, encouragement, or blessing right when they need it.

2. Try some apples and peanut butter.

The teenage years can be unpredictable, but you don't have to be.

The blessing I remember most as a teenager had to do with late-night talks over apples and peanut butter. After every dance, late-night game, or even just a night out with friends that stretched on all the way to curfew (or beyond), I knew that regardless of how the night went I'd have someone to talk to.

I would walk in the house, and my dad would be waiting for me with my favorite snack, apples and peanut butter. We'd sit at the kitchen table, and as I munched, he would ask me questions about my night.

Sometimes I'd have fun stories to share, or other nights, like the time I didn't get asked to prom or a mean guy at school called me fat, our conversations would be full of my tears. But no matter what was going on in my life, I knew there would be someone there at the end of the day who cared about what I was going through.

After I finished my snack and our conversation ended, my dad would hug me, pray for me, and give me his blessing.

Now, though I'm well into my thirties, my dad *still* waits up for me anytime I'm back in Arizona. We still sit down and talk about my night. And I still get a hug and a blessing.

These are by far some of the most meaningful and important

conversations I had during my teen years, and they have turned out to be some of the most meaningful and important in my adult life as well.

It may cost you some sleep and some extra money in snacks, but it will bring you and your child more blessing than you know.

I asked my dad once if he ever wanted to go to bed instead of waiting up to talk to me. His eyes got misty, and he said, "I asked my mom that same question once, and I'm going to tell you exactly what she told me . . . 'I can always go back to sleep . . . but I won't always be here to have these talks with you. There's nothing I'd rather do than talk to you.'"

3. Write a little note—it goes a long way.

Don't underestimate the power of a note. Does your child have a paper that he started the night before it was due? Does she have a big test that she is worried about? Is he trying out for a team? Feeling jittery about prom? Nervous about what her friends will think?

Write your child a quick note!

My sister, Laura, would start her term papers weeks in advance and would get a full night's sleep the night before they were due.

I didn't even know what my topic was going to be until after dinner the night before the paper was to be turned in.

But both Laura and I got notes of encouragement slipped under our door the night before we turned in our papers.

Even my sophomore year, when my dad had to drive my friend Nicole and me to Kinko's (before it was FedEx) at 3:00 a.m. to make copies of all our sources and footnotes (this was before the days when home copiers were available, the Internet was deemed credible enough to cite, and kids got to submit their papers electronically). I still found a note under my door telling me I was a great writer and the Lord had gifted me to use my words.

And there was another time, when I came home from cheer-leading tryouts to find small notes taped all around my room from my dad, mom, sister, and even the dog.

Again, these notes weren't long. Just one or two sentences. But I still have some of them hanging in my office and lying on my nightstand today.

4. Do your homework.

As your kids get older, they may become less excited about things you once did together, especially as they begin to test the waters with what they feel called to do in life. But don't get discouraged! There are still some powerful ways you can bless them—it just may take some research.

What is your child into? Music? Go to a concert, just the two of you. And give your child a blessing at dinner before you go.

Basketball? Go to a game, even if you're in the nosebleed section, and regardless of whether it's the local, college, or state champion team. Again, make sure to carve out some time over dinner or in the car to bless your child.

Science? Visit a museum or attend a lecture together, or line up a college visit complete with a lab experience.

Fashion? Go to a local show, watch *Project Runway*, or volunteer to help with your child's latest sewing project.

The bottom line is to meet your children where they are at. Even if you don't know anything about what gets them excited, do your research.

One of the best examples I've personally seen of this practice comes from my grandmother, and the story my dad shared about her bookshelf in chapter 11.

My grandma did her homework on what each of her boys was passionate about. She could ask them questions, talk to them at length about their passions, and had written notes in the margins of many of the magazines and journals based off their conversations.

She found a way to learn about them—to meet them where they were at—and encourage them when they were struggling in life or in their careers.

Your kids may change their minds fifty times before they land where the Lord has them. But you and your kids will not feel a single minute is wasted if you take the time to learn about what they love and encourage them as they learn as well.

Blessing Adult Kids

Here are some thoughts for blessing your children who are grown.

1. Keep using snail mail.

E-mails and texts are great, but there is something very special about a handwritten note.

Every week while Laura and I were in college, we would get a letter from home. Really, these "letters" were humorous greeting cards in which my parents would write one or two lines of encouragement before signing and sending them to us.

Often these notes would also include an article they had found that related to what we were studying, a picture, a gift card, or even (when we really needed it) some cash to help us get through the week.

I still have a box under my bed *full* of four years' worth of cards. Every single handwritten sentence from home helped make the hardest moments of college seem bearable.

2. Celebrate their first day of work.

I'll never forget my first day at my first job out of college. You know, your first "real" job.

The night before I was set to go to work, my parents came into my room. They had a note and a small wrapped package for me. Inside was a small antique piggy bank shaped like a small metal tin.

They told me, "Kari, no matter where you work or what you do, you are always worth more to us than any paycheck." They prayed for me and said a blessing over my new season.

I *still* have that piggy bank on my desk today, and there isn't a day that goes by that I don't look at it and think about the fact that no matter what I did or didn't get done that day, I'm worth *so* much more to my parents than my achievements or failures. (Which is especially handy, since I now am blessed to work with my dad.)

3. Keep exploring who they are.

You might assume that it doesn't matter as much to your adult children if you are interested in them and their lives, but that's actually the opposite of what they're thinking. They may not be seeking as much guidance from you as they were when they were younger, but they still want to know that you care about what's going on in their lives.

Take the game Twenty Questions from the previous section and adapt it for your adult children. For example, come up with twenty big questions (with three mini follow-up questions) that you can ask them about their work, life, interests, hobbies, and so forth. Note: This may require some homework. See the previous section under Do Your Homework for ideas.

For example, let's say your son works for a construction company, and you've done your homework and found out about a new development that could help with the longevity of pavement. You could ask one big question like, "I was reading the other day that a new type of asphalt has been developed that can last ten years without repaving. What are your thoughts on that?" Then you can ask three small follow-up questions like, "Do you think it would help or hurt construction companies? Is it something you would recommend to your clients? Do you think there is a better solution?"

Don't ask your children all twenty questions at once, but every week pick up the phone or grab dinner and ask a few questions . . . just to get to know them. Make sure to tell them at the end of your conversation that you love them, that you're proud of them, and that they have your blessing.

Some of you reading this may be having a hard time with where your child is currently at (see the last chapter in this section for more support on that). But even if your child is struggling or living a life that's different from what you pictured for him or her, try to pick questions that show your genuine care—not your disapproval of his or her decisions.

Meaning, if you don't like your child's job, significant other, or personal habits, keep questions about those topics off-limits for this conversation. You can still speak truth and share your opinion during other times of conversation. However, those things will fall on deaf ears and can even cause distance in your relationship if you don't take time to *build* the relationship as well (especially if you are coming out of challenges from the teen years).

Building a relationship means getting to know your child—and letting your child get to know you in a different way. Be vulnerable with him or her and spend time investing in the relationship by asking questions and listening—not sharing what *you* would do unless you're asked.

So if you really don't like your child's job and can't ask questions about it without voicing your opinion or disdain, skip that topic and pick something neutral. The more your children feel free in sharing with you, the more willing they'll become to let you speak into other areas of their lives as well.

4. Commit to weekly FaceTime.

With the exception of a few short months, I have not lived in the same state as my parents since I went to college. While we made it work during and after college, our relationship got even better with the blessing of FaceTime. There is nothing like being able to "see" your kids, and for them to "see" you. It also helps cut down on misunderstandings in communication that are all too common in texting and even phone conversations. While your millennial or Gen X kid may still favor texting, try incorporating FaceTime into your blessing routine at least once a month.

Helpful hint: smile—a lot!—while you have your kids on camera. And make sure you give them your blessing before you get off the call. It says in Proverbs that bright eyes make the heart glad (Prov. 15:30), and that counts for FaceTime too!

5. Make a care package.

There is nothing in the world like a care package. Imagine it: you get home, and sitting on your kitchen countertop is a box that contains some of your favorite things in the whole world, including a note from your parents telling you how valuable you are to them.

In reality, it may look more like your child picking this up from an Amazon locker, and the package may have a mixture of necessities (we can always use more socks!) and fun items. But no matter what's inside, it's a great way to bless your adult child—even if he or she lives in the same city as you.

Try to include things your child really loves—not just things that you want him or her to have. And don't forget a note of blessing as well!

If you want to take this idea to the next level, you can do what our good friend Shara did.

Shara not only picked up some of her son DeAndre's favorite things for her care package, but she wrote down *why* she picked each item specifically for DeAndre and turned each into a blessing. (Yes, we have officially awarded Shara the title of Blessing Champion of the World!)

For example, DeAndre loves chicken and waffles, so Shara got him a gift certificate to his favorite restaurant. In her card, she shared that she picked chicken and waffles not just because he loved it but because DeAndre "brings more joy, flavor, spice, and sweetness to [her] life than even the best chicken and waffle. And honey, that's sayin' something!"

It may sound simple, or silly, but Shara did that ten years ago. And to this day, DeAndre still gets tears in his eyes anytime he eats his favorite meal as he remembers his mother's blessing.

6. Give them a Blessing Coin.

Find a special time to give a Blessing Coin to your child. A Blessing Coin is something special that we have created to help you give your blessing. These coins have the five elements of the blessing on them and are both a great reminder for you to keep choosing to give your blessing and a great visible reminder for your child that he or she *has* your blessing.

To give your child the coin, schedule some time with him or her. Go to a game together, to dinner, to see a concert, to play racquetball, or even to shoot hoops in your front yard.

Near the end of your time together, share your blessing with your child and give him or her the coin. Tell your child something like this: "You are more valuable to me than any coin or any amount of money. This coin is something you can keep to remind you every day that you will *always* have my blessing."

You can find Blessing Coins at TheBlessing.com.

Blessing Your Grandkids

Before we launch into some creative and meaningful ideas for grandparents, let me (John) share with you something I remember vividly about my grandfather. We called it the Great Parakeet Fiasco, and it became a legend in our home.

I was in second grade. Our parakeet had escaped from its cage while we were at school. My grandmother was cleaning the parakeet's cage, and Tweetie (yes, we were creative in naming pets, including Mr. Cat) decided to make a break for it—and got past her hand and flew into the living room. Grandma ordered my grandfather to catch the runaway parakeet, which he did by throwing a dish towel over it and then taking it in his hand.

But then it happened. Tweetie was obviously scared and bit a large chunk out of Grandfather's right index finger. Almost spasmodically, Grandfather squeezed his hand and cried out, "Dumb bird!" (Or words to that effect.) My grandfather was an old carpenter and a hard-as-nails Texan. Tragically—and he truthfully didn't mean to—his hands were so strong, that spasmodic squeeze was all it took to send Tweetie to parakeet heaven. (Please, no e-mails on the theology of such a place.)

I share this tragic story not because it was funny. It wasn't. But what happened was almost as bad. My grandmother was not in the room when Tweetie expired. So my grandfather took the bird and put it back in the cage. He wrapped its feet around the wooden perch that stretched across the middle of the cage and then leaned the parakeet up against the side, hoping it would look like Tweetie had fallen asleep and passed away.

However, like any great cover-up, it didn't work. Pandemonium broke out when we got home from school, and a misshapen bird led to a reluctant confession. And here is why I share this very sad story.

There is simply no way to hide things—for long—from our

children or grandchildren. They are like God's little spies. And as God's Word says, "Nothing is hidden that will not become evident, nor anything secret that will not be known and come to light" (Luke 8:17 NASB).

That doesn't mean we have to be perfect grandparents. None of us are or will be. But kids remember our actions—positive or negative. And as we get older and realize more acutely that there is an expiration date on all our lives, it's important we realize that our children and grandchildren won't remember all the places we took them, but they will remember how we loved them.

So here are several small ways to bring the Blessing home to a grandchild's life.

1. Pick a household chore and team up with your grandchildren.

First, real men (and women) do chores. And hopefully your grandchildren will have parents who are wise enough to assign them some. If they're too young to do them, that's when kids want to do chores! But if they're old enough to do the chore, odds are they aren't going to like it.

Which is where you step in—not to do the chore for them, but with them. And while you're doing that task, talk to them about some chores you had to do as a child: the fun ones, the challenging ones. The time you got caught skipping out on a chore—and the consequences—or the thing that chore actually taught you. Your chores will very likely show you grew up in a very different world from today and your grandchildren's chores. And this will give you a chance to share your story—which is in itself a wonderful way of blessing each of your grandchildren.

I'm grateful for the stories that my mother told me about the pigs down in the mud and how they knew it was her when she was trying to feed them. Or my grandfather talking about falling asleep while driving the tractor and waking up when it ran into—and through—the neighbors' fence. It was another world. It brought me closer to both of them to hear their chores and challenges, and it remains a blessing to me to this day.

2. Declare a grandparent Anything-Goes Dinner national holiday.

You might talk with your children before the next time you're watching the grandkids to ask their permission to do this. (Or you can ask for forgiveness!) But one great way to bless kids is to declare a national holiday on whatever day you've got the kids for dinner. Announce it as National Anything-Goes Dinner Night and then head to the store. There, you let *them* pick out a main course, a something-else side to put on their plate, and a dessert. And since it's anything goes, get ready for chocolate milk for the main course, peanut butter mixed with jelly as their side, and macaroni and cheese for their dessert.

While they're eating, talk to them about how different things can still be good together—like how their grandmother and grandfather are different and the Lord has made them a wonderful mix. And how their mother and father are very different from each other, but they're wonderful together too. And, finally, how that grandson in front of you and the granddaughter on the other side of the table are very different from each other—but they're very loved as well. That's the message of 1 Corinthians 12. We're not all "eyes." We're not all "ears." But we are all placed in the body right where we belong.

It's a fun way to point out what you love about them—and how you can love someone (like their sister) just as much, even though you are very different from that person. This even provides a great opportunity to talk to your grandchildren about racial differences and help ensure that our next generation will step up and heal racial division and hurts in our country as well.

3. Just like air—teach them that God is always there.

Kids grow up in a flash. But even so, our time as grandparents is ticking on an even faster clock. One way to leave your grandchildren a picture of how your love and God's love will always be there—even when they can't see it—is to bring some balloons to the dinner table.

Make sure there's no choking hazard for little kids. With older kids, while still supervising them, have them each hold and blow up a balloon. Then, rather than having them tie the balloon, tell them instead to aim it at their grandmother (wherever she's sitting) or grandfather and "shoot" the balloon at them! Kids love watching those balloons shoot across the room! Let them do it several times until they're all blown out.

Then say, "Kids, let me ask you a question. Can you see air?" And of course, unless you live in Southern California, the answer for most kids will be no. Then share with them about what they've been doing with their balloons. "Did you know that air—even if you can't see it—has power? Just like how that balloon shot across the room. And air, even if you can't see it, is a part of space, just like the way air shapes a balloon when you blow into it."

Then tell them, "I want you kids to remember something, and that's the answer to a question. 'Is God real—even though you can't see him?'" They may say yes, or they may say no. But you can tell them, "Kids, just like air—God is there." You might even want to read them Colossians 1:15: "Christ is the visible expression of the invisible God" (PHILLIPS). "We can't see God the Father—but we got to see Jesus. And now, even though Jesus has gone back up to heaven, he is still real. And still here."

Next, you could also tell them what my grandmother told me. "John, the day will come when I'm not here and I'm up in heaven with Jesus." (She was dying of pancreatic cancer, and I was eight years old.) "Just because you can't see something, like Jesus or heaven, or my love when I'm up in heaven—they're all real."

4. Read them their own "hero's journey" book—with their name written all over it.

Here's a last suggestion on something small you can do with a child who needs some attention and has some time for you to read to him or her (think about *The Princess Bride* and reading to a not super-sick but still stuck-at-home kid). Read your grandchild a book (and if you can, purchase it as a gift) that has a pronounced hero or heroine in it. But each time that character's name comes up in the book, change that character's name to your grandchild's name.

Take the Chronicles of Narnia. The second book in that wonderful children's series is the *The Lion, the Witch and the Wardrobe.* (You can get it online for only a few dollars.) Let's say you have a granddaughter. In that book, Lucy is not only a main character but is very smart and brave. And so, too, will be your granddaughter (let's call her Heather). As you read, every time Lucy's name appears in the book, point to your granddaughter and substitute "Heather" for Lucy.

It's Heather who meets Mr. Beaver. It's Heather who runs from the White Witch. It's Heather who meets Aslan the great lion. It's a small way to say to a grandchild, "I see something special inside of you." And forever that book can be something on her shelf that makes her say, "My grandmother read me that book. And she thought I was as brave and kind as Lucy."

5. Finally, don't forget *your* kids.

Sometimes it's much easier to bless our grandkids than it is to bless our own kids. This is especially true in relationships with our adult kids where there may be layers of hurt or emotional distance.

However, by forgetting to bless our own children, we can inadvertently cause pain in that relationship and drive a wedge between us and them. Or we create a much bigger wedge—or, in some cases, a Grand Canyon–size hole.

So no matter how much fun you are having with your grandkids, don't forget their parents! Go back through this list and make sure that you are still taking time to bless your kids—just as much time as you spend blessing your grandchildren.

No matter what age or stage of life, we *all* need to know that we have the Blessing. Especially from our parents.

Okay, you've just read nearly thirty different ways you can give the blessing to your kids and grandkids today! That's pretty amazing.

But while we encourage you to steal and use every single one of those ideas, we also want you to get comfortable with creating your own.

Before we show you how to do that, let's jump into the Pictures Your Heart Remembers, Blessing Group Questions, and Making the Blessing a Lifestyle sections for this chapter.

Pictures Your Heart Remembers

As you read all these ideas for blessing your kids, what pictures come to your mind? Do you think about special moments you've already had with your kids? Do you think about moments you've experienced with your own family growing up? Do you think about missed moments or times when your family didn't give you their blessing? What excites you about giving the Blessing to your kids? What scares you? In the Bible, the Greek word for forgiveness literally means to "untie the knot." Do you need to untie any knots for yourself and give yourself some grace for missed opportunities or things you wish you'd done differently? Take a few minutes to write these things down and process them with the Lord.

Blessing Group Questions

1. What are some things that are holding you back from blessing your kids or grandkids? (e.g., lack of time, not knowing how, fear, etc.)
2. What is one way you can overcome the challenges above?
3. Did your parents create a lifestyle of blessing in your home growing up?
4. Do you feel your parents' blessing or lack of blessing has shaped how you are as a parent/grandparent and how you bless your kids/grandkids?
5. Reading the examples in this chapter, what stuck out to you? What challenged you?
6. What are some ideas you have for blessing your kids? Share them with your group.

Blessing Activity

Write down one blessing idea that stood out to you in this chapter. If you have more than one kid or grandkid, make sure to write down one idea for each of them.

Next, pick a time this upcoming week when you can do this blessing idea with your child or grandchild. Again, if you have more than one, take the time to do these separately with each of them one-on-one. Don't forget to add it to your reminders or calendar so you don't forget!

Share this with your Blessing Group as well to help keep you accountable.

Blessing for _____

Day: _____ Time: _____

Blessing Idea: _____
_____

Blessing for _____

Day: _____ Time: _____

Blessing Idea: _____
_____

Blessing for _____

Day: _____ Time: _____

Blessing Idea: _____
_____

Making the Blessing a Lifestyle

Okay, it's time to come up with some of your own ideas to bless your kids and grandkids. The categories below are a great way to get started.

You don't need to fill out all of these, but you can use them as a guideline to get your ideas flowing.

Try to come up with at least three ideas *total* for blessing *each* kid. Add them to your calendar—one a week for three weeks—so you'll have three weeks of blessing your kids ready to go! *Note: You can also go to TheBlessing.com to create a blessing plan for your kids.*

1. What are some activities/hobbies/passions that your child enjoys? (e.g., cars, football, reading, running, painting)

_____

_____

_____

_____

_____

2. What are some things you have done in the past that your child has really enjoyed? (e.g., time talking, throwing the baseball, making dinner together, eating a special snack)

_____

_____

_____

_____

3. What are some big things that your child has coming up in the next few months? (e.g., a birthday, a report due at school, a driver's test, college applications)

_____

_____

_____

_____

4. What are some things that you really love and appreciate about your child? (e.g., he or she is really caring, is a great big brother or sister, is super funny, is full of positivity)

_____

_____

_____

_____

5. What are some things that your child is struggling with? (e.g., Is your child having a hard time with a teacher at school? Is math really a struggle? Is that one friend leaving him or her out? Has the school bully made your child a target?)

_____

_____

_____

_____

6. What is something tangible that your child really likes (such as their favorite food, drink, or way to celebrate)?

_____

_____

_____

_____

7. Other:

_____

_____

_____

_____

Now look at the three things you've written in each category. Next to each item, brainstorm and write down at least one way you can turn each idea into a blessing. For more information on how to do this and suggestions for each category, go to TheBlessing. com and download this chapter's worksheet.

Finally, take each of the blessing ideas you've written and add them to your reminders or calendar. Do one a week for three weeks.

More Resources

For more ideas on coming up with blessings for your kids, grand-kids, or other relationships that matter most to you, check out our podcast, social media, or blog at StrongFamilies.com/blog.

If you want even more ideas for your kids specifically, you can find a ton in our books *Bedtime Blessings* volumes 1 and 2.

Chapter 15

Blessing Your Spouse

Another relationship that requires your blessing is your marriage. Blessing your spouse is just as important as blessing your kids. We've literally seen it change and repair thousands of relationships.

It's also hugely important for your kids to see. What we model matters. Modeling the Blessing in your marriage is a great way not only to help your kids feel happier and more secure in your home but also to set them up for success in their future relationships.

While planning a special event to give your spouse your blessing is a great idea and something you should do, the goal is to make giving your blessing an ongoing part of your marriage, not just a one-time action. To help take the stress out of this for you, we have tons of ready-to-use examples right here in this chapter.

Just as in the previous chapter, many of these ideas are things that my husband Joey and I (Kari) have done or that I've seen my parents or close friends model. Joey and I do *not* have a perfect marriage. There are a million things that we need to work on (999,999 are mine) and at least as many ways where we fall short. However, these are ideas that we've tried, learned from, or have seen work.

Practical Ideas

Okay, let's jump into some ways to make the Blessing a key and ongoing part of your marriage.

1. Create a blessing jar.

Get two mason jars. Put your name on one and your spouse's name on the other. Then cut two sheets of paper into forty small strips (twenty strips per sheet of paper).

You and your spouse each get twenty strips. Now write down twenty ways that your spouse can bless you, and have your spouse do the same.

For example, some of the ideas in my jar are: spend a night together without our cell phones, play a board game with me, bring me flowers, and hang up the curtain rods in the guest bedroom and office.

Some of the ideas in Joey's jar are: have chips and salsa for me when I get home, plan and make dinner, help me work on the yard, and take a drive with me in the truck.

Once a week, pick a strip of paper out of your spouse's jar and do what it says. Joey and I pick a random day that works for us (and we often pick different days).

If you take time to do this, you now have twenty weeks of blessings—things your spouse has said would bless him or her— that you can do! You can also add more blessing ideas as you think of them.

There is just one rule: you can't use any negatives. Meaning, you can't write things like "Take the trash out for me, for once in your life" or "Plan a date night . . . if you even care about me at all."

Similarly, when you actually go to complete the blessing you've picked out of your spouse's jar, you can't throw it back at your spouse in a negative way either, like, "See, I do listen to you!" or "Of course you would choose something that I don't like."

The goal is to *bless* your spouse in a way that means something to him or her—without questions, comments, or snide remarks.

Helpful hint: Be *really* specific. Does your spouse think date night means dinner and a movie, but you think it means a picnic and a long walk on the beach? Instead of getting frustrated or feeling disappointed, be specific about what kind of date night you want.

You may think it takes the romance out of it, but let me tell you—it doesn't.

Joey and I are very different, and when we first got married, I would "bless him" in ways that meant something to me. However, after a few months, Joey finally told me that not only did he not feel blessed but he actually felt discouraged.

That's when we started using the jar. I had no idea what really blessed Joey. In fact, when he outlined what did bless him (which mostly revolved around food), I felt in over my head. I'm not a great cook, and while I'm great at ordering out, that sucked the blessing out of it for Joey.

However, I realized (thanks to his ideas in the blessing jar) that Joey wasn't looking for a gourmet meal. He just wanted to feel taken care of—and something as simple as having chips and salsa (which, praise the Lord, doesn't require any cooking!) for him when he got home from a fourteen-hour day at work made him feel like I had his back and had been thinking about him during the day.

Joey's discovered the same thing about me as well. For me, it's all about quality time. However, when he first heard that, what he heard was *quantity* of time. But again, thanks to the blessing jar, Joey's come to realize I don't want hours of his time; I just need a few uninterrupted moments of conversation and connection during the day. Which again gave him hope that he could do it and, thanks to my "ask me three questions about my day" slip in the jar, gave him a clear place to start.

Give your spouse something specific to do, not just a ballpark idea or passing suggestion. Don't make him or her guess or try to read your mind. The reality is, most of us really do want to bless our spouse, and it can feel really overwhelming and discouraging to try something and have it fall flat.

So the more specific you are about what blesses you, the better. It'll give your spouse confidence and allow him or her to grow and get more creative the next time.

2. Leave a note.

Are you leaving for a trip? Does your spouse have a big day at work? Maybe a difficult meeting or conversation on the horizon? Is your spouse about to complete a long run or a personal challenge? Write your spouse a blessing note and leave it somewhere fun for him or her to discover.

My husband, Joey, is the best at this. Every fall, Joey's job sends him around the country with different teams during football season. It's a lot of fun, but it also requires many weekends of back-to-back travel. During this same season, my speaking schedule often picks up as well, and I'm busy flying around the country during the week to be at various events. We both love our jobs, and we both have said no to commitments when we feel they're just too much. However, the reality is, during the fall and winter season we are both gone a lot.

We've been doing this for four years now, so you'd think I'd be ready. However, last night, as Joey was getting ready to leave for this first trip of the season, I felt overwhelmed by the amount of travel and weekends alone that were still to come. Joey left at 4:00 a.m. for the airport, and by the time I rolled out of bed, I was feeling even more overwhelmed. So I did what any woman facing a crisis would do . . . I headed right to the coffee maker. My scowl immediately turned into a smile, and then into tears, as I saw a note in a coffee mug from Joey. He told me he loved me, he missed me already, and that we were not only going to get through this season but come out stronger and closer together. He also promised me a date night when he got home on Sunday (something from my jar that blesses me a lot).

To add to the blessing, he had also made me coffee and put it in a thermos right next to the coffee cup. Talk about husband of the year!

It was a short note, but it meant everything, especially on a morning like this. While the amount of travel or time apart isn't changing, my attitude and confidence about the situation certainly have. All because Joey took a few minutes to bless me.

What do you and your spouse have coming up where he or she could use some encouragement? Leave a note in her lunch, put it in his car for him to find in the morning, hide it inside her running shoe, or set it in his coffee mug (just don't forget the coffee!).

3. Share a nightly blessing.

We've mentioned giving your kids a bedtime blessing, but did you know you can do that with your spouse as well? In fact, we recommend it!

Every night, as Joey and I go to bed, we give each other a blessing. As we lie down, I'll turn to him and ask, "Why do you love me today?" and Joey will answer with one reason (or often more than one reason) why he loves and appreciates me, along with something specific I did that day that blessed him. Then Joey will ask me, "Why do you love me today?" and I'll respond with one or more things that I love about Joey and one way that he blessed me that day.

These are often little things, like "You did the dishes after dinner—thank you, that really blessed me," "You made dinner— thank you, that really blessed me," "You worked really hard on the house today—thank you, that really blessed me," "You spent time with me even though you were stressed and busy—thank you, that really blessed me," "You picked up the kids today—thank you, that really blessed me," "You played with the kids so I could have some downtime—thank you, that really blessed me."

There is only one rule: you *have* to answer, and it *has* to be positive.

No dirty positives, like "Thanks for emptying the dishwasher . . . for the first time in your life."

No rude compliments: "You *finally* mowed the yard . . . now the neighbors will stop complaining."

No other negative variations: "You washed the car—maybe now that will become a habit."

These negatives, and so many others, are why we recommend adding the words "thank you, that really blessed me" after the thing you shared. It cuts off the temptation to make it negative, and it really does bless your spouse (see the last bullet on the next page)!

Now, you may think this is silly and not something you would ever do. That's okay.

However, I would encourage you to see the bigger picture. Joey and I do this for several reasons:

- It's a great way to end the day—no matter how many disagreements we get into or how frustrated one of us is, taking a few minutes to think through the day and identify the *good*—the blessings can (and often does) change each of our mind-sets.
- Love is active—hearing "I love you" is great, but being given a specific reason why you are still loved, wanted, and valued *today* is something we all need at times. Especially if you are like me and tend to focus on what you didn't get done that day instead of the victories.

223

- Saying "thank you" is important—really! Studies have shown, again and again, that saying "thank you" reinforces *and* strengthens relationships. Some studies have even found that saying "thank you" encourages the other person to continue to pursue positive actions. Meaning, if you want your husband to keep taking out the trash or your wife to pick her clothes up off the floor, don't shame them when they don't— *thank them* when they do! The catch to this is you can't use a negative, and you have to be specific about what you are thanking your spouse for.

So if you follow our bedtime blessing formula—*one reason you love them + one way they blessed you today + thank you, that really blessed me*—you will encourage your spouse, strengthen your relationship, change your mind-set from negative to positive (or emphasize the positive), and reinforce behavior you'd like to see more of, all in one sentence!

Talk about a win!

4. Touch.

Just as touch is an important part of blessing your kids, it's just as important in blessing your spouse.

You don't need to violate PDA rules or make your kids groan in disgust unless you want to (and let's be honest, that's one of the best parts of being a parent!). However, you do need to keep appropriate meaningful touch a key part of your marriage.

Hold her hand, give him a quick shoulder rub, hug her when she comes in the door, put your arm around him during the movie, cuddle up while you lie in bed and share your bedtime blessing, dance together in the kitchen, put your hand on his shoulder in encouragement, kiss her.

One argument we get from readers about this is, "I don't

feel very affectionate." While this may be true, studies show that physical touch can actually lead you to experience affection.[1] As my dad always says, "Actions dictate feelings . . . not the reverse." Meaning, if you do it, you will begin to feel it. But if you wait to feel like doing it before you start, you may never start at all.

Appropriate meaningful touch doesn't just need to be done when you are alone. It's actually really great for your kids to see as well. Not only does it show them how to model it in their own lives,[2] but studies have shown that parents who demonstrate appropriate meaningful touch in front of their kids actually make their kids feel more confident and secure about their parents' marriage—and their homelife as well.[3] It literally makes them feel like they are a part of a happier home!

So you are not only blessing your spouse but also blessing your kids and setting them up for success in their future relationships.

5. Give a "just because" gift.

It doesn't have to be your spouse's birthday or a holiday to give him or her a gift. The key to this present is to get your spouse something he or she has mentioned or been wanting "just because."

Now, before you head off to the store to buy whatever just popped into your head, let me tell you how to make sure your spouse will see it as a blessing. Trust me, you will thank me later.

Joey, being the kind, amazing, wonderful, awesome husband that he is, decided to try this one day. We have been remodeling our house ourselves. Having no real idea of what we were getting into, our remodel has become more of a "demolish and leave it" situation instead of the DIY magic that Chip and Joanna Gaines so elegantly modeled on *Fixer Upper* . . . but that's another story. While there are a million things unfinished—including floors, ceilings, and one very persistent roof leak, the one thing that I had been begging Joey to get were new outlet and light switch covers. The ones that we had were either old, broken, discolored, or missing (as they had been taken off as we painted or removed walls), which made turning on the lights or plugging something in both a challenge and potential fire hazard.

So, on a bright fall day, Joey came in the door bursting with excitement, holding a beautifully gift-wrapped box with a large gold bow on top. Grinning with joy, I opened it excitedly only to find . . . outlet and light switch covers inside.

Before I share what happened next, I have to be honest with you. At that moment, I felt like I was living a real-life version of the movie *Father of the Bride* with Steve Martin. Specifically the scene where the fiancé gives Steve Martin's daughter a fancy blender as a wedding present. Did she want the blender? Yes, but the gift also caused them to temporarily call off their engagement, because not only did she feel like it was the furthest thing from being romantic but she felt like he was insulting her role in their marriage as well.

Now, I was determined not to storm out of the room or tell Joey that he clearly didn't understand how to give a gift—and I'm really glad I didn't. Because at that moment, he handed me a note.

The note said, "Kari, you are so full of energy and electricity that you power up our entire family. You add light to people who need it, and you light up my life as well. Love, Joey."

Y'all, my jaw dropped, and yes . . . I cried.

Looking back on that moment, I really believe that a disaster was averted by the note. In fact, I think the whole blender fiasco in *Father of the Bride* could have been averted if he'd handed her a similar note as well.

Now some of you may be thinking, *I don't get it. Didn't you want the outlet and light switch covers?* Yes. Yes, I did. However, what I wanted more was for Joey to get me something that made me feel loved, which is why I was initially disappointed with the gift when I opened it.

My disappointment immediately turned to joy when I realized that Joey didn't just see the outlet and light switch covers at Home Depot and bring them home . . . but that he specifically saw something special in me at the same time.

In fact, every time I look at our new, beautiful, matching, clean outlet and light switch covers, I'm reminded that my husband thinks I power up our family and add light to his life. I'm pretty sure that word picture Joey used will stay with me every single day we live in this house.

If you need extra help coming up with a word picture that will bless your spouse, you can reread chapter 9—or we have an entire book called *The Language of Love* that will walk you through creating your own word pictures step by step. You can check out our website, podcast, and social media for more tips on using word pictures in your relationships as well.

6. Do your spouse's chores.

I don't know how chores work in your home, but in ours, we often end up doing the same tasks each week to keep the house clean. Joey cleans the bathrooms, and I dust and vacuum.

One surefire way we've found to bless each other is by doing the other person's chores. Typically it looks like this: If Joey is out of town for work, I will clean the bathrooms as well as dust and vacuum. That way, when he gets home, we can relax together and spend time connecting—instead of working.

Joey has done this for me as well. He will dust and vacuum as well as clean the bathrooms. He's even gone so far as to have a romantic dinner waiting for me when I got home from the airport.

There is nothing like coming home to a clean house and an amazing meal and evening full of time and joy with your spouse. Not to mention that this is a super easy way to bless your spouse if he or she is busy with work, tired from a long week, or pitching in to help with something extra with the kids.

Give it a try! And add a note or meal to your blessing as well for an added wow.

7. Give your spouse a kid-free night.

Does your spouse look a little tired? Try blessing him or her with a kid-free night. We all love our kids, but sometimes we need time to ourselves to recharge.

A kid-free night can look any way your spouse wants it to: A night alone to read, take a bath, and relax. A night out with a good friend or to take a class. Or even just a night to have a bowl of popcorn and sole possession of the DVR.

The goal is to give your spouse a night off. You and the kids can go to Grandma's for the night. Or you can save up and give your spouse a night at a local hotel (a lot of hotels have great deals in the off-season).

Our friends André and Bianca took this to the next level. While Bianca was at a hotel with a good book and room service, André got the kids involved with creating a blessing for Mom.

When Bianca came home the next morning, she walked in to find a pancake blessing breakfast. André had made Mickey Mouse pancakes for her and the kids, complete with chocolate chips, and the kids each presented a blessing note and drawing to their mom.

A night of rest, some pancakes, and craft paper, glitter, glue, and markers were all it took to revive a really tired mama.

Bianca shared, "It was like I had fresh energy and joy over the season I was in. It's hard to feel tired all the time, especially when my kids are too young to go to school. I felt stretched in every direction, and I even was finding myself getting irritated and angry with them, and with André as well."

For Bianca, a night to really rest and take care of herself was exactly what she needed. It not only gave her fresh energy with her kids but strengthened her time and intimacy with André as well. Bianca loved this so much that the following year, she turned around and gave André a kid-free night as well.

As you can see, there are tons of ways that you can live out the Blessing each day with your spouse.

Let's jump right into the Pictures My Heart Remembers and Blessing Group Questions sections. Then, just like in the previous chapter, in Making the Blessing a Lifestyle we are going to help you come up with some blessing ideas of your own!

Pictures Your Heart Remembers

As you read this chapter on blessing your spouse, what pictures came to your mind? Did you think about special moments with your spouse? How about ways he or she has blessed you? What about moments between your parents or grandparents when you were growing up? Moments you've blessed or missed moments of blessing? Do you long for greater blessing in your marriage? Take a few moments to write out these pictures and process them with the Lord. You may even want to share them with your Blessing Group and your spouse as you work to keep living out the Blessing in your marriage.

Blessing Group Questions

1. What are some things that are keeping you from blessing your spouse? (e.g., feeling distant, not enough time, not knowing how, fear of rejection, etc.)
2. What is one way you can overcome the challenges above?

3. Is there anything else you need to do to be ready to bless your spouse? (This isn't about what your spouse needs to do. He or she may not change or do anything different; this is about you and getting the freedom you need to step toward and bless your spouse.)

4. What are three ways you want your spouse to bless you? (Make sure to put these in your blessing jar.)

5. What are three ways that your spouse wants to be blessed? (Ask your spouse, or copy his or her list. You don't need to guess here.)

Blessing Activity

From the list you got from your spouse in question 5, write down one blessing that you are going to give your spouse each week for the next five weeks. Add a date and time to it and put it in your phone or calendar to remind you. Share this with your Blessing Group as well to help keep you accountable.

Making the Blessing a Lifestyle

Okay, it's time to come up with some of your own ideas to bless your spouse. The categories below are a great way to get started.

You don't need to fill out all of these, but you can use them as a guideline to get you started.

Try to come up with at least three ideas *total* for blessing your spouse.

Add them to your calendar—one a week for three weeks—so you'll have three weeks of blessing your spouse ready to go! *Note:*

You can also go to TheBlessing.com/blessingplan to come up with a personalized, yearlong plan to bless your spouse in ways that are important to him or her.

1. What are some activities/hobbies/passions that your spouse enjoys? (e.g., cars, football, reading, running, painting)

_____

_____

_____

_____

_____

2. What are some things you have done in the past that have blessed your spouse? (e.g., made dinner, cleaned the garage, filled up the gas tank, washed the car)

_____

_____

_____

_____

_____

_____

3. What are some big things that your spouse has coming up in the next few months? (e.g., a birthday, a presentation at work, a run, a tough day—like the anniversary of a parent's death)

_____

_____

_____

_____

_____

4. What are some things that you really love and appreciate about your spouse? (e.g., my spouse is really caring, good with the budget, a hard worker, funny, full of positivity)

_____

_____

_____

_____

_____

5. What are some things that your spouse is struggling with? (e.g., is he or she feeling discouraged about what's going on at work? Is he or she struggling to connect with one of your kids? Does your

spouse feel like he or she needs to add in some healthy habits but can't seem to find the time?)

_____

_____

_____

_____

_____

6. What is something tangible that your spouse really likes (such as their favorite food, drink, or way to celebrate)?

_____

_____

_____

_____

_____

7. Other:

_____

_____

_____

_____

_____

_____

Now look at the three things you've written in each category.

Next to each item, brainstorm and write down at least one way that you can turn each idea into a blessing. For more information on how to do this and suggestions for each category, go to TheBlessing.com and download this chapter's worksheet.

Finally, take each of the blessing ideas you've written and add them to your reminders or calendar. Do one a week for three weeks.

As you try these ideas at home, we want to hear from you. Share your ideas, help others, and be part of creating a culture of blessing by e-mailing us, sharing your ideas with us on social media, or finding us in person at an airport near you (kidding—but we do travel a lot, so that could happen!).

Chapter 16

Blessing When You're Single

When it comes to our calling to bless others, without hesitation, so much of this book applies to singles. Like blessing your parents, or living out the five elements of the Blessing, or bringing the Blessing home to roommates or those at work who need it.

But in this chapter I'd like to focus on two areas where singles can be world-class in blessing others. And the first is in applying the Blessing with your siblings.

Blessing Your Siblings

When it comes to the Blessing, if there is one relationship that we can tend to overlook—or even take for granted—it's the relationship we have with a sibling. For my dad and I (Kari), the Blessing always starts at home . . . and it's no different here. There is something about a brother or a sister that can bring out the best in us . . . and also the absolute worst.

We see and hear about this all the time in families: "My brother and I are just so different." "My sister and I fight all the time." "We are family, but we aren't friends."

Even my sister, Laura, and I are polar opposites. We are physically different: I'm a very respectable five feet two (on a good day); she's five feet eleven (every day). Our personalities are different: I'm loud, outgoing, and with my job I am often leading up front. She's specific with her words, builds deep relationships with a few people, and serves where most people can't see. How we process things is different: I'm a "just pick something, it'll work out!" type of processor. Laura takes her time and thinks through every angle of a situation before coming to a decision. What we like to do is different: I like quality time over dinner or a family game night. Laura likes to go to a movie. Pick a category, relationship preference, or strength, and we are probably on opposite ends of the spectrum.

However, we do have one big thing in common: Jesus.

No matter how different we are—and the fights, challenges, conversations, tears, and so on that have accompanied those differences—we keep finding common ground in Jesus. And we keep choosing to take steps to bless each other. Even when it's not easy.

Hopefully, you and your sibling grew up in a home where you got the Blessing. If that wasn't the case, it's not all on you to try and make up for a parent's lack of the Blessing. But what you can do is give your sibling a tremendous gift—*your* blessing

The reality is, your sibling(s) will always be your family. They should be your biggest advocate, and you should be theirs. While this may not be the current reality in your relationship, the good news is, no matter where your relationship is at today, it's never too late to start giving them your blessing. It just may be the tipping point that can lead to a breakthrough in your differences—and the creation of a deep and lifelong friendship.

So what are some ways that you can start blessing your sibling(s)?

1. Don't hold back on your words.

One thing that I've noticed with Laura and me is we tend to hold back on saying positive things because we are family. I know she's always going to be there—so I tend to just assume that she knows how much I love her and how proud I am of her.

But just like we've shared in the rest of this book, if we don't say it, people don't know it. And even when it comes to our siblings, we can't just assume. In fact, when I started to change my perception about intentionally blessing Laura, our relationship changed. We got closer, spent more time together, and even developed a deep friendship—one that goes beyond "just family."

So how can you start using words to bless your brother or sister? Start by challenging yourself to never miss an opportunity to "say something."

Did you see something today that reminded you of them? Text them a picture—with a quick blessing attached. Did they bring an amazing dish to the family picnic? Thank them for doing that—and add a quick blessing. Your blessing doesn't need to be about food, but use it as an onramp to share about something positive you see in them.

Did they get a promotion at work? Send them a gift card, take them to dinner, or find another way they enjoy and celebrate with them.

If you don't live near your siblings, don't worry. You can still bless them.

Laura and I have lived in different states for twelve years, but we still work hard to find ways to bless each other. Sometimes she sends me a gift for a big accomplishment. Sometimes I call her and just listen while she processes a bad day. Other times we get on a plane and show up when there's a big celebration—or a big heartbreak.

The bottom line is, whether you live close to your siblings or far away, there are a million ways that you can choose to step toward them. They don't need to be grand gestures. You just need to start—and keep making that choice.

2. Remember important days.

Another way you can bless your siblings is to remember days that are important to them.

Is New Year's a big day for them? Send them a blessing. Is their birthday or anniversary coming up? Send them a blessing. Do they have a big interview or presentation this week? Send them a blessing.

The best way I've found to do this is to put big-days-for-Laura in my phone. I even set a reminder a week before if I need to send her a gift or a card. That way on the big day she knows she has my blessing.

Another thing that's helped me is figuring out which days are actually important to Laura. While tests and exams cause me to go into a tailspin of anxiety, they aren't stressful for Laura at all. But giving a Club Talk at YoungLife in front of two hundred high school kids is something that causes her stress levels to rise. So I'd skip the text on test day but make sure to send her one—or more—texts with encouragement and my blessing the week of her Club Talk.

For your siblings it may be that their birthday or their kids' birthdays are a huge deal. Or maybe it's work- or school-related. Or perhaps it's a date that reminds them of the loss of a loved one. Whatever the dates are, planning and figuring out what days are important to them can take work. But it is worth every second. When you show up physically or emotionally on a day when they need you, it can make all the difference in the world in your relationship as well.

So stop and take a few minutes to write down some important dates that matter to your siblings. Put them in your phone—with reminders ahead of time if you need to. Don't forget to send them a blessing when you get that reminder in the weeks and months ahead.

3. Speak their language.

When it comes to giving your blessing, it's important to remember *who* you are blessing. If you recall with the blessing jar example from the last chapter, it's because each person has a different definition of what actually blesses them.

One thing we see again and again with siblings is that we often try to bless them the same way we would want to be blessed. And we are shocked, offended, and angry when they don't feel blessed by it.

So when you go to bless your siblings, you need to make sure you are speaking their language.

Do they want to talk over coffee or a meal instead of seeing the latest *Star Wars* film? Do they feel blessed when you fill up their gas tank or help them with a project? Do they light up when they talk about cars, woodworking, photography, horses, running, or another hobby?

Whatever it is that blesses them, do that. Just don't forget to find a time to give them your blessing as well.

It can feel uncomfortable when you break out of the norm and meet someone where they are at. You may not even enjoy the hobby, movie, or activity that you do with them. However, this isn't for you. It's for them. You are doing this to step toward them, to support them, to show them that you love them, and to bless them in a way that means something to them. So feel free to have an uncomfortable or less than ideal afternoon. Just keep in mind that whatever you lose in time or enjoyment, you will gain back exponentially in relationship.

(Helpful hint: if you really don't like the movie or activity, don't make that the focus of your time together. You can be honest and say, "it's not something I would have chosen." But work really hard to keep your negative words or attitude out of your time together. And I bet if you try really hard, you can find at least one thing that you actually enjoyed. Focus on that. Share that. And who knows, maybe you'll even find something new that you enjoy as well.)

4. Be consistent.

Your relationships with your siblings will most likely be the longest ones you will ever have. You'll know them longer than your spouse, they will most likely outlive your parents, and they will still be your siblings when friendships come and go.

That said, the key to keeping the Blessing a part of your longest-running relationship is to be consistent. This is especially important if you have tension in your relationship, or don't have a strong friendship yet. Consistency is key and is a major thing your brother or sister will be looking for as you go. So how can you build blessing consistency into your relationship with your siblings?

One way is to start small. It can be really temping to go "all out" and try to do big gestures and lots of blessings at once. However, the key to consistent change is to make small, two-degree changes. Then after you've mastered one two-degree change, you can add another two-degree change, and so on. While this may not seem as exciting or appear on the surface to be as effective, it works.

If you need more help on small changes, we have an incredible book on our website called *The 2 Degree Difference* that can help you live out small, sustainable changes.

But let's come up with one small, two-degree action you can do right now to bless your brother or sister. For me, I'm going to call Laura once a week for the next month. Even if it's a five-minute call, I'm going to choose to pick up the phone and not hang up until I've given her my blessing. That's it! One small, two-degree thing that I can do consistently. Next month, I can add to that with another small thing. But for this month, all I'm going to do is pick up the phone and bless her once a week. Okay, now it's your turn. What is one small thing that you can do consistently to bless your siblings this month?

Write it down, add it to your calendar, and take action. It's a great and easy way to build consistency when it comes to blessing.

Blessing Your Friends

We all have that one friend who is just the *best* at blessing others. You know who I'm talking about. The one who shows up with a home-cooked meal, your favorite movie, and their healing essential oil blend—just because you "sounded stuffy" on the phone.

Or the friend who drops everything on a Saturday (their only day off) to help you finish that one home project that you just haven't been able to get done.

Or the friend who seems to notice any person who needs a ride to the airport or could use help moving, volunteers for everything, and at the same time is able to make an award–winning homemade dessert for your weekly small group.

I am not that friend.

In fact, it has taken a lot of time, work, effort, and, quite frankly, failure to learn how to be even a fraction of that for those in my life. However, one thing I have realized is that the more I just take the time to be there for people—no matter what that looks like—the better my friendships and relationships become.

This section is *not* designed to make you feel like you need to be "Superhero Best-Friend Bob" or "Superhero Best-Friend Betty." But it *is* designed to help you discover some areas where you can take the time to be there and bless those you love. After all, in my home, and probably yours as well, friends are family.

1. Look for opportunities.

While looking for opportunities to bless may sound like a simple thing, it can actually be pretty challenging. It requires us to be present, aware, and observe what's going on with our friends. It also requires us to listen to what they are saying and turn it into action. However, if we are able to do this, we can come up with some of the most meaningful and timely blessings imaginable.

Did your friend have a bad week? Bring him his favorite coffee or snack. Did your friend just get her dream job? Take her to her favorite restaurant to celebrate. Did your friend's car just get totaled? Offer to pick him up or take him to work.

There is no limit to the options, or the needs, that are out there. The key is making the time to take action. It's a choice. And we can all choose to step toward our friends, especially when they need our blessing.

2. Text them as you think about them.

One thing that has helped me immensely in blessing my friends is to stop the second the Lord puts a friend on my heart, or the second I think about someone, and text or call that person.

If I wait or assume I will do it later, I often get busy with life, and I forget. Not because I don't love my friends or don't want to bless them. But I'm forgetful, busy, and, as I shared, still very far from being Superhero Best-Friend Betty. So my secret is to text or call the moment I think about it. It's also been amazing to watch how the Lord has used some texts to bless a friend at key time that I had no idea about.

Ready to take action? Put down the book, write down a blessing, encouragement, prayer, or truth, and share it with the first friend who comes to your mind. Repeat as often as you can!

3. Don't forget the holidays.

For a lot of people, the holidays can seem very far from "the most wonderful time of the year."

Some people are dealing with loss, others with broken families, and still others with not being able to fly home and be with their families for Thanksgiving or Christmas.

But the holidays create an amazing opportunity for blessing.

Every year since I can remember, my parents would spend the entire months of November and December asking each of their friends, and even acquaintances, what they were doing for the holidays. My parents would then invite them to come to our house for Thanksgiving and Christmas and celebrate with our family. It was always shocking how many people they had asked who had no plans and no holiday invitations for those two important days.

One year we had twenty people—none of them immediate family—over for Thanksgiving. Another year we had only two. The number was never important. What was important was that each person knew we wanted them there. That each person knew they were important. And, yes, that each person knew they had our blessing (something we do around the table at Thanksgiving, Christmas, and even the Fourth of July).

This tradition of blessing has led to incredible friendships, and even healing for some who were mourning loss of family, loved ones, or broken relationships at home.

We even have one family, the Crowells, whom we have spent every holiday with for the past thirty years. It has been one of the closest and most special friendships for both of our families (parents and kids alike) for decades. All because my parents asked, "What are you doing for the holidays?"

4. Take action.

In my twenties I had the incredible blessing of getting to live with two amazing families. These families not only changed my life but taught me what it looked like to take action with blessing.

My first lesson in blessing came two days after I moved in with the Narciso family. At the time, Adam and Jenny had two

243

amazing daughters; one was three and the other was only six months old.

Both girls were incredibly cute, sweet, and amazing. They also required a ton of love, care, energy, and support.

Being a single girl in my midtwenties, I hadn't spent a lot time of time around kids, other than in my babysitting days in high school. And being fresh out of college, I certainly hadn't lived in a house with kids since I was a kid myself.

So I was understandably surprised when I realized that the sweet little six-month-old never slept through the night. Some nights she would cry for a few hours at a time. Other times she would cry through the entire night—only to fall asleep at 6:00 a.m.—the exact time that the three-year-old would wake up!

But every morning, Jenny would get up with the girls, make breakfast, and spend the rest of her day caring for them—all while functioning on little to no sleep. The most amazing part to me was how kind, loving, and positive she was about it.

However, it was evident that she was exhausted. Adam would come home and help—but by the end of the day, they were both worn out and knew that in a few hours they would both be up again trying to get their baby back to sleep for the night.

So what does this have to do with blessing? Everything.

I began to notice there were things that I could do—without Jenny having to ask me—that would help her.

I would do the dishes after she cooked for the girls. I would clean up the table or sweep the floor after a particularly messy meal. I would offer to bring her coffee, groceries, or a treat if I was going somewhere.

While I wasn't perfect at it, and at times, I know I could have done more, I realized that I didn't need to wait for someone to ask me to help. I could see a need, meet that need, and turn it into a blessing.

244

Do you know of a mom who isn't getting enough sleep? Offer to babysit and give her an afternoon off. Do you know of a married couple who could really use a date night? Offer to babysit for free. Is your mom's gas tank half full after you borrowed the car? Fill it up for her. Does your roommate normally take out the trash? Do it for him as a blessing.

You don't need to wait for someone to ask. You can see a need, meet a need, and turn it into a blessing.

Remember, it's not about someone noticing or about getting a thank you afterward. It's about blessing people where they are and in ways they need someone to show up for them. Siblings and friendships are just a few of the relationships where you can choose to live out the Blessing. For an extra bonus, leave them a little note of blessing as well.

Before you move on to the next chapter, which is all about living out the Blessing with your parents, take a few minutes to work through the Pictures Your Heart Remembers, Blessing Group Questions, and Making the Blessing a Lifestyle activity below.

Pictures Your Heart Remembers

As you read this chapter on blessing when you're single, what pictures came to your mind? Do you think about special moments with your brother(s) or sister(s)? Or hurtful moments where the Blessing has been absent? Do you feel hope and joy about building stronger relationships? Or do you feel discouraged and frustrated? Take a few moments to write down these pictures and process them with the Lord. You may even want to share them with your Blessing Group or a friend as you work to keep living out the Blessing.

Blessing Group Questions

1. When you think about blessing your sibling(s), what comes to your mind? Does it feel like an easy thing to do? Or do you think there are some challenges that are preventing you from stepping toward them? (If you have more than one sibling, make sure you share about each of them.)

2. Do you think your feelings noted above are preventing you from blessing them? Why or why not?

3. What is one way that you can choose to step toward and bless your sibling(s) this week? (Make sure to ask your group next week to check to see that you took action on this.)

4. Is there anything else you need to do to be ready to bless your sibling(s)? (This isn't about what your brother or sister needs to do. He or she may not change or do anything different; this is about you and getting the freedom you need to step toward and bless them anyway.)

5. What is the best blessing a friend has ever given you? Why did it mean so much to you?

6. Who is one friend that you can choose to bless this week? What is one thing that you know would bless them?

Blessing Activity

In the space below, write down the name of each of your siblings, as well as one friend who you know could use the Blessing this week. Next to their names, write down one way that you can bless them this week. Add a date and time to it and put it in your phone or calendar to remind you. Share this with your Blessing Group as well to help keep you accountable. If you aren't sure what will bless your siblings, the following section will help.

Blessing for _____

Day: Time:

_____

Blessing Idea:

_____

Blessing for _____

Day: Time:

_____

Blessing Idea:

_____

Blessing for _____

Day: Time: .

_____

Blessing Idea:

_____

Making the Blessing a Lifestyle

Okay, it's time to come up with some of your own ideas to bless your siblings and your friends. Earlier in this chapter we talked about "speaking their language" when it comes to blessing, and these categories below are a great way to get started doing just that.

Fill in as many blanks as you can for your siblings, and even for your friends. We have blank copies of this worksheet at TheBlessing. com so you can print one out for each of your siblings and friends as well. Use this as a cheat sheet for coming up with blessings that are unique to that person.

If you don't know the answers, don't be afraid to ask. Do some research. It will make a big difference in your relationships if you do.

Don't forget, after you come up with your ideas, add them to your calendar—one a week, for three weeks, so you'll have three weeks of blessings ready to go! This is another great two-degree tip for consistency with blessing.

1. What are some activities/hobbies/passions that they enjoy? (e.g., cars, football, reading, running, painting, dance, horses)

_____

_____

_____

_____

2. What are some things you have done in the past that have blessed them? (e.g., made dinner, remembered a birthday, celebrated a victory, washed their car, did the dishes)

_____

_____

----

3. What are some big things that they have coming up in the next few
   months? (e.g., a birthday, a presentation at work, a run, a tough
   day—like the anniversary of a parent's death)

----

4. What are some things that you really love and appreciate about
   them? (e.g., they are really loyal, the first to celebrate others, great at
   solving problems)

_____

_____

5. What are some things that they are struggling with right now? (e.g., are they feeling discouraged about what's going on at work? Are they struggling with a friendship or a relationship? Do they feel like their job is a dead end and they have to start over?)

_____

_____

_____

_____

_____

6. What is something tangible that they really like (such as their favorite food, drink, or way to celebrate)?

_____

_____

_____

_____

7. Other:

_____

_____

_____

_____

_____

_____

Okay, now look back over your list, and put a star next to three items.

Next to each item with a star, brainstorm and write down at least one way that you can turn each one of those ideas into a blessing. For more information on how to do this and suggestions for each category, go to TheBlessing.com and download this chapter's worksheet.

Finally, take each of the blessing ideas you've written above and add them to your reminders or calendar. Do one a week for three weeks.

If you want even more ideas on how to bless your siblings or friends, check out TheBlessing.com, our podcast, or find us on social media. Don't forget to share your ideas with us as you try these and live out the Blessing at home.

Now that you've learned how to bless your siblings and your friends, it's time to live the Blessing in another important relationship—with your parents.

Chapter 17

Blessing Your Parents

For many of us, blessing our parents is not something we are used to doing. Not to mention that if we grew up in a home where our parents didn't give us their blessing, it can be downright uncomfortable.

However, whether your parents blessed you or have chosen to withhold their blessing, you can make the choice to step toward them. Not out of codependency or guilt. But once you have received God's blessing, you can choose to give it to others.

Keep in mind that when you give your blessing, it may or may not be reciprocated, so keep your expectations with Jesus, not on their response. Regardless of the response of others, we are still called to "untie the knot" in forgiveness, choose to step toward them, and love them like Jesus.

As you are reading, if you find that this chapter is particularly challenging for you, we'd encourage you to get some additional support. Join one of our online trainings at StrongFamilies.com, find a great counselor, reread chapter 13, or share and process with your spouse, close friend, or Blessing Group. It's okay if this chapter is hard or brings up the fact that you may not have received your parents' blessing. But you can keep choosing movement toward life by continuing to choose to bless others, including your parents.

One other thing to keep in mind is this: many of us tend to be closer to or relate more easily to one of our parents. We'd encourage you, if you can, to make sure you are choosing to bless both parents, even if you don't feel as connected to one as you do the other. You can even add stepparents, in-laws, and bonus parents to this as well.

Practical Ideas

Let's jump in. Here are some simple ways that you can begin to add the Blessing into your relationship with your parents.

1. Say thank you.

You would be surprised how seldom parents hear these two super small but very important words. They may have heard it frequently from little-kid versions of ourselves after they handed us a juice box and said the phrase that made us all roll our eyes in unison: "What do you say?"

Cue annoyed little kid's voice: "Thank you."

But it's pretty clear these forced thank-yous don't bring about the joy and blessing that a real thank-you can.

The truth is, a simple thank-you really says a lot more. And taking the time to thank your parents, even for something small, is an open door to begin to forgive (if that's needed in your relationship) and to bless in bigger ways.

You can pick something small, like, "Thank you for picking up my kids today" or, "Thank you for wiping the counter for me." And then you can work your way up to bigger and more personal things as you feel comfortable.

The goal is to practice saying it . . . for as many reasons as you can think of. Make it a personal goal not to let any good thing go unthanked when it comes to your parents.

2. Write to them.

Whether it's a note, a list, a sticky note, a long letter, or even a book, take some time to verbalize your blessing to your parents and write it down for them.

For example, when I turned thirty, I wanted to do something to bless my mom. I was not an easy child to raise, and I put my parents through the wringer in more than one scenario.

This led to tension, specifically with my mom, for most of my teenage years and well into my twenties. As a newer Christian, and as someone who was really trying to live out the Blessing, I decided to do something to thank her and let her know that I wanted her to continue to speak into my life.

So, for a few months before my thirtieth birthday, I worked hard on a book for her. The end product was my first book, titled *You Were Right*. Inside the book was a list of literally everything I could think of that my mom had been right about for the past thirty years. And, y'all, I hate to admit it, but there were *a lot* of things my mom was right about.

The day of my thirtieth birthday rolled around. Joey, knowing that I had written this book, had surprised me with a flight home so I could be with my parents. I nervously handed my mom a printed copy of the book and began to read it to her out loud. My heart swelled with joy as I watched her cry happy tears over a gift I'd given her.

It was worth every second—and even a few of the mistakes it took to get me to that point in my life.

Now, before you think, *Okay, there's no way I'm going to write a book. I don't even know where to start*, don't worry! While a book is great, the reality is a simple note can have just as powerful an effect. As my mom always says, "A little note goes a *long* way." The key is to start.

3. Offer to help.

If you're anything like me, there is something about going home or being at my parents' house that immediately puts me right back into "kid mode." I may be able to function (most days) like a responsible, aware, semicompetent adult in my own home, but put me back at Mom and Dad's and it all goes right out the window. Over the years, I've had to work really hard to snap out of kid mode and realize that I have a unique opportunity to bless my parents during the few days out of the year that I'm back home with them. That usually comes in the form of offering to help them.

For my mom, there is no greater way to bless her than to help her around the house. It may be unloading the dishwasher, watering the plants, dusting, vacuuming, or any of the other millions of chores that I used to do in high school, but if I offer to help her—and if I actually complete the task, without any hint of my old whiny high school self—she feels like she's won the lottery.

For my dad, it's all about time with him. If he's going to run an errand or walk the dogs, I offer to go. That way, not only do we get some time together but *he* feels like he's won the Blessing lottery.

While the kid-mode part of me would rather lie on the couch and enjoy a few days off from adulting, I have never regretted the time I've taken to bless my parents. And we've had some of our best conversations and biggest moments of blessing in our relationships during those times as well.

4. Share with them, and then ask what they think.

I'm not talking about sharing something material, although you can do that too. I'm talking about sharing something emotional.

Now, in relationships where this isn't safe, skip this suggestion. But for most of us, we can choose to share more than we do currently in our relationships with our parents. The best part is, you get to choose the topic and what you share.

Here are some suggestions for you: Pick something relevant. What is something that you are dealing with now? Is the budget tight? Is there a coworker who for some reason thinks you are the worst? Is there a decision you're trying to make? This doesn't need to be a big thing. In fact, if this idea of sharing is new to you, feel free to start small.

Once you have your situation, bring it up with your parents. Tell them what's going on, and follow that by asking, "What do you think about that?" or "What would you do in that situation?"

The first time you do this, your parents may be so shocked you are asking for their opinion that they may not know what to say. That's okay! Next week find a new situation and keep asking. Let them know that you really do want their input.

Now, there is only one rule: when they give you their input, even if it is the polar opposite of what you would actually do, thank them.

This does *not* mean that you need to do what they said. And by no means should you lie and tell them you are going to do what they suggested if you aren't. You are an adult, and it's okay to feel the way you do and take any action you choose. *But* . . . they just shared a part of their heart with you—so thank them for choosing to do that and for choosing to invest in you in that way.

If you repeat this scenario again and again, in most cases you will see some pretty amazing changes in your ability to relate, respect, and communicate with each other.

5. Don't get annoyed.

Many of us have a standard way of relating to our parents. Unfortunately, for many of us, this often looks the same way it did when we were teenagers. We get annoyed about the same things.

We get frustrated with the same things. And we respond the same way we did when we were kids.

The great news is, we are able to change this! If you find yourself getting annoyed with that one thing your parent does that just drives you crazy, you can choose to bless instead.

One of our good friends, Marci, and her husband, Jackson, shared their story with me the other day. Marci and Jackson were spending time watching a football game with Jackson's parents. In Seattle, the Seahawks are a way of life, and Jackson's family frequently hosts big events for all their family, neighbors, and friends to attend. During these Seahawks events, the game is blaring, kids are running around, and it's borderline chaos and mayhem.

Jackson's dad is pretty hard of hearing, and communicating with him in a quiet setting can sometimes be a challenge. However, during one of these gatherings, it is virtually impossible.

But this particular day, during the game and even during commercials, Jackson's dad kept asking his son questions. Questions about his life, his job, his interests, his new car, his latest home project—you name it. Jackson would answer, but because of the volume of the game, the size of the crowd, and his hearing loss, Jackson's dad would inevitably have to ask him to repeat his answer.

After about the third round of this, Jackson's replies began to get shorter and snippier. By the end of the first quarter, he had even started to pretend that he didn't hear the questions his dad was asking.

During halftime, Marci pulled her husband aside. "Honey, can I share something with you?" she asked, hoping that between the full plate of nachos in his left hand and an overflowing plate of wings in his right, he would stop chewing long enough to hear her heart.

"Sure, my love," Jackson replied with a smile.

"Well, I've been watching you and your dad the whole game . . ."

She paused nervously. "And, Jackson, I think you are really missing the fact that your dad is trying very hard to bless you."

When Jackson didn't say anything, Marci continued. "I know you get really frustrated having to repeat yourself, but, honey, he really can't hear you. And I've watched him patiently and expectantly ask you question after question, even when you've been short or rude to him. But now you are just ignoring him, and you can tell he's hurt, and he was really trying to connect with you."

At this point in the conversation, Jackson had put down both plates of food. Then Marci gently grabbed his hands.

"I know this probably isn't easy to hear, but just last week you were saying that you wished you and your dad talked more. He's literally trying to give you exactly what you've been praying for, but you can't see it because of your frustration. Jackson, you are an amazing husband, son, and father. I just don't want you to miss this moment."

Jackson wiped tears from his eyes and asked his wife, "What do I do about it? You're right. I was getting frustrated. And he was trying to connect with me. But now he's stopped asking me questions."

"Honey, all you have to do is start asking him some questions in return," Marci said with a smile.

The rest of the second half wasn't about football. It was about Jackson and his dad communicating and relating with each other.

Marci watched them with happy tears in her eyes, and everyone in the room could feel the joy in her husband's and father-in-law's hearts—joy that went far beyond any Seahawks win. Which, Jackson wanted me to inform you, they did do that day.

On the drive home, Jackson asked Marci to help remind him that his dad wanted to connect with him, not annoy him, next time they were in a loud situation and his dad began to ask him to repeat his answers. This day marked a huge shift in Jackson and his dad's relationship—all because Jackson was willing to see that his frustration was blocking his father's attempt to bless and connect with him.

Remember, it's okay if this chapter is either hard or uncomfortable for you. Keep pressing in. Get more support. And keep choosing to bless. Before we move to the next chapter, let's take a few minutes to go over the Pictures My Heart Remembers, Blessing Group Questions, and Making the Blessing a Lifestyle sections below.

Pictures Your Heart Remembers

In the Pictures Your Heart Remembers section of chapter 3, we had you stand outside your home and look in. Now we'd like you to go inside your home. Once again, imagine that you are ten years old and you are inside your home growing up.

As you read in chapter 1, my dad never got the Blessing from his father, even though he chose to continue to bless him—again and again and again.

There are many of you reading today who are in the same situation.

Even if you did grow up with the world's most amazing parents and received the Blessing every day, there can still be areas or wounds that need to heal when it comes to your parents.

Take a few minutes to journal through the following scenarios. Share these with your Blessing Group, spouse, or counselor.

What did your home look like when you were roughly ten years old? Write down everything you can think of. Who was there? What were the smells? What did it look like? What were the feelings in your home? Was the Blessing present or available to you?

259

_____

_____

_____

_____

_____

When you think of your parents, what pictures come to mind? Start with pictures from when you were young and then move toward the present. Try to list as many as you can. (Write down everything you can think of. Happy pictures, sad pictures, painful pictures, etc. One positive example for me: I think of my parents at my wedding. My dad beaming and crying as he walked me down the aisle, and my mom rocking the dance floor as she danced with Joey in her special mother-in-law/son-in-law dance. One painful example for me is the day I was old enough to realize that my dad sometimes had to travel for work. While he wasn't gone long, I vividly remember feeling his absence when he was. I was six, and I can still tell you what I was wearing and where I was standing when it all clicked in my brain.)

_____

_____

_____

_____

Journal with Jesus. Ask him to help you rewrite those pictures in your heart. Ask him to show you where he was in all of this. Then take the painful or challenging pictures you've written above and rewrite them, but with Jesus standing right beside you in every single picture. Share what you think he felt and how he loved you in that time (even if you can't see it yet) as you write. Ask him to help you untie the knot. Declare and read your blessing from chapter 13 out loud and ask him to help you choose blessing—for yourself and for your parents.

_____

_____

_____

_____

_____

Blessing Group Questions

1. Are you currently in the habit of blessing your parents (or in-laws)? Why or why not?
2. Do you ever find yourself getting annoyed, angry, frustrated, or (insert other emotion here) with your parents (or in-laws)? Is there a way to look at that annoying/frustrating thing differently or even turn it into a blessing? Hint: Ask your spouse or Blessing Group for help.
3. What is holding you back from blessing your parents (or

in-laws)? What is one thing you can do to overcome that challenge?

4. Brainstorm some of your own ideas for blessing your parents (or in-laws), or steal one or more of the ideas you liked from the chapter and add your own spin. Share them with your group.

Blessing Activity

Pick one of your ideas from question 4 above, and set a date and time to give this blessing to your parents (or in-laws). Share this with your Blessing Group to help keep you accountable.

Making the Blessing a Lifestyle

Use the categories below as a way to come up with your own blessing ideas for your parents (or in-laws). Remember, you do not need to fill in all the blanks, but do try to fill in at least three ideas total.

Don't forget to do this twice—once for each of your parents, if that's an option.

1. What are some activities/hobbies/passions that your parent enjoys? (e.g., cars, football, reading, running, painting)

_____

_____

_____

_____

_____

2. What are some things you have done in the past that have blessed
   your parent? If you haven't done anything like this before, is there
   something you can remember your parent appreciating when
   someone else did it for him or her? (e.g., made dinner, cleaned the
   garage, filled up the gas tank, washed the car)

_____

_____

_____

_____

3. What are some big things that your parent has coming up in the
   next few months? (e.g., a birthday, a presentation at work, a run, a
   tough day—like the anniversary of a parent's death, divorce)

_____

_____

_____

_____

4. What are some things that you really love and appreciate about your parent? (e.g., he or she is really caring, good with the budget, a hard worker, funny, full of positivity)

_____

_____

_____

_____

5. What are some things that your parent is struggling with? (e.g., Is he or she feeling discouraged about what's going on at work? Is he or she feeling lonely? Does your parent feel like he or she needs to add in some healthy habits but can't seem to find the time?)

_____

_____

_____

_____

6. What is something tangible that your parent really likes (such as their favorite food, drink, or way to celebrate)?

_____

_____

_____

_____

_____

7. Other:

_____

_____

_____

_____

_____

Look at the three things from these categories that you've written.

Next to each item, brainstorm and write down at least one way that you can turn each one of those ideas into a blessing. For more information on how to do this and suggestions for each category, go to TheBlessing.com and download this chapter's worksheet.

Finally, take each of the blessing ideas you've written above and add them to your reminders or calendar. Do one a week for three weeks.

Part 4

Turning Hurt into the Blessing

Chapter 18

Blessing Others, Even When It Hurts

I don't know about you, but there have been several seasons in my (Kari's) life where blessing others is not something I've felt able to do. It may be something physical or emotional, but there are times when it hurts to bless. However, each time I'm ready to throw in the blessing towel, I think of my friend Brooke.

I met Brooke at the very end of my freshman year in high school. It was the week of cheerleading tryouts, and I'll never forget the moment Brooke wheeled into that gym. Every head in the room turned to watch her as she took her place in the group and confidently began to learn the moves we would need to perform to make the squad.

Brooke was born with cerebral palsy, something that has not only made using a power wheelchair necessary for her but has impacted her speech and muscle movement as well.

To add to the challenge, as a soon-to-be senior, Brooke would need to qualify for varsity in order to make the squad, as seniors weren't allowed to be on the junior varsity teams.

There were whispers, doubts, and even awe and confusion as the beautiful girl in a power wheelchair completed the first day of tryouts.

By day two, those whispers and doubts had turned to astonishment.

269

And by day three, astonishment had turned to cheers and encouragement.

On the last day of tryouts, when it was time to perform in front of the judges, Brooke showed up with a huge smile and a bow in her hair, and knocked the judges' socks off.

Brooke went on to not only be a key and very loved member of our squad, but she helped us compete and win second place at the state competition that year.

Brooke may have cerebral palsy, but she's never let that stop her from pursuing what the Lord has called her to—or from blessing others. Since meeting Brooke that day, I've watched her do many things, including make the varsity cheer squad, give the graduation speech at the Walter Cronkite School of Journalism and Mass Communication at Arizona State University (where she also won the Walter Cronkite Outstanding Undergraduate Award for Excellence in Journalism), write an incredible book called *The Little Butterfly Girl*, and run powerful workshops to help people share and find healing in their stories.

In the fourteen-plus years I've known her, I've never seen her give an excuse not to show up or to stop blessing others. Even when it hurt. And I've watched her hurt, a lot.

Brooke not only agreed to share some of her story but to also walk us through how she still chooses to bless, even when it hurts. I can't think of a better expert on this topic, and I pray that you are as encouraged and challenged by her story as I am.

Blessing When It Hurts
by Brooke Brown

"What in the world can I do for them when I need so much help myself?" Sound familiar at all?

It's a question I've asked more times than I'd like to admit. I'll be the first to say I understand how easy it is to become consumed with your own physical and emotional needs when you live with a disability, health condition, or some other ongoing struggle in life. I was born with cerebral palsy (a developmental condition that affects my muscles and speech) and I need assistance to do almost all my daily living activities. The spasticity and high tone in my body cause me to be totally dependent on my power wheelchair for mobility. Having my muscles be as tight as they are is frequently quite painful, along with the arthritis and TMJ I've developed.

All these factors make it difficult to nurture meaningful relationships. I can't go to social events or meet up with friends unless they, or someone else, are willing to drive my van. Talking on the phone can be incredibly frustrating unless the other person can understand me really well already. There are a million other things I could mention, but you get the idea. While I've felt useless, left out, isolated, and lonely on many occasions, I've also learned I have to make the choice to bless others even when it hurts or I don't feel able.

But what does that look like? These are some things I believe anyone living with persistent challenges can still do to bless others.

Ask God to Help You Illustrate His Grace

In other words, ask him to give you the strength to get up and try instead of complaining and wallowing in your hardships. Commit to doing the things that ease your pain and make you more productive.

In my case, this means being faithful about going to Pilates and the gym every week to exercise my muscles so they hurt less, which allows me to put more energy into my work. Making an effort in this way is a blessing to others, because watching you persevere will encourage them to do the same with their own struggles.

Whenever You Are Able, Reach Out and Meet in the Middle

In my situation my friends have to come to me much more frequently than I can come to them. This can sometimes put extra strain on finding time to spend together, which may make it feel like a chore rather than nurturing fellowship. So I do my best to take advantage of the times my assistant is working and I can return the favor for once. If it doesn't work out, at least I can be a loving and listening friend they can always call, text, or e-mail for support.

If you're unable to do as much for your friends as they do for you, they will be blessed by the extra effort you put into whatever you *can* do.

Let Your Love and Gratefulness Be Known—Often

I rely on the help of others to accomplish nearly everything I do, including going to the restroom and getting dressed. While helping me "do life" has been a full-time job paid by the state for most of my assistants over the years, I still want them to feel loved and appreciated. So I make it a point to develop a friendship with each of them. That way, work will be a safe and encouraging environment, especially when they have major drama going on elsewhere (which seems inevitable in the caregiving industry). Even though some friends laugh and shake their heads at me, I always point out the little things they do for which I'm keenly grateful.

If you have awesome people who help you "do life" when it hurts the most, tell them how much you appreciate them . . . every day! Take them to coffee or lunch once in a while. Give them tokens of thanks. And most of all, invest in their lives and be understanding when personal stuff comes up for them. Your support will be a profound blessing.

Continue to Use Your Gifts, Even When It's a Struggle

I'm certain the Lord gave me my storytelling, writing, and presentation skills as a tool to bless others. It's humbling to see my work change hearts. However, the physical act of typing is difficult because of my fine motor impairments and the fact that spending long periods at my computer aggravates my pain spots. Therefore, my work takes a lot longer to complete than I'd like, but I choose to keep going. At the end of the day, it's what makes my spirit come alive because I'm fulfilling God's calling on my life. It often seems as though the more I persevere, the bigger impact my stories have on audiences. It just takes serious determination and prayer.

If your pain affects how you bless others with your gifts, don't give up.

Pray for endurance. Ask God for help. I promise he'll be there to lift you up.

So What Can We Do?

Okay, if you aren't crying yet, I certainly am. Brooke's pain isn't minimal. And neither is yours. As you read Brooke's words, I hope you experienced the grace she has for herself and the grace she has for others. I hope and pray that you are able to extend that same grace where it's needed as well.

Before you move on to the next chapter, which talks about what to do if you need to ask someone for the Blessing, take a few minutes to go through the Blessing Group Questions and the Making the Blessing a Lifestyle section.

Blessing Group Questions

1. Have you had a season where it honestly hurt to bless? If yes, what did that look like? If you haven't, do you know someone who has? Share what that looked or looks like for that person.
2. Did you have grace for yourself in that season? Why or why not?
3. Did you have grace for others in that season? Why or why not?
4. What are some ways that you can bless and encourage someone you know who may be in a season of hurt right now?
5. If you are in a season of hurt, how can you begin showing grace to yourself and blessing others where you are at?
6. Is there anything else that came to mind for you as you read Brooke's story?

Blessing Activity

Complete the following section. Make sure to share your answers with your Blessing Group to help keep you accountable.

Making the Blessing a Lifestyle

If you are in a season of hurt:

1. Write down one way you can bless someone right where you're at. Plan a time to give that blessing.

2. Write down one way you can show grace to yourself in this season.

3. Write down one way you can show grace to others in this season.

If you have a loved one in a season of hurt:

1. Write down one way you can bless your loved one in this season. Plan a time to give this blessing.

2. Write down one way you can show grace to yourself in this season.

3. Write down one way you can show grace to your loved one in this season.

Chapter 19

I've Blessed Them, and It's Not Working

While my dad and I (Kari) get a number of e-mails, messages, and notes about the change and transformation people see as the result of giving the Blessing, there is another type of message that we get as well. This is the message that says, "I've blessed them, and it's not working. Help me!"

Often this message comes to us from parents who are brokenhearted over their teen or adult children who have chosen to walk away from the Lord or are struggling to accept the truth about who they are in Christ.

For me, these messages are personal. Mainly because this was my story too.

You would think that a girl whose dad literally wrote the book on the Blessing would never struggle, never walk away from the Lord, and would live a perfect, happy, well-adjusted life, right?

Well, you would be very, very wrong. One of my favorite parts about speaking to groups across the country and getting to write with my dad is sharing this part of our family's story. We both think it's important to talk about because we are not perfect. Our family isn't perfect. And life, unfortunately, isn't perfect.

We also think it's important to share because while the Enemy intended these things for evil, the Lord has completely restored them for *good*. And if this is something you are struggling with, we know he can do that in your family as well.

While I grew up with the Blessing and two parents who made sure I knew I was loved every single day, I struggled with believing it for myself. God seemed really abstract to me, while the world kept presenting me with "tangible" ways to have value each and every day.

Over time, I decided that maybe the world had a better idea about where I could find my value. That's when things began to fall apart.

I got into some horrible relationships, developed some horrible habits, and made some really horrible decisions. A few months after I graduated from college, I did something my parents would never have expected. I eloped.

This was not the best choice for many reasons, but it seemed especially ironic for a young woman whose dad was in full-time marriage and family ministry.

The marriage was a disaster. The man I eloped with was abusive in every sense of the word. He was unfaithful. And it became clear very quickly that he had no desire to work on any of these issues in our marriage.

I tried everything, but nothing changed, and I became more and more depressed, isolated, and broken.

Many things led to this point in my life, and since I share a lot more about my story in other books and I want to focus this chapter on you, I will keep it brief here. One night, I did reach my breaking point.

I cried out to the Lord and told him, "If you are real, I don't care what you do or how you do it, just get me out safely." There was an immediate answer, and several weeks later I was on a plane to start a new life in Tacoma, Washington.

Since that time I've gone through a lot of healing, made many more mistakes, and have had a ton of breakthroughs. And after several years of working on me, I also met and married my amazing husband, Joey, and have watched the Lord redeem more areas of my life and heart than I ever thought possible.

One of the biggest takeaways I hope you get from this story if you are a parent is *you're not responsible for the choices your children make.*

While your children are living in your home, you do have some say and authority over what they are and are not able to do. They may try to go around your authority or even break it outright, but while they are in your home, you do have some say.

But there is still an important variable here. Whether they are in your home or have already left home, it is up to them to choose who they are going to be.

You can *do* all the right things. You can *say* all the right things. You can *be* all the right things. And they can *still choose* to walk away from the Lord.

Let's pause, because I know some of you reading this are now asking yourselves the question, *Then why should I even bother giving them my blessing? Does this book even work?*

Yes. Absolutely, positively yes.

Let me tell you why.

When I *did* come home, when I *did* want to change, when I *did* want to live for the Lord, when I *did* want to get help, *I knew I could* because I had my parents' blessing.

In fact, when I finally came clean with my dad about all the things I'd been doing, he told me, "Kari, it's not about where you've been, it's about where you are going." And he gave me his blessing.

That unleashed me to move forward, to move to Tacoma, to get counseling, to find great friends, and eventually to meet Joey. This all led to the most redemptive wedding—and marriage—I ever could have imagined.

And it gave me permission to make mistakes along the way—of which there have been many, and some just as big and painful as mistakes I'd made in the past. But I knew that no matter what I did, I had my parents' blessing. I had the Lord's blessing. And that changed *everything*.

My dad and I share both sides of this story in our upcoming book. However, know that he and my mom spent a lot of time praying, processing, crying, venting, in counseling, and choosing to bless me even when it was hard.

It wasn't a pretty process. It wasn't a fun season. *But* God is *bigger*. God is *faithful*. God loved me more than my parents ever could. And he never, ever stopped pursuing me. No matter how far I tried to run.

God loves your children too. And he will *never, ever* stop pursuing them. No matter how far they try to run.

It may be ugly. It may be painful. It may end differently than my story did. But God is still there. He still loves you. He still loves them. And he can still work all things together for good.

If you are in a season like my family was, know this: we are praying for you. We don't say that half-heartedly or carelessly. We really do, every day, because we talk almost daily to amazing families who are dealing with really rough things.

Also know that you do not have to do this alone. In fact, please, please don't. Find a great counselor, someone who can help you process through the pain, boundaries, and healing that you need. Doing this *now* will help you be able to tell your child someday, Lord willing, "It's not about where you've been, it's about where you are going"—instead of saying, "It's about time" or "Yeah . . . we'll see if you can follow through for once" or any other reaction that can spill out when we are in pain and dealing with a break in trust.

It will also help you if your story turns out like our sweet friend Jennifer's. Jennifer's oldest son, Todd, was injured during a football game his junior year of high school when a bad tackle damaged his spinal cord. Even after three surgeries, he still struggled to regain the amount of normal motor function and range of motion in his legs that he'd previously had. Todd could still walk but could no longer run, dodge a tackle, or stand for very long without pain. This damage—and the chronic pain that went with it—would be something that Todd would have to live with the rest of his life.

During this time of surgery, recovery, and the family trying to figure out what they could do long term, Todd developed an addiction to the opioid medication he was given.

When it became clear that his situation wouldn't improve and this was his new daily reality, Todd dived even further into his addiction. By what would have been his freshman year of college, Todd was headed to rehab (as mandated by his parents) instead of to the local university with his friends.

After rehab, things looked positive. But several months later, Jennifer began to see the warning signs of relapse. This pattern repeated four more times over the following years. The last time, Todd checked himself out of rehab after only four days and never came home.

He moved from couch to couch, drug house to drug house. He lived on the streets and would only call or show up when he wanted money or needed a place to sleep. One night, Todd even broke into his parents' home while they were on vacation and stole everything of value, including a ring that had been Jennifer's mother's.

This was when Jennifer started going to counseling. She was broken. She was devastated. And she had just about given up hope.

Over the next six months, Jennifer and her husband did some hard work. They established boundaries; they worked through their own pain. They learned to surrender Todd to the Lord, and they worked through the guilt they were feeling, the blame they were carrying over Todd's actions.

Jennifer shared a little with us about that season: "I went from being incapacitated by grief, sorrow, and fear—to trusting God. The circumstances hadn't changed, and it was still challenging, but I gained a peace that I had never experienced before. It was supernatural. My husband experienced it too. That peace gave us what we needed during that time and for the hard months that followed."

As you may have guessed, it was a few weeks into their sixth month of counseling that Jennifer got "the call."

"I can still tell you where I was standing, what I was wearing, and what I was doing at that very moment. In fact, I was in the middle of making my favorite chili. I couldn't make that chili again for almost five years," Jennifer said. She went on:

> When we learned that Todd had passed, we were devastated. But again, as we prayed together and cried together, that supernatural peace came over our hearts. It didn't take away the loss we were feeling, but it gave us what we needed to keep moving forward—which in and of itself was a miracle. If that call had come six months earlier, I would have never been able to do any of the things that I did after that phone call. I would have been completely debilitated, and I don't know if I ever would have come out of that place.

Jennifer and her husband continued to mourn, heal, and find peace. And they also continued to choose to heal through counseling, support groups, and their Blessing Group as well.

Today Jennifer is an amazing counselor who helps other families who are dealing with addiction. And God has turned her story of pain into blessing for others. She shared:

> I still miss Todd. Every day. But I feel so strongly that God has redeemed Todd's story as well as ours. By helping other families,

something I know Todd would have loved, God has used him to free others and point them to Jesus. He has saved lives. He has provided hope. And he has continued to bless us as we wait to rejoice with him in heaven someday. That is how we remember Todd. We praise the Lord every day for the way that he has healed us and used this for good.

We hope and pray that you never experience what Jennifer did. Or even what my family did. But we want you to know that even if your child never walks away, walks away for a while, or never chooses to come "home," God is not done with your story. And he is not done with your child's story either.

Pictures Your Heart Remembers

We know that this chapter brings up a ton of emotions for anyone reading it. We all have been impacted by loss, and our greatest fear as parents is having something like this happen to our child. Before we go any further, take a moment to journal and process with the Lord the emotions that you are feeling right now. Are you rejoicing over a child who came home? Heartbroken over a child who has walked away? Afraid that your child is going to make a decision like this? Whatever it is, let's spend some time giving it to the God who provides *peace*. Ask him to give you that supernatural peace, the kind that surpasses all understanding.

Blessing Group Questions

1. Are you in a season where your child is struggling to believe or has rejected your or God's blessing?

2. What came up for you as you read this chapter? You can share what you journaled above with your group.

3. What are some ways that you can continue to turn to the Lord in moments where it can be hard to feel peace over your kids?

4. What are some ways that you have seen God show up in your kids' lives?

5. Do you feel like you need more help processing where you are at as a family? What steps can you take this week to get the support you need?

Making the Blessing a Lifestyle

If you are dealing with a tough situation with your family, take the time to find a great counselor. Ask friends for references, then try out a few to find the right one. Please do not go through this season alone.

If you'd like us to pray for you specifically, please e-mail us directly at TheBlessing@StrongFamilies.com.

Now that you know what the Blessing is and how to make it an active part of your relationships, in the next chapters we will look at what we can do if we didn't get the Blessing ourselves, and how to start healing some of the painful consequences of such withholding. This section might be especially helpful to you if you or someone you love is struggling with a lack of blessing in your life.

Chapter 20

What If I Didn't Get the Blessing?

It should be clear by now that helping a child receive and accept the Blessing is of tremendous importance. But perhaps you have come to realize that you grew up in a home that withheld the Blessing, and this realization has left you feeling hopeless. If so, take heart. You have the wonderful opportunity to overcome the past by extending the Blessing to your own children.

In this chapter we'll deal with some first steps in what to do if you missed the Blessing. But this is a topic worthy of going into in much more detail, which Dr. Tony Wheeler and I (John) will do in a book called *The Blessing Cry*.

There is help here in this book, in our Blessing Courses, and on our website and podcast, where you'll find more of the outstanding work Dr. Wheeler has done in being our go-to expert in reversing the curse and really bringing Jesus' love into the life of someone who missed the Blessing.

So know then that missing the Blessing is worthy of a whole book and more focus than we can share in this book. But start here—and start with the reality of understanding just how missing the Blessing can affect us.

Life Without the Blessing

We have already looked at several examples of the challenges faced by people who missed out on the Blessing when they were children. Let's examine a little more closely the ways that being deprived of the Blessing can show itself later in life. Without the Blessing, children can become . . .

The Seekers

Seekers are people who are always searching for intimacy but are seldom able to tolerate it. These are the people who feel tremendous fulfillment in the thrill of courtship but may have difficulty sustaining a relationship of any kind, including marriage. Never sure of how acceptance feels, they are never satisfied with wearing it too long. They may even struggle with believing in God's unchanging love for them because of the lack of permanence in the Blessing in their early lives.

The Shattered

These are the people whose lives are deeply troubled over the loss of their parents' love and acceptance. Fear, anxiety, depression, and emotional withdrawal can often be traced to missing out on the family blessing. This unhappy road can even lead a person to the terrifying cliffs of suicide, convinced he or she is destined to be a "cipher in the snow."

The Smotherers

Like two-thousand-pound sponges, these needy people react to missing their parents' blessing by sucking every bit of life and energy from a spouse, child, friend, or entire congregation. Their past has left them so empty emotionally that they eventually drain those around them of the desire to help or even listen. When this happens, unfortunately, the Smotherers understand only that they are being rejected. Deeply hurt once again, they never realize that they have brought this pain upon themselves. They end up pushing away the very people they need so desperately.

The Angry

As long as people are angry with each other, they are emotionally chained together. Many adults, for instance, remain tightly linked to their parents because they are still furious over missing the Blessing. They have never forgiven or forgotten. As a result, the rattle and chafing of emotional chains distract them from intimacy in other relationships, and the weight of the iron links keeps them from moving forward in life.

The Detached

Quite a few children who have missed out on the Blessing use the old proverb, "Once burned, twice shy" as a motto. Having lost the Blessing from an important person in their lives once, they spend a lifetime protecting themselves from it ever happening again. Keeping a spouse, children, or a close friend at arm's length, they protect themselves, all right—at the expense of inviting loneliness to take up residence in their lives.

The Driven

In this category, line up extreme perfectionists, workaholics, notoriously picky house cleaners, and generally demanding people who go after getting their blessing the old-fashioned way: they try to *earn it*. The thwarted need for affirmation and acceptance keeps these driven people tilting at a windmill named "accomplishment" in an illusory attempt to gain love and acceptance.

The Deluded

Like their driven counterparts, these people throw their time, energy, and material resources into the pursuit of anything they hope will fill that sense of emptiness inside. But instead of focusing on achievement, they look for social status, popularity, attention, and plenty of "toys." They never quite understand that the Blessing is a gift that cannot be bought. Only counterfeit blessings are for sale—usually at an exorbitant price—and they last only as long as the showroom shine on a new car. So these folks are constantly feeling the need to trade in one fake blessing for another.

The Seduced

Many people who have missed out on their parents' blessing look to fill their relationship needs in all the wrong places. As we mentioned in an earlier chapter, unmet needs for love and acceptance can tempt a person to sexual immorality, trying to meet legitimate needs in an illegitimate way. Substance abuse and other compulsive behaviors can also fall into this category. A drink, a pill, or a behavior is used to cover up the hurt from empty relationships in the past or present, and an addiction can easily result.[1] One study of compulsive gamblers (especially those struck with "lottery fever") found that more than 90 percent of the male subjects had "dismal childhoods, characterized by loneliness and rejection."[2]

Hope for Healing

Do any of these descriptions sound even a little bit familiar? Perhaps you or someone you love has struggled to cope with the feelings or behaviors we have described—or someone else has pointed them out to you. (Sometimes it's hard to see in our own lives what is abundantly clear to others.)

If any of these scenarios ring true (or partially true), don't worry. There is hope and help for anyone to leave the ranks of those above and join the ranks of "the blessed." In fact, every missed element of the Blessing can be regained. Rather than being locked into repeating the past, we all can find freedom to grow into the people God wants us to be.

In the rest of this chapter, we suggest some important steps that can begin the healing process. We are not offering a simple formula nor guaranteeing an instant cure. However, in counseling men and women all across the country, we find that many who have started with these principles have received hope and healing.

In our experience, the road to blessing begins with the very difficult first step of being honest with ourselves.

Honesty: The First Step Toward Healing

Several years ago, I (John) counseled with the parents of a very disturbed twenty-one-year-old named Liam. He was angry and belligerent, occasionally violent, and his mental problems placed a tremendous burden on his family. And it was immediately apparent to me that they should have sought help long before they did.

These problems had first begun to appear after a car accident when Liam was eleven years old. The accident occurred soon after the family moved to Texas. Before the accident, when they lived in Michigan, Liam and his family had gotten along beautifully. In fact, they had been a model family at their church and in their community.

When Liam's behavior began to change following the accident, his concerned parents took him to specialist after specialist. They always received the same diagnosis: their son's problems had no medical solution. Perhaps time and understanding would work things out.

Instead, ten years after the accident, Liam was getting progressively worse. But his mother, who loved him dearly, refused to recognize the severity of his problem. "It's just not that bad," she kept saying. "We just need to be patient."

Even when Liam was angry and sullen, she would spend hours trying to reason with him and read him verses of Scripture to make an impression on his life. Again and again she prayed that this "thorn in the flesh" would be removed and that their lives would be restored to what they were before the accident.

In an attempt to alleviate the mounting pressure because of Liam's behavior, she would often set up family socials and special holiday events. She wanted to re-create a time when the whole family could be "all together again, just like in Michigan." However, as soon as Liam arrived on the scene, he would ruin the party with his sulking and his outbursts.

Still, the mother held on to her denial. Her husband and the rest of the family could think what they wanted; she *knew* that things would get better. Life would once again be just like it was "in Michigan." She even dreamed about it—until one day her dreams turned into a nightmare.

Liam's father was nearing retirement, and the couple, who had saved up for years to buy a place in the mountains, was really looking forward to it. So six months before Dad officially retired, they called a Realtor about putting their house on the market.

Their children knew about the plan and were excited for them—except Liam. Though he had been living on his own for several years, he still made his parents' home his headquarters. This was almost a necessity because his violent temper had driven off every roommate and all but the staunchest of friends.

When Liam came to his parents' home one night and saw the

For Sale sign in their yard, he went berserk. He banged on the door repeatedly, but his parents were not home. Finally he pulled up the sign from the front yard and used it to bash in the front-door window. Then he proceeded to tear up the house.

Liam's parents returned home several hours later to find the place in shambles—chairs overturned, lamps smashed, a potted tree ripped from its place and replaced by the "For Sale" sign. Upstairs and down, the house was a wreck.

Yet of all the damage Liam had done to the house, one thing in particular broke his mother's heart. Liam had gone to the hall where all the family pictures hung and cut every one of them to pieces. From baby pictures on up to their last family portrait with all the grandchildren, each one was torn beyond repair.

Liam's mother, like every parent, treasured her children's pictures. They were priceless to her, especially the pictures of the family before Liam's accident. To her, those photos were a sign of hope that one day things would be just like before, just like "in Michigan."

Liam's mother finally had to recognize and acknowledge that wasn't going to happen even if Liam made a dramatic recovery. She was forced to come to grips with the past and take responsibility for her present problems, instead of living with the dreams that Liam's problems would go away or trying to convince herself that the last ten years of Liam's outbursts really weren't that bad.

How does this story apply to those who have missed out on the Blessing? Like Liam's mother, many will try to explain away and put off admitting the obvious in their lives. Drawing imaginary pictures of their pasts or denying the real problems that exist can often keep them from honestly facing their pasts and their parents. By protecting themselves or their parents, they effectively block their own healing.

Liam's mother refused to make the painful acknowledgment

that her son had a serious problem, and she ended up suffering even more. People who put off coming to grips with their pasts often reap the same kind of harvest, a harvest where pain is multiplied and sorrows doubled, all because they refused to face the legitimate pain that comes with facing the truth.

Shining a Spotlight on the Past

John 8:32 is a Scripture verse that we require our counselees to memorize. It records the words of Jesus: "You shall know the truth, and the truth shall make you free." The truth about which Jesus speaks in this verse refers to knowing him in all his purity. Christ offers no cover-ups, no denying there is a problem when there really is one. When we know the truth, we walk in the light that exposes darkness and shows the way to freedom.

Many of us need to turn on truth's searchlight and shine it on our pasts. Only then can we be free to walk confidently into the future. Jorge was able to do this, and it paid rich dividends in his life.

Jorge was four years old when his parents told him a new little brother or sister was on the way. As with most four-year-olds, nine months seemed like nine years as he waited for his new playmate.

The day finally came when Jorge's mother left for the hospital, and he knew he wouldn't have to wait much longer. That next day, Jorge went with his father to the hospital to see his new baby sister. However, when Jorge came into his mother's hospital room, he had a surprise. He had *two* baby sisters, two beautiful twin girls who were already the apples of their mother's eye.

Jorge was certainly not loved any less when the twins came home, but life was certainly different. He now had to share his parents' time and attention with not only one sister but two. When the twins got older, things became even worse from Jorge's perspective. The same people who stopped his mother to comment on how cute the little girls were in their double stroller rarely lifted their eyes to notice an older brother longing for the same affirmation.

Jorge's parents loved him deeply. In no way did they intentionally try to overlook Jorge or cater to the twins. And Jorge loved his sisters. He was the perfect big brother, looking out for the twins and showing them the ropes when they got into school. Yet as the years went by, even the special bond between the twin girls became a minor source of jealousy for Jorge. He just could not compete with the special closeness between his two look-alike sisters, and it bothered him.

Long after he and his sisters were grown and out of the house, Jorge attended one of my seminars and heard for the first time about the family blessing. In many ways, Jorge knew that he was loved and accepted and that his parents tried hard to provide him the Blessing. Yet in his heart of hearts, he questioned whether he had really received it after the twins were born. For years he had a nagging insecurity in his life that he could trace directly back to this fact.

Jorge knew that all his family would soon be gathering at his parents' house to celebrate the holidays. After the conference ended, he also knew that he needed to deal honestly with his feelings of missing out on at least a part of the Blessing. With every bit of courage he had, Jorge decided he would bring up the subject with his parents.

The first morning he was at his parents' home, the opportunity arose. The three of them were alone at the breakfast table; everyone else had gone out shopping for Christmas ornaments or a last-minute present.

Jorge began talking with his parents by sharing with them

much of what he had learned about the Blessing at the seminar. The concept was new to them as well, and they perked up and got right into the discussion.

Jorge then took several minutes to praise his parents and thank them for the way they had put several elements of the Blessing into practice. Finally, in a loving, nonaccusatory fashion, he shared one of the deepest secrets of his heart—his feelings of missing out on part of the Blessing after the twins came along.

As soon as Jorge began sharing his concern, his mother began to cry. Jorge immediately tried to comfort her and told her he wished he had never brought it up. "No," said his mother. "Please don't be sorry. I've wanted to talk about this for so long. I've always thought it might have bothered you, but I didn't know how to bring it up."

Almost instantly Jorge and his parents were drawn into unity. They cried and laughed and hugged one another as if they had just come together after years of being apart. In a way, they had.

That night the now-grown children and their parents sat down for a family council, something they hadn't done in years. The topic of that morning's breakfast conversation was shared with the twins, and they had their chance to cry, to share, and to reaffirm their love for their brother and their parents. Any nagging guilt they had felt over the situation was now resolved and turned into gratitude for a courageous older brother.

Jorge's willingness to share his feelings honestly with his parents and his twin sisters made a big difference—if ever a part of the Blessing had been missing in his life before, it was certainly present now. Even his employer noticed the difference when Jorge returned to work after the holidays a far more confident man.

We can't stress how important it is to be honest with your feelings regarding missing the Blessing. It is the important first step to healing and restoration.

The Gift of Understanding

The next recommendation I (John) would make to anyone who has missed out on his or her family's blessing is to understand as much as possible about his or her parents' backgrounds. Following this one bit of advice can free many people from wondering why they never received the Blessing—something I discovered firsthand.

For years I felt pain about the relationship I had with my father. It would often be years between our visits, and he never made contact on his own initiative. His silence trapped a layer of hurt in my life that seemed untouchable . . . until I met Uncle Max.

He was my father's uncle—my great-uncle—but I didn't even know he existed until I went away to college in Texas. As I mentioned earlier, Max Trent was the head librarian at Southern Methodist University in Dallas. And as I got to know him, I took a big step toward really understanding my father—because Uncle Max told me so many stories I had never heard before.

I discovered what life was like at home when he was growing up. I learned much more about his war years and the personal and alcohol-related problems he had suffered as a result of those years. I learned that he had been deserted by his father, just as he had later deserted us.

Learning all these things was like turning on a light in a darkened room. I had often wondered why my father resisted communication with us. Now I saw numerous experiences that had shaped his behavior. I had never understood certain patterns he developed—and then I discovered they actually ran generations deep.

What I learned from Uncle Max was something I hope all children will take into consideration. In the vast majority of cases, parents who do not give the Blessing to a son or a daughter have never received it themselves.

Andrea, like me, took this advice to heart, and it totally changed her perspective of her father. Andrea heard about the concept of the Blessing at a singles' retreat where I spoke. For years she had struggled with how distant her father seemed. He was always cordial to her, and he never raised his voice with any of the children. But what was missing left Andrea with nagging questions about whether she had received the Blessing. Besides an occasional hug, her father had not demonstrated, to her way of thinking, any of the five elements of the Blessing she had learned about.

Andrea was still living at home, and she took the first opportunity she could after the retreat to talk to her father about what she had learned. What Andrea found out in that conversation turned out to be a key to understanding her father.

After her father had listened to his daughter talk about the Blessing—he was always a good listener, just not a good talker—he cleared his throat and shared with Andrea something of his past. Andrea had never met her grandparents on her father's side. They had both died a few years before she was born. And as her father had been an only child, Andrea had no aunts and uncles to pass down the family stories. So what her father told her now was news to her.

Andrea's father had grown up in England. His parents had even held claim to a small title of nobility. And they had their son raised with all the dignity and care afforded any English citizen of high birth. During his early years, he had a nanny who helped raise him, while his parents kept the respectable distance considered proper for teaching children discipline and manners.

His relationship with his parents was so formal that anytime he addressed his father, it was to be prefaced by Sir. There was no Dad, Daddy, Papa, or anything of the kind in this household. Sir was the proper form of address. Not surprisingly, appropriate meaningful touch was strictly taboo in that household, and words of praise were as rare as hen's teeth (which, in case you weren't raised on a farm, really are quite scarce).

295

In the course of one hour, Andrea learned more about her father's background than she had in the nineteen previous years. As a result of seeing how her father was raised, she gained a new compassion and understanding for his actions toward her and her brothers and sisters. She even found out that, compared to his parents, her father felt he was trying fanatically hard to make sure each of his children received the Blessing. And all the time she thought he was withholding it.

If we will stop and take the time to look beyond our parents' actions during our childhoods to their pasts, it will be time well spent. We may even come to realize they need the Blessing as badly as we do. And that realization can be the catalyst that frees us to seek the Blessing from a more dependable source.

We shouldn't look down and lose hope if we grew up without the Blessing. We should look up, instead, to the incredible provision of a blessing that can leave our lives overflowing, the kind of blessing that can even replace a curse with contentment.

Pictures Your Heart Remembers

Let's spend some time in this chapter reading through each question for the group study. They are all so heavy and potentially filled with pictures and memories. Work through the questions in a way that enables you to share your thoughts with your group.

Blessing Group Questions

1. You read about different ways you can find the "return address" to present hurtful behaviors—by tracing that address back to missing the Blessing. Of that list shared in this chapter (Seekers,

the Shattered, Smotherers, the Angry, Detached, Driven, Deluded, Seduced), is there a ninth category you'd add from your personal behavior?

2. When it comes to this chapter and the idea of missing the Blessing, we need to face something that is uncomfortable head on. The story here of Liam's mother not wanting to admit their family had a huge, real problem with their son is one of pushing off or avoiding that very difficult conversation. Can you share a time when you had the courage to take that step into being uncomfortable—and how the Lord helped you through, no matter the outcome?

3. Understanding is a huge part of dealing with missing the Blessing—not as a way of building a case for someone's irresponsible or uncaring behavior, but of at least shining a light on the *why* of that behavior. For me (John), it helped to understand some of the terrible pictures my father carried from the Pacific theater in World War II. Can you share about a relationship where understanding brought with it a way to "untie the knot" or at least realize from where the person's hurt had come?

4. I (John) know a counselor who is always telling people, "Look for the need behind the deed." How does that saying offer people a way to help them deal with missing the Blessing?

5. False beliefs can freeze us in a place we don't have to stay. Is there something false you believed about yourself as a result of missing the Blessing that you know today, in the light of Jesus' love and grace, isn't true or in control of you?

Chapter 21

Your Next Step Is Living the Blessing

When is the end a beginning? We pray you've had an encouraging, meaningful, life-building time with your Blessing Group. But what's next? Here are several things we'd recommend for you to keep moving forward in giving and living the Blessing. Because, again, it's not just a one-and-done thing.

First, have your Blessing Group or Team get a certificate together in both living the Blessing and helping those who have missed the Blessing. Kari and I have created an online course specific to the Blessing. If you're ready for another step, this is a great one to choose. The first part will help you in giving and living out the Blessing, and the second (with Dr. Tony Wheeler) will help in encouraging you personally if you missed the Blessing. Just go to TheBlessing.com and look for the Blessing courses.

Second, as a group, pick out a *second place* where you'll start showing up and blessing people.

Your home needs to be the first place where you live out the Blessing. But if your group is asking, "What's next?" a great thing to do is to keep meeting together by stepping into a second place. For example, there may be a senior citizen's home nearby. Go over and meet with the staff, see if they need volunteers to encourage, read to, or bless some of the residents. Yes, you might have to go through a background check (as you would if working with children today), and it might seem inconvenient, but there are so many lonely people in these homes who never get a visitor. If you just show up and start looking for ways to speak into their lives, you'll be amazed to see what the Blessing can do in a place where people are often losing hope and longing for someone to love them like Jesus.

Serving seniors is just one option. Your group could also volunteer at a school or church. We know one group who talked with their church's children's director and volunteered to stand at the door and give a quick blessing to each child before the kids headed out of the room and back to Mom and Dad. It's become a favorite thing for the children—they would line up, get their blessing, and then run out to Mom and Dad all fired up and talking about the blessing they got. This led to some great talks with parents and a whole church who started learning to bless—all because a few people stood at the door and blessed kids before they ran out.

Be creative and pray for doors to open to start living out the Blessing. Again, the first place to bless is at home, but be looking for that second place as well.

Third, bring a Blessing speaker to your church to launch a Blessing Challenge.

Kari, Dr. Wheeler, myself (John), and others on our team head out to local churches all the time to teach about the Blessing and launch a challenge for parents to start blessing their kids and grandkids. At TheBlessing.com you can find out how to bring one of our Blessing speakers to your church, men's event, women's event, or even workplace event.

Fourth, read another book together as a group.

If your group liked going through this book, then here are two books that would make a great "next step" in going deeper on two of the five elements of the Blessing: giving a spoken (or written) message and attaching high value to others.

Thanks to Focus on the Family, Kari and I have just revised and updated two award–winning classic books. Each one is designed *specifically* to help you go even deeper and gain more skills in one of the elements of the Blessing. The first will instruct you in how to use your spoken or written words to bless others, and the other will increase your ability to attach high value to others by helping them see their strengths.

The Language of Love will help you become skillful and powerful in using word pictures to bless others. It lays out the concept that you read about in chapter 9, where we shared how Jesus so often used word pictures (stories and parables) to express truth in a way people would never forget and also deeply understand.

The second book we recommend you go through with your group is *The Two Sides of Love*. Like many of our books and courses, *The Two Sides of Love* came directly out of looking for ways to help people go deeper on one of the elements of the Blessing. Again, this book has been updated and revised and even comes with a code for you take an online assessment, called the Connect Assessment, that can help you and those you love *see* their strengths and *value* the strengths they see in others.

Finally, look for webinars, tools, great ideas from others, and more at StrongFamilies.com, the world headquarters of people wanting to live and give the Blessing.

There are many more examples, stories, and support to help you live out the Blessing in the relationships that matter most to you. All you need to do is go to TheBlessing.com/bonuschapters to get the free e-book. Each of these chapters has Pictures Your Heart Remembers, Blessing Group Questions, and Making the Blessing a Lifestyle sections for you as well.

If you notice a relationship that we didn't cover, we'd love to come up with ideas to help you! Just e-mail us at TheBlessing@ StrongFamilies.com or send us a message on social media. We are always creating new content, and we would love to come up with something specific to help you. So stop right now, go to TheBlessing.com/bonuschapters and download your free e-book to keep living out the Blessing.

Whatever you do, keep moving forward in blessing others— and in finding out more about how Jesus can bless your life as well.

A Final Blessing Story

We started this book with two stories of people who missed the Blessing, but we'd like to close this book with the story of a couple who decided they were going to keep giving the Blessing—no matter what. That's our prayer for you, that you'll find ways to keep reminding yourself that the Blessing is your "job," and that you'll lean in and bless others—just as this couple did whose son couldn't hear a word they said.

Years ago my wife, Cindy, and I were teaching about the Blessing at a conference for physicians and their spouses. That's when we met little Aaron's mother. She came up quietly. She shared her story softly. Yet it left a profound impact on our lives—that is, after Cindy and I had stopped crying and thanking God for what we had heard.

It seems that several years before, this woman and her husband (both physicians, by the way) had traveled from out of state to attend a similar conference of ours. They left their precious three-year-old son, Aaron, at home with a babysitter. While they were gone, Aaron began to spike a fever. The babysitter called, then called again. But the cell phone reception wasn't great in the hall, and it took them some time before they could return her call. By the time they did talk, the sitter was terribly worried about their son, particularly because his fever was so high.

Imagine two doctors, thousands of miles from their hurting son, unable to do anything to help. Needless to say, they left for home immediately, but by the time they got there, little Aaron had been diagnosed with viral meningitis and sustained profound hearing loss as a result of the fever. The parents, of course, were devastated when they got this news. But they determined their son's hearing loss wouldn't stop them from blessing him—not for a single day.

Up until the day their son lost his hearing, this couple had done something that they had seen in one of our videos. The video showed Cindy and I singing that simple little blessing song we had made up for Kari and Laura when they were little to wake them up in the morning. We would hug them as we sang:

Good morning, good morning, how are you today?
The Lord bless you and keep you throughout the day.
We love you, we love you, we love you, Kari (or Laura).

Aaron's mom and dad had thought our song was cute and adopted it as a way to bless their son in the mornings. Ever since he was tiny, they had been singing, "We love you, we love you, we love you, Aaron."

But now Aaron couldn't hear that good-morning song or blessing. So they immediately set out to learn the words in sign language. That way, as Aaron grew older, he wouldn't miss a day of them sharing that he was special and valuable to them, that God had a special future for him, and that his parents would always be committed to him.

I think of all the children I have met whose parents never bothered to say "I love you" even once to them, who never told them anything about their future except words like, "Don't take algebra. That's for the smart kids." Parents who would never take the time to write a blessing letter, no matter how much it could mean to their child.

And then I hear stories like Aaron's—stories about parents who are going to give the Blessing to their child no matter the challenge. And that's our blessing for you: that you keep the Blessing going. That one million parents like Aaron's will step up to the plate and hit it out of the park by passing on the Blessing to their own child . . . and many others.

And may a million more lives be changed in the process.

Notes

Chapter 1: The Importance of Asking Why

1. Simon Sinek, "How Great Leaders Inspire Action," TEDxPuget Sound, video, 17:58, September 2009, https://www.ted.com/talks/simon_sinek_how_great_leaders_inspire_action.

2. Teammates such as Dr. Tony Wheeler, who works across the country with us, teaching how we can deal with missing the Blessing, and Brooke Brown, who is world-class at helping people get up each day focused on blessing others even through extreme pain. You can find out more about both of them as well as learn how to invite Kari or me to speak to your church or group (or via Zoom to your small group) by visiting TheBlessing.com.

Chapter 2: Celebrating with Your Blessing Team

1. "Ex-Marine Baz Gray Completes Solo Trek to South Pole," BBC News, January 7, 2019, https://www.bbc.com/news/uk-england-devon-46780829.

2. John Trent, "LOGB Strengths Assessment," Strong Families, https://StrongFamilies.com/logb.

3. Some of the best and most beautiful journals for capturing these thoughts can be found in a small shop in Seattle in the Fish Market, right across from the original Starbucks. Deneen Shank creates affordable, beautiful handmade journals. Check out No Boundaries Homemade Journals at www.noboundariesbooks.com.

Chapter 5: A Life-and-Death Choice

1. Francis Brown, S. R. Driver, and Charles A. Briggs, eds., *A Hebrew and English Lexicon of the Old Testament* (Oxford: Clarendon Press, 1974), 311, "live." See along with James Strong, *Strong's Exhaustive Concordance of the Bible* (Hendrickson Publishers), citation 2416. The word *life* carries definitions such as "to be quickened," "running,"

"springing," and to "troop." We are "alive" when we are animated to "get moving" and, like a "troop" of soldiers, move or step toward an objective.

2. Brown, Driver, and Briggs, *Hebrew and English Lexicon*, 559. "Death": "to depart, to remove, to step away." The New Testament word for "death," *thanatos*, also carries this idea of stepping away.

3. Brown, Driver, and Briggs, 139.

4. Brown, Driver, and Briggs, 457. "Honor": "to be heavy, weighty, honored." The idea of coins on a scale can even be seen in one way this word is translated: as an "offering."

5. Brown, Driver, and Briggs, 886b. "Curse": "to be slight, of water, be abated." To see a picture of this in Scripture, go to Genesis 8:3, where the flood waters are "cursed," literally meaning, "the waters abated." It is, in part, pulling away life-giving water from someone that we curse them.

Chapter 7: The First Element: Appropriate Meaningful Touch

1. Robert Salt, "Affectionate Touch Between Fathers and Preadolescent Sons," *Journal of Marriage and the Family* 53 (August 1991): 545.

2. Job 41:15–17; also see Brown, Driver, and Briggs, *Hebrew and English Lexicon*, 621.

3. Salt, "Affectionate Touch," 545.

4. Salt, 545.

5. Salt, 545.

6. The blessing of Ephraim and Manasseh also had a unique spiritual message. When Jacob "crossed" his hands and blessed the younger with the older son's blessing, it was a picture of God's election.

7. Charles F. Pfeiffer, Howard F. Vos, and John Rea, eds., *Wycliffe Bible Encyclopedia* (Chicago: Moody Press, 1975), 750.

8. Harvey Richard Schiffman, *Sensation and Perception: An Integrated Approach* (New York: John Wiley & Sons, 1982), 107.

9. Dolores Krieger, "Therapeutic Touch: The Imprimatur of Nursing," *American Journal of Nursing* 75, no. 5 (May 1975): 784.

10. "We need four hugs a day for survival. We need eight hugs a day for maintenance," says Virginia Satir, noted family therapist and author,

quoted in *UCLA Monthly*, Alumni Association News, March–April 1981, 1.

11. Marianne D. Borelli and Patricia Heidt, *Therapeutic Touch* (New York: Springer Publishing, 1981), quoted in *Reader's Digest*, January 1992, 21.

12. Tiffany Field, Touch Research Institute at University of Miami School of Medicine, quoted in "A Conversation on Touch in Early Development," *Current Health* 13, no. 2 (1986): 13.

13. Saul Schanberg and Steven Butler, *Symbiosis in Parent-Offspring Interactions* (New York: Plenum Press, 1983), 41.

14. L. W. Linkous and R. M. Stutts, "Passive Tactile Stimulation Effects on the Muscle Tone of Hypotonic Developmentally Delayed Young Children," *Perceptual and Motor Skills* 71, no. 3, part 1 (December 1990): 951–54.

15. F. B. Dresslar, "The Psychology of Touch," *American Journal of Psychology* 6, no. 3 (1984): 316.

16. Marcia Mark and Perla Werner, "Agitation and Touch in the Nursing Home," *Psychological Reports* 64, no. 3, part 2 (1989): 1020.

17. Mark and Werner, "Agitation and Touch," 1023.

18. Robert M. Sapolsky, *Stress, the Aging Brain, and Mechanisms of Neuron Death* (Cambridge, MA: MIT Press, 1992), 73.

19. James Hardison, *Let's Touch* (New York: Prentice-Hall, 1980).

20. Helen Colton, *The Gift of Touch* (New York: Seaview/Putnam, 1983), 102.

21. Edgar Wycoff and Jill Holley, "Effects of Flight Attendant's Touch upon Airline Passengers' Perceptions of the Attendant and the Airline," *Perceptual and Motor Skills* 71, no. 3, part 1 (December 1990): 932–34.

22. Colton, *Gift of Touch*, 49.

23. Arthur Janov, "For Control, Cults Must Ease the Most Profound Pains," *Los Angeles Times*, December 10, 1978, part 6, 3.

24. Marc H. Hollender, "The Wish to Be Held," *Archives of General Psychiatry* 22 (1970): 445.

25. Alfred Edersheim, *The Life and Times of Jesus the Messiah, Part Two* (Grand Rapids: Eerdmans, 1972), 329.

26. Sidney Jourand's study, quoted in Tiffany Field, *Touch* (London: Bradford Books, 1988), 22.

Chapter 8: The Second Element: A Spoken or Written Message

1. Gary Smalley, *The Key to Your Child's Heart* (Waco, TX: Word Books, 1984). See the chapter on "Balancing Loving Support Through Contracts," 77–107.

2. Jack Burtin, "Goodbye . . . Be Good to Each Other," *USA Today*, August 19, 1985, 1.

Chapter 9: The Third Element: Attaching High Value

1. Brown, Driver, and Briggs, *Hebrew and English Lexicon*, 139.

2. That is why Psalm 95:6 translates the word *bless* as "to bow the knee" when it says, "Come let us worship the LORD and bow before Him" (literally, "bless him").

3. J. D. Douglas, "Lion of Judah," *New Bible Dictionary* (Grand Rapids: Eerdmans, 1971), 742.

4. Some circles dispute how Solomon, with all his many wives, could be a model for a godly marriage. One can see a commentary on the Song of Solomon for a fuller explanation, but in brief here are two reasons why we feel Solomon's story can still help any married couple today. First, Solomon did not begin to take foreign wives and concubines until later in life, after his visit by the queen of Sheba. Song of Solomon is dated by most scholars as being written early in his reign as king. More important, any person, including Solomon, could leave his first love when he stops walking with God. During Solomon's later years, when he took many wives, his fellowship with God was certainly not where it was when he asked for the gift of wisdom.

5. S. Craig Glickman, *A Song for Lovers* (Downers Grove, IL: InterVarsity Press, 1974), 48.

Chapter 10: The Fourth Element: Picturing a Special Future

1. M. J. Cohen, *The Jewish Celebration Book* (Philadelphia: The Jewish Publication Society of America, 1946), 108.

2. Jay Stifler, *The Epistle to the Romans* (Chicago: Moody Press, 1983), 119.

3. While we do not recommend the book because of its secular bent and conclusions, William S. Appleton's *Fathers and Daughters* (New

York: Berkley Books, 1984) has a number of chilling studies that
have been done on the destruction that happens when a father has a
poor relationship with his daughter.
4. We would like to extend our special thanks to Dr. Jeffrey M. Trent,
associate professor of medicine, University of Arizona, for putting
this example into "everyday English" for us.

Chapter 11: The Fifth Element: An Active, Genuine Commitment

1. For a helpful discussion on this point, see Charles Swindoll, *You and Your Child* (Nashville: Thomas Nelson, 1977), 27–32.
2. Gary Smalley, *The Key to Your Child's Heart* (Dallas: Word, 1984), Chapter 2, "Expressing Loving Support—The Most Important Aspect of Raising Children."
3. Dewey Roussel, "Message of the White Dove," *Reader's Digest*, September 1984, 29.

Chapter 12: First Steps: A Written Blessing

1. "Dad's Letter Offers Parable for Eldest Daughter," AZCentral, June 3, 1998, http://www.azcentral.com/specials/special25/articles/0603goldwater.html.
2. "Dad's Letter," AZCentral.
3. A personal letter shared with me by the engineer in question.

Chapter 13: Your Blessing

1. John Trent, *The 2 Degree Difference: How Little Things Can Change Everything* (Nashville: B&H Publishing, 2009).
2. "21 Bible Verses About Being Chosen," Knowing Jesus, accessed November 30, 2018, https://bible.knowing-jesus.com/topics/Being-Chosen.
3. "10 Bible Verses That Show Your True Value," accessed November 30, 2018, Amazing Facts, https://www.amazingfacts.org/news-and-features/news/item/id/13320/t/10-bible-verses-that-show-your-true-value.
4. Dawn (contributor), "21 Bible Verses for When You Need to Feel God's Love," Seedtime, December 13, 2016, https://christianpf.com/bible-verses-about-gods-love/.

5. Isa. 43:1 NIV.

6. Isa. 43:1 NIV.

7. 2 Cor. 6:18.

8. Rom. 8:31–39 NLT.

9. Deut. 31:6.

10. John Callahan, "7 Bible Verses Reminding Us That God Has Given Us a Purpose in Life," Christian Post, accessed November 30, 2018, https://www.christianpost.com/news/7-bible-verses-reminding-us -that-god-has-given-us-a-purpose-in-life-137732.

11. Jer. 29:11 NIV.

12. Deut. 30:3–13 THE MESSAGE.

13. Isa. 42:16 NIV.

14. John 15:16.

15. Luke 15:11–32 NIV.

16. Ps. 139:13–14 NIV.

17. Jer. 29:11 NIV.

18. Mark 16:15.

19. John 13:34 NIV.

20. Rom. 8:31–39 NLT.

21. John 7:37–38 NIV.

22. Isa. 40:29–31 NIV.

23. Ps. 30:11–12 NIV.

Chapter 14: Blessing Your Kids and Grandkids

1. "Babies Understand Mother's Tone of Voice Not Their Words," Telegraph, January 9, 2012, https://www.telegraph.co.uk/news /health/news/9002249/Babies-understand-mothers-tone-of-voice -not-their-words.html.

2. Lori Kase Miller, "The Benefits of Introducing Baby to Music," Parents, October 2014, https://www.parents.com/baby /development/intellectual/the-benefits-of-introducing-baby-to-music/.

3. Joshua A. Krisch, "When Do Babies Understand Facial Expressions?," Fatherly, July 24, 2017, https://www.fatherly.com/health-science /science-facial-expressions/.

4. "What's in a Smile?," Raising Children, July 9, 2015, https: //raisingchildren.net.au/babies/connecting-communicating /bonding/whats-in-a-smile.

Chapter 15: Blessing Your Spouse

1. "Marital Affection: The Foundation for a Healthy Family," *Health Journal*, February 1, 2014, http://www.thehealthjournals.com /marital-affection-foundation-healthy-family/.

2. "Marital Affection," *Health Journal*.

3. Jenn Morson, "How Much PDA Is Okay in Front of Your Kids?," What to Expect, August 10, 2017, https://www.whattoexpect.com /news/first-year/how-much-pda-okay-front-baby-kids/.

Chapter 20: What If I Didn't Get the Blessing?

1. An excellent book we recommend that deals with the impact family influences can have on both the creation and cure of substance abuse is Jeff VanVonderen, *Good News for the Chemically Dependent* (Nashville: Thomas Nelson, 1985).

2. Richard A. McCormisk, "Affective Disorders Among Pathological Gamblers Seeking Treatment," *American Journal of Psychiatry* 141, no. 2 (1984): 215.

About the Authors

John Trent, PhD, a noted speaker and author, is president of StrongFamilies.com and serves as the Gary D. Chapman Chair of Marriage, Family Ministry, and Therapy at Moody Theological Seminary. He and Gary Smalley have won Gold Medallion writing awards for their books *The Blessing* and *The Two Sides of Love*. Dr. Trent has also written several children's books, *I'd Choose You!* based on *The Blessing* and the Gold Medallion award-winning book on children's personalities, *The Treasure Tree*. Learn more about creating the Blessing culture and lifestyle at TheBlessing.com.

Gary Smalley was one of the country's best-known authors and speakers on family relationships. In addition to writing *The Blessing* and *The Two Sides of Love* with John Trent, their book *The Language of Love* (newly revised and updated) won the Angel Award as the best contribution to family life. His national infomercial, "Hidden Keys to Loving Relationships," has been viewed by television audiences all over the world.

Kari Trent Stageberg is the CEO of StrongFamilies, her dream job since her dad, John Trent, started the ministry in 1998. More than twenty years later, after personal faith and relationship struggles, Kari was restored and healed through the power of the Blessing. Today she is a speaker, cohosts the StrongFamilies and *Live Blessed, Girl* podcasts, helps nonprofits through her partnership with the Nonprofit Consulting Shop, speaks, and pursues writing through her blog, MyBelovedDaughter.com. She lives in Tacoma, Washington, with her amazing husband, Joey.